MIND AND OTHER MATTERS

Brian Smith

A Life Story

Grosvenor House
Publishing Limited

All rights reserved
Copyright © Brian Smith, 2020

The right of Brian Smith to be identified as the author of this
work has been asserted in accordance with Section 78
of the Copyright, Designs and Patents Act 1988

The book cover is copyright to Brian Smith

This book is published by
Grosvenor House Publishing Ltd
Link House
140 The Broadway, Tolworth, Surrey, KT6 7HT.
www.grosvenorhousepublishing.co.uk

This book is sold subject to the conditions that it shall not, by way of
trade or otherwise, be lent, resold, hired out or otherwise circulated
without the author's or publisher's prior consent in any form of binding or
cover other than that in which it is published and
without a similar condition including this condition being imposed
on the subsequent purchaser.

A CIP record for this book
is available from the British Library

ISBN 978-1-83975-140-0

Front cover – sunrise over Fishtail mountain, Nepal.

To my wife, Ann. This is her story as much as mine.

I owe a big vote of thanks to Jill Rundle, our friend of nearly 70 years, and an avid reader. Without her encouragement it is doubtful if I would ever have finished this book, given the difficult circumstances I found myself in over the last three years. Her advice and helpful criticism were absolutely invaluable.

Thanks also to my own close family, to whom I showed early versions of the first few chapters. They, too, were very generous in their praise, which spurred me on to complete it. I hope they enjoy the finished product.

Foreword

I started writing this in 2009 when my wife, Ann, was in a psychiatric hospital for over three months with very serious depression and then at home under my care for a further year or more struggling to overcome this dreadful illness. Writing this gave me something to focus on and an escape from the stresses of caring for her. Because I enjoyed reading other people's autobiographies I hoped others might find mine interesting, too, and my family and friends would have a better understanding of what my life and Ann's have been about. I hope, in particular, it will raise awareness of what a dreadful curse mental illness is.

I have tried to throw light on a life which started in poor circumstances, before the 2nd World War, in a country and world which was utterly different to today's, and is now coming to an end in relative affluence, having had some exciting and rewarding experiences on the way, plus a lot of challenging, troubling and difficult ones, too.

Whilst this is very much a personal story I have set it against the changes and events through which I have lived. My early life was in Belgrave, the working class area of Leicester, before moving on to Birmingham and Coventry, and then becoming part of the drift to the south-east in the swinging '60s. There is no single theme that runs through my working life. I was often invited to change tack and take on a new challenge and readily agreed. At one early job interview I was asked where I expected to be in ten years time. I said that I had no idea. It depended on what turned up, I said. And so it proved. As an innovator and risk-taker all my life I have been fortunate to be involved in a number of significant new initiatives and developments and to work with many talented and prominent people. I count myself very lucky.

I have tried not to make this a "technical" report of the work I have done, although it is difficult not to include some of the detail if it is to be understandable. I hope I have pitched it about right.

If this was just about my work, though, you might stop reading this now. Be reassured, it is not. I have tried to capture the times I have lived through, the personal and other problems that Ann and I have faced, of which there were many, and the enjoyment I have found in my family and social life. If I can capture the essence of all this it might be a good read. I leave you to judge.

February 2020

The Unfolding Story

Leicester
    1. War & Peace   1
    2. Salad Days   26
    3. Growing Pains   47

Birmingham
    4. Independence   68

Coventry
    5. A Flying Start   85
    6. A Family Man   110

Welwyn Garden City
    7. Blossoming Out   129

Marylebone
    8. Health Matters   141

Lambeth & Kennington
    9. The South Bank Show   157

Harlow
    10. Now We Are Four   173

Whitehall
    11. Your Move, Sir Humphrey   184
    12. From The Inside   193
    13. Making Government Policy   212

The City
    14. Birth of a Regulator   238
    15. Troubled Minds   267
    16. Honoured, Ma'am   290

Welwyn Garden City
    17. Leisure Time   321
    18. Black Clouds & Silver Linings   333
    19. Close of Play   348

Chapter 1

Leicester
War and Peace

I was conceived in the summer of 1935, probably at one of my parents' favourite haunts outside Leicester, such as Barkby, Beeby, Scraptoft, Swithland Woods or Bradgate Park, all within an easy bus or bike ride from home. My parents, Bill and Evelyn, were married four months later in October and I was born on 11 March 1936. Although the majority of first-born children were conceived out of wedlock at that time, only 4% were actually born before marriage, such was the social stigma attached to giving birth to a bastard, as the child would then be called. It served as a powerful incentive to young couples to get married, which my parents did, so giving me a better start in life.

Mum and Dad lived close to each other in the Belgrave area of Leicester, Mum in Harrison Road and Dad in Jermyn Street. These regimented, treeless streets all looked very similar – row upon row of terraced houses built in the early Victorian era for the growing number of workers needed for Leicester's booming hosiery, footwear and light engineering industries. Leicester's population rocketed in the 19th century from only 17,000 in 1800 to 219,000 in 1900. It has gone on growing rapidly since and is now over 400,000.

Most of the houses, like Mum's, had no front garden. The front door opened directly from the pavement into the front room, which would be kept neat and tidy for special occasions and for receiving visitors, but not for everyday use. In practice it was hardly ever used. The back room was where the family lived, ate and the younger children had a weekly wash in the bath tub in front of the coal fire. For older children and adults there were excellent public baths a few streets away, all gleaming white and steamy.

There was a good reason for living in one room: it meant that you only had to heat one room in the house – a major factor in keeping your living costs down. There was a technique for keeping the fire alight overnight by putting damp "slag" on it before going to bed. Chimney fires were fairly common in the neighbourhood, so everyone had the soot-blackened chimney sweep regularly to clean them. A sheet would be stretched across the fireplace and wooden poles pushed through one by one until the chimney sweep told the children to go outside and shout when the brushes suddenly appeared from the chimney pot on the roof, to great excitement. The bedrooms in winter were freezing cold. Although there were fireplaces in the bedrooms they were seldom lit, unless someone was ill. There was a toilet and a coal house in the minute "yard" at the rear. Going to the outside toilet in the night, particularly in winter, was just not done, so everyone had a "potty" beside their beds, emptied every morning.

Some streets, though, were just a little bit "posher" and my dad's family lived in one of these. It had a miniscule front "garden" and steps up to a rather nice front door, inlaid with coloured glass. This opened into a narrow, attractive hallway decorated with pretty tiles on the floor and walls and coloured glass above the door. The rooms were a bit bigger, too, and the front room had a bay window. Although Belgrave was a relatively poor area the houses in the streets where Mum and Dad lived were all privately owned, well built and well maintained and the area had an aura of honest respectability about it. People did not feel threatened by crime or anti-social behaviour. Everyone got on with the hard job of earning a living and raising their family.

When Idi Amin expelled the Asian community from Uganda in 1972, and Edward Heath's Tory government allowed 27,000 of them into this country, Leicester City Council tried to discourage them coming to Leicester, taking out an advertisement in the "Uganda Argos" saying that Leicester's public services were stretched to the limit, but this only served to publicise Leicester as a possible destination and some 5,000 descended on the city. It was mainly in this part of Leicester that they settled because housing was cheap. As their families grew the time soon came when there were fewer indigenous white people living in the Belgrave area than Asians and my dad would say that we did not live in England any more, but in the middle of the Indian Ocean.

The transformation is now complete. Over half the city's population is non-white. By 2017 there were 55 mosques, 18 Hindu temples, nine Sikh gurudwaras, two synagogues, two Budhist centres and one Jain centre. The city has become synonymous with multiculturalism. Cinemas in which I spent much of my youth watching British and American films now show only Asian films and the shops cater almost exclusively for the Asian community, with beautiful saris, sparkling footwear and exotic food on display in their windows. It is all much more colourful now than in my days there, but alien to my old way of life. Some of my brother's family still lived there and seemed to accept it without any grumbling. There appears to be no great resentment between the communities, which I find a bit surprising, given the impact it has had on the area and on the way the white community lives. That's not the case in many other parts of the country, where immigration has become a huge political issue and a festering sore that threatens to erupt at some point.

The streets were well served with small local pubs, often on street corners. The Jubilee, on the corner of Harrison Road and Acorn Street, where we lived later, became my dad's local and his second home, as it was for many of the men in the neighbourhood. The air inside would be thick with smoke, because the majority of men smoked cigarettes. Those who didn't would inhale almost as much as those who did. They would spend the evening talking and playing dominos or cribbage. Most would not drink a lot, because that cost too much. It was for each other's company that they went there. This was before the days of television and Sky Sports screenings. If they stayed at home they would be huddled together with the rest of the family, often a large one, in one small room, listening to the radio or reading and the men just wanted to escape for an hour or so. The women, with a few exceptions, did not have that option and my mum would not dream of spending the evening that way. She was too busy dealing with the family's needs or working to earn extra money. In some streets there would be a small footwear or hosiery factory nestling unobtrusively amongst the houses. My mum worked for years at Hartshorn and Jesson's in Acorn Street, just two minutes walk from her family home. We would later live in that street.

Mum and Dad were not poor, but when I was young they were often short of money and unable to pay bills or buy necessities, particularly when Dad was out of work. I can recall visits with Mum to the pawnbroker to raise some cash or being asked to take some clothing or other material to the "rag and bone man" to exchange for money - the thinking was that he would be more generous to a fresh-faced young lad, I think.

When Dad was working he would give Mum £5 per week and that had to cover everything - paying the mortgage, the insurance premiums and the household bills, maintaining and running the house, putting food on the table, clothes on our backs and bringing up three children. There were no supermarkets or large retail local shops then and much of what we needed was supplied by tradesmen who came round the streets in vans or on horse and cart. Many times I would be sent to the front door to ask the grocer, the baker, the milkman, the coalman or other tradesman if we could put off paying until next week or to say that Mum wasn't at home – when she would be hiding in the pantry. Dad kept the rest of his earnings to spend on beer, which relaxed him; on betting, which led to his downfall; and on cigarettes, which killed him.

Mum and Dad lived largely separate lives. I always thought they got married simply because Mum was pregnant, not because they had lots of interests in common and enjoyed each other's company, but I might be wrong. They never showed outward signs of affection, so I did not even know if they loved each other, but they generally got on well together. They were both very likeable people in their different ways. Recently, however, I came across a photo of Mum and Dad on holiday, on the back of which Mum had written of her broken heart after he died and lamented how much she missed him. She had kept those feelings well hidden when they were both alive. There were some spectacular disagreements, however. Dad went too far one Sunday lunch time, after he had been out drinking, bridling Mum once too often about her plain cooking. She smashed his plate of roast dinner on his head. She was an extraordinarily tolerant and kind person, but even she had her limits.

Mum was the backbone of the family. She kept it going through sheer hard work and guts. She was born in 1911 and christened Evelyn May Langley. She was one of twelve children - seven boys and five girls. Her father worked in a nearby shoe factory and died of cancer at the age of 64. Her mother never really recovered from his death. She was ill much of the time until she died, aged 73. I have only vague recollections of them. I did not see nearly as much of them as my own grandchildren see of me, but Mum always talked of them very fondly. She said they were a close and happy family and, although quite poor, the children were always well fed and cared for, but life became very hard when their dad's shoe factory closed. Mum's seven brothers all fought in the army in the Second World War and miraculously all came home alive, but some carried injuries or had medical problems. I met them occasionally, but knew none of them very well.

We had more contact with two of Mum's sisters, Vera and Florence (Flo). They married two brothers, Bob and Eric Durden. We saw most of Vera and Bob and their son, Colin, my cousin. They lived opposite the Carlton Cinema, in which I spent many happy hours. Flo and Vera were as different as chalk and cheese. Flo was a lovely, kind and friendly person, but Vera was not my cup of tea at all. She looked as if she had something nasty permanently under her nose. Every question seemed to be probing and inquisitorial and her whole manner slightly disapproving and judgemental. It did not help that she had a high pitched, strangulated voice, which was difficult to hear. Her husband, Bob, was a dear. He was a bus driver and keen gardener. I enjoyed his company, but he was under Vera's thumb. I don't think Vera needed or wanted to work and she seemed to look down on my mum, who did.

Mum left school when she was 14 years old, as the vast majority of children did then, and started work at Hartshorn and Jessons, which made boots and shoes. Their factory, in Acorn Street, was just round the corner from her parents' house. She was a shoe machinist and a very good one. She soon became the firm's Sample Machinist, entrusted to make the shoes that would be shown to the sales representatives of firms they hoped would buy their shoes.

Dad was also from a large family. He was born William Henry Smith in 1908. His mother had been in domestic service, but was now a full-time mother and housewife. She had a slightly refined, aloof air about her, as befits someone who had rubbed shoulders with superior people and knew how to behave "properly", but she was very kind to me. Dad's father was a Chief

Inspector for Leicester Corporation Water Works and was probably instrumental in getting my dad a job there. Dad had three brothers and six sisters, of whom no less than five died suddenly of heart attacks – two in their twenties - as did his own father. Dad trained as a plumber when he left school at aged fourteen and later became an Inspector for Leicester Corporation Water Works, travelling from site to site in and around Leicester on his bike. He was always being called on by neighbours and family to tackle leaks etc. Many a Sunday he would be headfirst down a hole trying to get to grips with a burst pipe or sorting out other problems.

I had a bit more contact with the aunts and uncles on Dad's side than on Mum's. They were generally more outgoing and enterprising. Dad's youngest brother, Alan, had his own watch and jewellery shop and he spent a lot of time at our house, partly because he shared dad's interest in horse-racing, which only encouraged my dad in his gambling vice. When I was about five I was an angelic, curly-haired page boy in a white trouser suite at Uncle Arthur's wedding. One of the bridesmaids, my aunt Margaret, collapsed and died soon afterwards with a heart attack whilst picking her baby out of the cot. On a happier note, I can still recall a visit to a farm run by another of Dad's relatives (on his mother's side) in the Leicestershire Wolds on a lovely warm autumn day. Outside the back door of the old farmhouse there was a deep well and a buttery in which all manner of fruit had been stored – apples, pears, plums, damsons etc. On opening the door the smell was pure nectar. I spent the day exploring the farm and climbing trees in the orchard to pick more fruit to take home. It was a day that has stuck in my memory.

Dad was a gregarious man, who liked other people's company. He would talk to anyone and everyone as he walked down the street, and he usually did. He had a joke or a funny remark for every occasion. He was also meticulous about his appearance in public, particularly on Sundays when he would wear a dark suit, an immaculately ironed and starched white shirt and red tie with a white handkerchief sticking out of his coat's lapel pocket. I think he must have got this from his mother. He was not at all interested in sport, although he claimed he played tennis when young until he fractured his arm very badly. He never went to the cinema or the theatre or read books or listened to the radio. He had no interest, therefore, in the things that interested me, so we had little in common. His passions were horse and greyhound racing and playing cribbage at local pubs or clubs. There were no betting shops in his day. The law then required bets to be placed only on racecourses, and he would go regularly to Leicester Racecourse or on coach trips to other courses with his younger brother, Alan, and his friend, Ernie Robinson, our travelling grocer, who I helped on his van to earn some pocket money. Market Rasen in Lincolnshire was my dad's favourite course. In practice, working men would place bets regularly with various illegal bookmakers in the neighbouring streets and I would take the bets for dad and his friends and collect his winnings, if any!! I'm sure the police were aware of this, but turned a blind eye.

On rare occasions we would go out for the day to a Point-to-Point race meeting, organised by local Hunts, which met regularly throughout Leicestershire, the home of hunting. I enjoyed these. It was all very informal, the down-to-earth farming community and the upper class hunting fraternity mixing with city outsiders like us and all sharing the thrill of horses thundering passed at great speed. When I had reached my teens Dad started taking me with him at Sunday lunchtime to whatever club he currently favoured. He frequented the Conservative Club, the Liberal Club and the Trades & Labour Club – a true floating voter, or drinker!! It was the last one, on Gypsy Lane, that I remember best. There would be a series of singing, dancing and comedy acts, a bit like a music hall, but not the same quality. It was not dreadful, but I thought it a waste of two or three hours when I could be out with my friends. Dad realised this and stopped taking me.

Mum, on the other hand, was a fairly shy person, but quite determined and competitive. The first question she would ask me on returning from some sporting or other competitive activity was always "did you win?" and, if the answer was yes, she would say "good" and smile contentedly. She had no time to get involved in any sporting activity herself, nor was she physically capable, but she did like going occasionally to the cinema when we were all older. She was a great romantic and loved getting carried away into a fantasy world. It must have been a relief from the hard grind she had to endure. She was a keen reader and loved playing cards. When I was in my mid-teens she would ask me to partner her at local whist drives and, so she says, we often won. She would take us on trips into the countryside at different times of the year. In the autumn we would go "gleaning" for grain in the fields around Beeby in east Leicestershire after the wheat, barley, oats etc had been cut and harvested. We would feed this to our hens over the winter. I loved being in the open air, walking amongst the stubble in golden fields and collecting the ears of wheat and barley that the harvesters had left behind.

In the spring and summer we would take the bus out to the Charnwood Forest area of north-west Leicestershire. This is very attractive, unspoilt and hilly countryside of spectacular granite outcrops, dense woodland and pretty stone villages. Swithland Woods was a favourite spot, especially in spring when it was bathed in bluebells. Bradgate Park was another: it is a large area of open, natural parkland, owned and managed now by Leicester City Corporation and is a paradise for children in the summer holidays. It is heaving with people at weekends. It was the home of Lady Jane Grey, who was the uncrowned queen for just nine days in 1553 before being arrested for alleged treason and executed, allowing Henry VIII's daughter, Mary, to become queen. The remains of her house are still standing. A fast flowing stream, ideal for paddling, runs through the park and a large herd of deer roam the hills on the far side of this stream. It is great place for walking and playing games. Years later, when mum was old and able to walk only short distances, we would revisit this park and it brought back happy memories for her.

For the first eighteen months after marrying Mum and Dad rented rooms off Harrison Road for just fifteen shillings per week (75p in today's currency) before buying a house in Rotherby Avenue for £500. It had a cul-de-sac at our end and opened onto waste ground at the other, which we called "The Bog". This would become a place of endless adventure and recreation for us. Our house was in the middle of a terrace, with two rooms plus a kitchen downstairs, two bedrooms plus a box-room upstairs and small gardens at the front and the back. Crucially it had an inside toilet, which was quite upmarket for the Belgrave area. Mum had to go back to work nine months after I was born because she now had a mortgage to pay and could not rely on dad's earnings because he was so often ill and off work. The next door neighbour, Mrs Churchill, acted as child minder. My brother, Terry, was born three years after me and my sister, Sheila, one year and ten months after him. Terry and I shared a double bed when Sheila was born and we remained there until I left home.

Mum stayed at home after Sheila's birth, doing work at home. The shoe factory supplied her with a sewing machine and brought her the cut out leather every few days and collected the finished shoes. Her life was an endless round of caring for the children, doing the shopping, the cooking and the household chores whilst also earning money through her machining work. I don't know how she did it. There were no washing machines or other labour-saving appliances then. Wash day, usually Mondays, involved putting hot water into a large aluminium "Dolly tub", similar in size to a beer barrel, adding the clothes and pummelling them with a wooden "Dolly" until they were judged to be clean. They were taken out, rinsed in the sink and then passed, one by one through a mangle, comprising two cylinders, which were turned with a hefty handle until all the water had been squeezed from them. The wet clothes were either hung on a clothes line in the yard outside or placed in front of the fire on a "clothes horse" and left to dry. It was like being in a sauna.

Respite of a kind came after a few years because Dad's health deteriorated. His heavy smoking left him with chronic breathing problems, making it difficult for him to ride his bike in order to carry out his Corporation inspection work. He had a lot of time off work before eventually giving up and staying at home to look after us whilst Mum went back to work. That immediately reduced their income, so typically Mum did additional work at home in the evenings and weekends. One of these jobs was to sew buttons onto a card for which she was paid threepence for 48 buttons (just over 1p in today's currency). I would take them every weekend to the company's offices in the town centre. Eventually Dad did resume work, becoming an insurance agent for the Prudential, doing door-to-door collection of premiums – working class families generally chose to pay in cash every week. With both Mum and Dad in full-time employment the financial pressures on Mum eased. She was able to find enough to meet our school expenses and our leisure activities.

As I grew up I spent more and more time outdoors. In fact I practically lived outdoors. After the war ended and the black-out was lifted children would continue playing under the street lights after it got dark until our parents called us in. In our younger days we would play in the street or down on The Bog, where a large bomb crater had filled with water, forming a good-sized pond on which we played "pirates", floating on an old bed mattress. As we got older we ventured further afield into the countryside. There was no TV or computer or I-Pad or X-Box to keep us in the house. There was the radio, but that was not a sufficient pull to get us back indoors except at certain times of the day when particular favourite programmes were on – the children's programmes in the late afternoon or "Paul Temple" and "Dick Barton, Special Agent" in the early evening, which became compulsive listening. We made our own entertainment. The games we played changed as we got older, but there was always cricket and football. Trying to win coloured glass marbles off each other by rolling them in the gutter and hitting your opponent's was a great favourite. The large ones were highly prized. A bit trickier was the art of flicking cigarette cards from between your first and second fingers to knock over and cover your opponent's cards, which you then kept.

This was a time when boys and girls collected things, of which cigarette cards were the easiest. Most men and many women smoked heavily and the different brands tried to keep their customers by offering cards with each packet, which their children would collect or use for playing games. Some children's comics did the same and I still have my collection of The World's Best Cricketers provided every week by "The Adventure -The Paper for Boys". I also collected stamps and built up quite a good collection in my loose-leaf album. I specialised in countries of the British Empire, which then comprised a quarter of the world's population in over fifty countries. I drew meticulous coloured maps of each country and added basic facts, such as size, population, capital city, languages spoken, etc. I had nothing of great value, getting most of them from a shop in the city centre which offered large brown envelopes full of used stamps, costing next to nothing. I got others as presents at Christmas and birthdays. My brother, Terry, liked to come to the shop with me and help me stick them in the album. I left the album with him when I left home, but it vanished without trace, as did the British Empire itself after the war.

Another little hobby of mine was to make models. We had a cat, which I liked for most of the time, but not after it destroyed my beautifully constructed model galleon made out of matchsticks, which I had stuck together. I had made the mistake of using fish glue, which the cat found irresistible.

From an early age most children in the street had bikes, bought second hand from a local dealer. Cycling was not then the hazardous experience it is today. Few people had cars and lorry traffic had not yet taken off – that came after the railways were severely cut back following Dr Beeching's report in 1963 and the first motorways were built. Initially we would just ride in the street or down on The Bog, where we created our own race track, much like the ones created for mountain bike racers today. When we were about nine or ten we went further afield, riding through The Bog and out onto Barkby Lane to the villages of Barkby Thorpe and Barkby, about two miles away. First stop was often an orchard at Barkby Thorpe where we would go scrumping for fallen apples, then onto Barkby, a pretty little village with a brook running through the centre, where we would park our bikes and walk beside the brook and over fields to a bridge and a pool. Most of us could not swim then, but we splashed about and enjoyed ourselves. The pool was probably over six feet deep in the centre. Later, when I could just about swim, I would join everybody else in swimming across the pool, because not to do so would lose you credibility with the rest. We did not recognise the danger inherent in this, but there was, of course, and we were lucky to get away unscathed.

Being young and out in the country on one's own laid you open to all kinds of other potential problems. We had one upsetting experience when a group of us were waylaid by a much older boy in Abbott's Spinney, near Barkby Thorpe. He threatened and bullied us and ended up pouring water from the stream down each of our backs, before letting us go. Our parents were furious when we reported what had happened. Dad found out who it was and took me to where the boy lived, which was right outside my Junior School, and confronted him. He asked me to say if he was the perpetrator. I wouldn't, mainly because I feared reprisals, I think, or perhaps I was just a coward. Nothing more came of it, but it was an unsettling experience. That did not stop me going out on my bike, though, and I was soon going much further afield to Swithland Woods and Bradgate Park, about seven miles away. I was climbing one of the large granite outcrops at Woodhouse Eaves one day when an authoritative voice warned me that what I was doing was dangerous and asked me to come down. It was Mr Joels, one of my history teachers, who lived there.

The Bog really came into its own in 1947 when it was transformed into a winter wonderland. It is generally reckoned to be the worst winter ever experienced in the UK. Snow fell from mid January to late March with drifts of ten feet or more and bitterly cold nights. Leicestershire and Northamptonshire, in the centre of the country, were particularly badly affected with over a hundred villages completely cut off. The village of Caldecote recorded a temperature of -23.3 degrees C.

Life on the Bog, however, was bliss. The snow lay several feet deep and was perfect for building our own igloos, which survived for weeks. We had great snowball fights and created long and wickedly slippery slides down the hills and played there for hours.

For the country, however, the situation was dire. Roads and railways were blocked. Coal supplies were insufficient to keep power stations running, so they closed, leading to cuts in electricity supplies for industry and households. Vegetables were frozen in the ground, leading to widespread food shortages. Over 25% of our sheep stock was lost. Then, to make it even worse, it thawed and there was widespread and severe flooding. It was the wettest March for over 300 years. The Labour Government, and Emmanuel Shinwell, the Minister of Fuel and Power, in particular, were severely criticised and it probably led to the shift in public opinion resulting in their defeat in 1951 to the Tories. After surviving the long years of war it seemed cruel to have to endure this. Fuel was in short supply and Mum and I would queue for hours at the Gas Works to buy coke to keep our fire going. The queues were very long and I got freezing cold waiting. We had taken an old pram to carry it in, but it was not ideal for such a heavy load and we struggled to get it home through the ice and snow.

Our other source of regular amusement was the cinema. In the 1940s all films were in black and white, but colour became more common from the 1950s onwards, led by the popularity of Hollywood musicals, which I absolutely adored. Saturday morning children's cinema was a regular event. We would laugh at Tom & Jerry cartoons and at Laurel & Hardy or Abbott &

Costello films. We would be thrilled by stories of space travel with Flash Gordon and by the American, Wild West adventures of Roy Rogers (and Champion, his Wonder Horse), Gene Autry or The Lone Ranger. They were all basically the same formula – the good guy versus the bad guy, with the good guy coming out on top, which was very reassuring for young, impressionable youngsters.

When I was older I would start going to evening performances. The cinema was very popular, with some 30 million attendances each week. Queues for tickets formed long before the performance was due to start. There was no advance booking, so you got there very early if you were particularly keen to see something, and people would be turned away when all the tickets had been sold. At each performance there would be an A film and a B film with the Gaumont British or Pathe News sandwiched in between. The news would be delivered in megaphone style as if every item was a momentous public announcement, quite unlike the casual style of modern TV announcers. The B films would be shorter and usually British. The A films were mostly British or American with the occasional French or Italian film. Children could go to U-rated films unaccompanied, but had to be with an adult to see A-rated films. If I wanted to see an A film I would ask someone I knew in the queue if they would buy a ticket for me, which they often did. Films were usually shown for only three days, so there would be huge queues outside the cinema, come rain or shine, to get in to see a particularly good film. The cinema industry was booming, and there were a lot of very good films made. I spent many happy hours there.

I was three and a half years old when the Second World War started and nine and a half when it finally ended. My clearest and most painful memory is of the celebrations to mark VJ Day in August 1945 when Japan finally surrendered after atomic bombs were dropped on Hiroshima and Nagasaki. There was a spontaneous celebration in the street and an enormous bonfire was built with an effigy of the Japanese Emperor on top. It was spectacular and burnt all night. The next morning a huge pile of embers were still smouldering, stretching right across the road and someone started a game of "dare", challenging others to ride their bikes over the bonfire. I came a cropper, falling straight into the glowing embers and badly burning my hands and legs, particularly my knees. I spent the next few weeks going to the hospital every day to have the dressings changed. Removing the bandages and dressings was excruciatingly painful and I dreaded the journey on the bus knowing what was in store when I got there. I bore the scars on my knees for years after. To add insult to injury I was not fit enough to join in the street party and celebrations to mark the ending of six years of war.

I can remember clearly the bombing raids in November 1940, when the sirens would wail and we would hurry down to the damp and musty-smelling Anderson air-raid shelter, which filled the whole of the back garden. It was dug about four feet into the ground, lined with concrete walls and topped with a curved corrugated iron roof, covered with sandbags. There were bunk-beds to lie on and blankets to keep us warm, but the raids were usually over in a few hours when another loud wail would signal the all-clear. The Germans targeted both Coventry and Leicester in 1940, because both had significant manufacturing industries, but the devastation in Coventry was much, much worse than in Leicester. There were reports of seeing a bright red glow in the sky, from as far as twenty miles away, on the fateful night when Coventry was devastated.

Both our small front and rear gardens had been converted to war-time use. There were posters everywhere exhorting the nation to "Dig for Victory". The blockade imposed on our shipping by German U-boats made it increasingly difficult for us to import food from across the Atlantic, so great efforts were made to be as self-sufficient as possible. With the majority of able-bodied men fighting the war, women took over their role on the land, creating the Women's Land Army. Dad did his bit by growing a few vegetables in the front garden and keeping chickens in the back. They provided a plentiful supply of eggs and every now and then Dad would kill one by wringing its neck and hanging it on a hook on the wall, where it would twitch and convulse uncontrollably for hours. If Dad killed more than one I would help Mum pluck their feathers, covering the floor of the back room inches deep in a soft down. I was happy to go along with this until my favourite hen, Genie, a lovely Rhode Island Red, was killed. I went right off chicken.

Part of the Bog, the waste ground at the end of the street, was converted into allotments and Dad took on one of these. He found the physical effort of digging difficult because of his bad chest, so I helped him and became really keen, buying chemical fertilizers from Woolworths to encourage my vegetables to grow. After the war, when I was about eleven, I entered some of the vegetables I had grown into the Belgrave Allotment Society's Annual Show and won a prize. That was the start of my interest in gardening, particularly of vegetables, which I have retained all my life.

Dad had been declared unfit for military service because of his chest and was appointed an Air Raid Patrol (ARP) Warden instead. He took it very seriously, going out every night at dusk to make sure that all curtains (lined in black) were closed and the blackout rigidly enforced. Any chinks of light would provide enemy aircraft with clues about what was down below. There were no street lights, of course, which meant that we could not play out in the street in the winter months, which was annoying. It would be six years before they would be turned on again. There was an official ARP notice board in our front garden providing news about the war effort and appeals from the Government for the public's help. Dad enjoyed the attention that this role brought him.

With London about to undergo heavy nightly bombardment from German bombers the Government mounted the second phase of its evacuation programme, moving thousands of children to safer parts of the country. In the summer of 1940 a long line of children, each with a label attached to their coats, walked slowly down our street, stopping at every house, asking its occupants if they were prepared to take in any children. It is hard to imagine that happening now given the current climate of suspicion about abusive behaviour, but 1940 was a desperate time. Mum took two brothers, Jimmy and Donald, for which she got an allowance of eight shillings per week (40p in current money). She was so soft she would have probably have taken them all if she could. We had no spare bedrooms. My younger brother, Terry, moved into Mum and Dad's bedroom and I slept in our double bed with Jimmy and Donald. They were older than me, but as far as I can remember we got on pretty well.

They came from Kensington and had wealthy parents. I can remember them receiving huge parcels, packed with sweets, chocolate and other goodies that made me green with envy. They were very generous and gave us some of it, probably under instructions from their mother. When she came to collect them, a few months after they arrived, she came in a car and wore a fur coat. I expect Mum was overawed. She looked a bit like a film star to me. Their early departure may have had something to do with a dramatic incident involving one of the brothers. A large group of evacuees and older boys, plus us, were walking along a footpath by the River Soar, about a mile from our home, when Jimmy and Donald reached out to grab some bull rushes, which they had probably never seen before, and Jimmy fell in. Fortunately, he was rescued easily enough, after some initial panic, and no harm was done, but everyone was a bit shaken and we all got a dressing down from our parents. This episode, plus the fact that Leicester was itself being bombed, may have decided their mother that the dangers of staying with us were as great as Hitler's bombing of London, so she came to collect them.

The old adage that "You don't miss what you've never had" certainly applied to us in the war. There was a lot that we did not have, but it was not until we got them after the war that we realised what we had been missing. Everyone can remember the excitement of the first time that the vans carrying Fyfe's bananas arrived and oranges and lemons appeared in the corner grocery shop. These were unknown exotic fruit to us then. There was a shortage of everything, including petrol, fuel and clothing, as well as food, so the Government issued ration books, specifying each person's entitlements, and there was a certain amount of sharing of coupons to allow someone to buy something they needed in exchange for something that the other person needed. Even when the war ended the rationing continued for a long time because the country was in a desperate state, effectively bankrupt, and only kept afloat by huge loans from the U.S.A.

The continuation of rationing became a big political issue and the Conservatives cleverly exploited public dissatisfaction, particularly among the middle classes, to win narrowly in 1951, portraying the Labour Government as too controlling. Rationing finally ended in 1954, fifteen years after it was first introduced. Street lighting had returned earlier, in April 1945, so we could enjoy playing out in the street after dark, but it was not until 1953 that shops were allowed to have their windows lit at night. I can remember going into town to witness this new phenomenon with my friend, Colin Atkins, and experiencing a strong feeling that a bright new future was opening up, which was probably no more than the optimism of youth, but Harold MacMillan latched on to that mood later, proclaiming to the electorate that "You never had it so good" and winning a convincing victory in 1959, the third in a row for the Tories. He would also proclaim that "the winds of change" were blowing through the British Empire as British rule ended and each country grasped their independence. In its place the British Commonwealth was born with our new Queen Elizabeth at its Head. Looking back on those war years it all seems a pretty Spartan existence, compared to what followed, but at the time it did not feel at all bad. Material things are not the answer to happiness.

Christmas then was a much simpler affair, not the highly commercial extravaganza it has since become. Mum would save up throughout the year in the various "Christmas clubs" run by local shopkeepers so that there was always traditional Christmas food on the table and toys in our "stockings". We had traditional Leicestershire fare of Melton Mowbray pork pie and Stilton cheese for breakfast on Christmas Day, which would be frowned upon now in our high cholesterol and calorie-averse society. I could always rely on getting at least one book, or "annual", such as Adventure, The Wizard, Hotspur, The Beano or Rupert Bear, and some fruit and chocolate. Mum and Dad would make some of the presents themselves. When I was a bit older and the myth of Father Christmas had been punctured I can remember watching Dad make a simple fort for my brother, Terry, out of plywood and Mum making soft toys for Sheila plus clothes to fit them. We hung up trimmings, mostly hand-made paper-chains which we made from coloured paper and glue, but I don't remember having a Christmas tree or lights. Playing cards at Granny Smith's was a highlight. She had a large round table which was ideal for games like Newmarket. We would be given a small pot of money – farthings, half-pennies and pennies - to use for placing on the various key cards and there was great excitement when you claimed one of these or scooped the kitty by playing the last card.

Christmas was also a time for earning a bit of money through carol singing. In the days just before Christmas

I would go round the neighbourhood in the evening, either on my own or with friends, singing carols outside the houses, knocking on the door and hoping for a donation. Today that would all be done for charity, but our efforts were all private enterprise.

Chapter 2

Leicester Salad Days

The only clear recollection I have of Belper Street Infant School is of lying down for an afternoon nap and being covered with a warm blanket. I don't know if this was a regular event or a one-off because I was not well, but it has stuck in my memory. I was very happy there and at my next school, Northfield House Junior School, which I went to in 1943 when I was seven. It was just under a mile away on Gypsy Lane and I would walk there and back with my friend, Tony Phillips – few children then were taken to and collected from school by parents. It had an attractive central courtyard with a covered walkway round the four sides and flowerbeds and a small fishpond in the middle. It had its own playing field on which we would play football and cricket matches. I took seven catches in one match fielding close to the bat and waiting for the batsmen to pop the ball into the air.

In my last year there we had to take an examination to determine where we went next. This was the 11 Plus exam, introduced at the end of the war by the Coalition Government following the passing of Rab Butler's 1944

Education Act, which brought in free education and created state-funded Grammar Schools. I was totally unaware of the huge significance of this event, as were my mum and dad, but I certainly know now. On the day the exam was to be taken someone from school came to our house to find out why I had not turned up and then waited to take me back with them – I had been out late playing with friends and overslept. I'm sure every middle class parent in Leicester with an eleven year old child would be well aware of the significance of these exams, but not my parents. The importance of education was lost on them, and on most other working class families in the area. Education was simply what you did until it was time to go into a factory. Fortunately for me someone at school was looking out for my interests and made sure that I sat the exam, which I passed.

I would have had a very different life if I had not, similar perhaps to my brother, Terry, who was constantly ill, did not pass the exam and went to a Secondary Modern School. He did well there, but not well enough to make a difference. He left school early and spent all his working life in a local shoe factory. He was relatively poor the whole of his life and died young. What a contrast with my good fortune. Had there not been an 11 plus exam he might have fared better and not been stigmatised as a failure. It was because of his experience that I have always been against selection at aged eleven. It is simply too arbitrary. Although many did well out of this system, including me, it seems so unfair to those that did not. I was very supportive, therefore, of the Labour Government's introduction of Comprehensive Schools in the 1960s.

I had to choose between three Grammar Schools in Leicester. Wyggeston was reckoned to be the best, we were told, and had many famous old-boys, including the Attenborough brothers, Richard and David, who were a bit older than me. Alderman Newton's was the next best, followed by The City Boys Grammar School. I put them in that order. I went for interviews with Mum or Dad to each one. Dad came with me to the Wyggeston one and completely ruined any prospect I had of getting in there. He had an argument with the headmaster about the kind of treatment I would get, given my background, compared to someone whose parents were well-healed and professional. I don't know why he did this, but I squirmed in my seat as the meeting went on and was glad to get out. Mum came with me to the others and I was accepted at Alderman Newton's.

Alderman Newton's was a very good school. It had been founded in 1784 by Gabriel Newton, a former Mayor of Leicester, and it had many illustrious former pupils. More recent ones included Lord (C.P.) Snow, the novelist, academic and Government advisor. He was one of the many from the school who would go to Christ's College, Cambridge. He was a Parliamentary Secretary to the Minister of Technology in Harold Wilson's Labour Government in the nineteen sixties and first came to prominence for his strong views on the breakdown of communication between the two cultures of science and art – he complained that scientists never read Charles Dickens and those versed in the arts knew no science. He will be better remembered for his "Strangers and Brothers" series of novels, of which "The Master" is the best known. The first one, set in a Midlands city, which is clearly Leicester, tells the story of a rather precious, head-in-the-clouds group of young men and women, led by the charismatic lawyer, George Passant, who spend their weekends at a farm. That rang a lot of bells for me. I would later spend many weekends at a farm just outside Leicester with the charismatic Bert Howard, the Head of History at the school, playing games and engaged in endless discussion. The link between these two seems more than coincidence. The clincher is that the book is dedicated to H.E.H. (Bert) Howard.

Other old-boys include Prof. Sir J.H. (Jack) Plumb, who also went on to Christ's College, where he became a Fellow and finally its Master. I would meet him at Christ's and again in Leicester over the next few years. Other recent ones were Sir Edwin Nixon, who would become Chief Executive and then Chairman of IBM, UK for over 25 years, and Sir Alan Walters, the advisor to Prime Minister Margaret Thatcher and architect of her controversial monetarist economic policy, with devastating results for the country's industrial base.

The school was in the city centre, close to the cathedral and guildhall. It was in the very uninteresting old Wyggeston School building, having moved there in 1920 from its former site just down the road in Greyfriars. That school became the Girls' Grammar School, to which my sister, Sheila, would later go. Greyfriars would achieve fame in 2014 when Richard III's body was discovered near there. He had slept at The Blue Boar Inn in Leicester the night before the Battle of Bosworth, some ten miles away, where he was killed, stripped naked and brought to Greyfriars, which was then a monastery, and hurriedly buried there. It lay undiscovered for 530 years. Leicester is now capitalising on its find.

The school was very well run and formal. The day started with morning assembly at which there was a short service and a lesson for the day, read by the Head

Boy or a Senior Prefect. The Headmaster made any necessary announcements, including the results of school sporting events, such as cricket and rugby matches, and gave us our marching orders for the day. The Masters all wore their black academic gowns and we wore green blazers and short grey trousers. Outside school we had to wear our green caps at all times. Failure to do so would lead to a detention if a Master or Prefect caught you. Senior Prefects took detentions, which were for one hour after school. I would later do this duty and there was never any dissent from those detained. Discipline was very good. Prefects were also in charge of the long refectory tables at lunchtime, arranging for the collection of plates etc. Masters sat at an elevated long table at the end of the room at right angles to ours and were waited upon. I really enjoyed lunches. The food was very traditional – usually meat and two vegetables plus a hot pudding with custard and not a pasta dish or salad in sight. It was much better than anything I got at home and I lapped it up. Outside, in the playground, there was a long glass-fronted notice board, which acted as a school newspaper. A Senior Prefect was appointed as its editor and the contents were changed regularly. My friend David Crawley would later have that job and I became a regular contributor, writing reviews every week of films and plays I had seen.

Before the first term started I had to go to the school to collect books and be shown around. I had no idea how many there would be so I took a suitcase, which was far too big. Everybody else had a school satchel and I felt very conspicuous and embarrassed and a bit of an idiot. Not a good start. However, once the term got underway I felt very much at home. I loved everything about school, especially the lessons, which I revelled in. Because I was highly motivated I did well. We were placed in classes according to our surnames in the first year, but thereafter we were streamed according to ability. I won the mathematics prize in the first year and went into next year's top stream, where I finished first in the end of year exams, winning both the Form and French prizes. I won one or more prizes each year after that – physics, mathematics again, and several others. Prize-giving day was a big event, held at the very grand De Montfort Hall with its twenty or so huge columns at the front. The Headmaster gave a review of the year and a visiting dignitary made a speech and awarded the prizes, which were always books, except for my last award, which was a cheque for £50 to help me pay for books and other expenses when I went to university – that was a very large sum in those days and I was extremely fortunate to be given it. Mum and Dad would come to the prize-giving and glow with pride when I went forward to receive my awards.

The top stream was further divided in the third year and I went into the fast stream, which effectively did two years in one, missing out the fourth year with the aim of sitting the School Certificate exam at aged fifteen and the Advanced Certificate at seventeen. This allowed some to sit the Cambridge Entrance Examination at seventeen and re-sit it at eighteen, if necessary. It did not quite work out like this because the government changed the rules. It scrapped the School Certificate and brought in the General Certificate of Education, but you now had to be sixteen to take its first (Ordinary Level) exam, so I could not take it in the fifth form. We did take the papers, though, as if it was a valid exam, and I passed in all ten subjects, but officially it did not count. I took it again next year in the Sixth Form, by which time we were half way through our Advanced Level course, so we only took five "O level" subjects. Grades were not published then but the Headmaster told me that I did well. The rest of my time in the Sixth Form would prove eventful and difficult.

For social purposes we were placed in one of four Houses, each named after a part of Leicester. I was in Highfields, whose Senior Housemaster was Bert Howard, the Head of History and a towering presence in the school. He would have a malign influence on me later. In my first year he had picked me out as someone to cultivate and he chose me to captain the House cricket team. The posh boys in the team were surprised and I can remember one of these questioning my decisions in the first match and trying to undermine my authority, but I earned my stripes and the team's respect because I knew my cricket and was good at it. We played each of the other Houses in a spirit of healthy rivalry. I ended on a high note, scoring a match-winning 50 in my last year. The Houses also played each other at rugby and competed in athletics, and I took part in these, but cricket was always my first love.

I was selected for the school's first year cricket team and got into the school's first XI when I was fifteen. We played matches twice a week, on Wednesday afternoons and Saturday mornings, and had a weekly net practice/coaching session after school, so it was a big commitment. We had a full fixture list, travelling some distance by coach to all the other Grammar Schools in Leicestershire and also to Nottingham, Derby, Kettering, Coventry, Nuneaton and Oakham outside the county. It was all a big adventure to me. Within Leicester itself we did not play Wyggeston, which was a pity, because we were a good team and would have given them a close game.

We did play City Boys Grammar School, whose ground at Grace Road was also the one used by Leicestershire County Cricket Club, where I would spend much of the summer months. I was so proud to use the same changing room as some of my cricketing heroes and to go out to bat through the same white wicker gate that they used. In one game there, soon after getting into the first team, I played a match-saving innings of 25 not out. Bert Howard was in charge that day and clapped me in as we came off the field. The next day, at assembly, the results were read out by the Headmaster, including my score. I was glowing, a big halo hovering over my head and a smug grin on my face. Mr. Joels – "Joey" - saw me and swung his gown with something hard on the end, which thudded into my head, shouting "Smith, take that smirk off your face". My moment of glory had not lasted long.

I had another painful experience when playing Hinckley Grammar School who had a very fast opening bowler. I opened the batting and spent half an hour trying to avoid being injured. On a good wicket I might have succeeded, but theirs simply wasn't good enough for such bowling and eventually I took a painful blow on my wrist trying to fend off another ball that reared up. I had to "retire hurt" but, after all the remaining wickets had fallen and with only a few overs left, I decided to bat again and try to play out time. It was one of those "Wilson of The Wizard" moments. I shielded the last batsman from the bowling and we survived to draw the game. I was taken straight to hospital and found that I had a hairline fracture of my wrist, so that was the end of cricket for me for that season.

The geography master, Reg Cain, was the school's cricket coach. He was very easy-going and could easily be diverted into talking cricket in the middle of his lessons, which we did as often as we could. He was also a very good batsman, scoring over 1,000 runs in a season for Leicester Town, the leading club in the area at the time. It played on the old County ground on Aylestone Road. I played there once when he asked me if I fancied a game for the Town's second team. I think he was just trying to be kind and encourage me. He was a very good coach and taught me a lot. I was a batsman, either opening the batting or going in at three or four, and an occasional off-break bowler. He encouraged me to bowl more and I overheard him remonstrating to the first team captain that I was not being used enough.

I modelled my batting on Leicestershire's elegant opening batsman, Maurice Hallam, described in Wisden, the cricketers' bible, as "the finest opener never to play for England". I modelled my bowling on Leicestershire's brilliant Australian off-spinner, Vic Jackson. He formed a formidable spinning partnership with Jack Walsh, another Australian, who bowled left arm leg breaks and the "Chinaman" – an off-break bowled with a leg-break action. He turned it prodigious distances and the cricket was always entertaining when he was in action. Jack was also a great hitter, who would have done well in the modern one-day forms of the game. He would often play a whirlwind, cameo innings. Each year a few county matches were played at club grounds around the county within easy cycling distance for me. These grounds generally have shorter boundaries, so hitting sixes is easier. He hit several in a quick-fire 106 against Essex at Loughborough in 1948, which thrilled the crowd because it was so unusual in those days.

Cricket was my great obsession during my grammar school years and I would spend the summer school holidays and Saturdays watching Leicestershire play at Grace Road. A junior ticket for the whole year cost only ten shillings and sixpence, or 52.5 pence in today's money - what a bargain. I would cycle there, a round trip of about six miles, armed with my sandwiches, a bottle of water or lemonade, and a bat and ball for playing in the lunch and tea intervals. In good weather it was sheer bliss. You had to be dedicated to support Leicestershire, though, because they were either bottom or next to bottom of the County Championship year after year, vying with Somerset for the bottom spot. How the fortunes of both these teams would change over the coming years. Somerset found Ian Botham, England's greatest all-rounder, and imported two of the world's leading players, West Indians Viv Richards and Joel Garner, which rocketed them to the top of the table.

Leicestershire's transformation was less spectacular. Charlie Palmer, a modest former teacher, who had spent much of the war in a Japanese prison camp, took them briefly to the top of the Championship table for the first time ever in August 1953. It was a moment to saviour so I got the bus to Trent Bridge, Nottingham just so that I could see them walk out as leaders. I was a proud supporter. They could not keep it up, though, and finished third, but this small, dapper, unassuming man, who wore glasses and was almost bald-headed, set Leicestershire on the upward path to becoming champions. Over the next few years the county turned to a succession of famous ex-England stars to keep up the momentum. Ray Illingworth, the ex-England captain, would lead them to their first Championship title in 1975. They would win it again in 1996 and 1998.

I started going regularly to county matches in 1947, when I was eleven. This was the year when Dennis Compton of Middlesex set the cricket world alight and tore up the record books. He scored 3,816 runs that year, including eighteen centuries, at an average of 90.85. He was unstoppable. He was the "Brylcream Boy", the first sportsman to exploit his fame commercially, his perfectly combed head of hair plastered on posters all over the country. He was the most exciting batsman ever, improvising outrageously and scoring incredibly quickly. He batted with flair, freedom and gaiety and would have made a fortune in the modern game. He was a joy to watch.

One year later I saw the Australians, led by Don Bradman, who scored 81. They were generally acknowledged to be the greatest Australian touring side ever and did not lose a match, beating a strong England side convincingly. It was Bradman's last tour and he needed only four runs in the last Test Match to average over 100 during his career. He was given a standing ovation all the way to the wicket, but was bowled fourth ball for nought by an Eric Hollies leg break – a terrible anticlimax for the great man.

I was an avid autograph-hunter, hovering outside the players' changing rooms or waiting in the car park long after other spectators had left. The players were generally happy to sign my book and often added a little message. Over the years I built up a very good collection with many famous names in it, but sadly it was lost when I left home.

Over the next sixty-plus years I would play rugby, soccer, basketball, tennis, squash, badminton, golf and bowls and go running, too, but none come close to matching the appeal and challenge of cricket. It has everything. It demands courage and determination to face a hostile bowler hurling the ball at you at nearly 90 mph, often on a dodgy wicket, or great patience and concentration faced with a spin bowler trying to out-fox you on a "sticky dog" of a wicket. It demands lightening reflexes to catch a ball in the slips when you have only a split second to react, or to judge how to catch a high ball in the outfield dropping out of a dazzling sun in a swirling wind. It demands athleticism and technical skill to bowl for long spells and test the batsmen's ability to play you. The state of the wicket and the weather will often determine how a match is played and the art of captaincy is to be aware of these factors in order to get the better of the opposition. I could go on endlessly about what makes it so special. The modern game demands shorter matches with lots of runs scored very quickly, because that is what spectators want, apparently. That has its attractions and I do enjoy it, but for me it is the battle of wits and skill, played out over a longer period that makes cricket particularly special.

Outside the cricket season I would support Leicester City Football Club. It cost very little for juniors to stand on the terraces and we were encouraged to go right down to the front. I went with friends walking with the good-natured crowd from the city centre to the ground in Filbert Street. There were sometimes close to 40,000 people, but we felt perfectly safe. There was none of the trouble between home and away team supporters which bedevils the modern game.

Leicester City was not a great side, but they had some very good players. In 1949, when I was thirteen, they were struggling to avoid relegation from the Second Division, but had a wonderful run in the FA Cup. They reached the Cup Final and played Wolverhampton Wanderers, then one of the country's leading clubs. I saw every one of their cup matches, home and away, but not the Final. I was at the semi-final at Highbury, Arsenal's ground in London, to see them beat Portsmouth, travelling on a supporters' coach with friends. I can still recall the excitement of the whole occasion. Portsmouth were the league leaders and Leicester were given no chance by the pundits, but the Cup often throws up giant-killers and Leicester trounced them 3-1. Don Revie, Leicester's young star, scored a great goal and generally outplayed the Portsmouth defence.

I was very disappointed not to get to the Cup Final, so I wrote a letter to the Secretary of Leicester City Football Club explaining what a great supporter I had been and asking if he could get the autographs of the players as compensation for missing the game. Immediately after the match, which Leicester lost 3-1, I got a reply, enclosing a large souvenir brochure telling the story of Leicester's run in the Cup. The centre pages had large photos of the two teams and each player had signed his name. You can imagine how I treasured it. Sadly, it went missing, along with many other similar possessions, when I left home.

The Wolves team had two big heroes of mine, the England captain and centre-half, Billy Wright, and the right-half, Bill Slater. Bill Slater played for England as both an amateur and a professional and was, to my mind, the finest example of an English sportsman that you could hope to find. He was extraordinarily talented and the words "fair play" might have been created for him. He was the role model every sportsman should try to emulate. Six years later I would end up having football and basketball coaching from him.

Over the years Leicester's fortunes have fluctuated, but they have always been a good FA Cup side, losing again in the Final a few years later to Tottenham Hotspur. They have been a very good breeding ground for England players, too. Don Revie would go on to have a successful career as an England player and then England's manager. Centre forwards Gary Lineker, Alan Smith, Frank Worthington, Emile Heskey and more recently Jamie Vardy all played for England, as did goalkeepers Gordon Banks and Peter Shilton. Gordon became something of a legend for his heroics in goal when England won the World Cup in 1966. Then, in 2015/16, this Cinderella club had a fairy tale season. Having conjured up a miraculous escape from relegation the previous season they continued that form to confound everyone by winning the Premiership with a team that cost peanuts. Not only did they win, but they did it by playing the most exciting counter-attacking football, putting their wealthier rivals to shame. It was hailed as one of the greatest sporting achievements of all time.

The school played rugby, as did all grammar schools and I played for the school at all levels, but I did not really enjoy it. I was quick and could accelerate fast, so I was put on the wing, but I was frozen stiff for most of the match through sheer lack of activity. Schoolboy rugby is rarely a fast running and passing game, so the ball comes to the winger only once or twice a game and then rarely in a way in which you can do well, particularly if your fingers are frozen. I did not shine at rugby there. Some years later, when I was working, I would play at scrum half and then fly half, where you are in the game all the time, and I did enjoy the game then, but my schoolboy experience was pretty miserable. The other reason for not enjoying it was Mr Morris, who took rugby coaching and organised the school teams. He was a small, grumpy Welshman with a glass eye and he did not like me. The feeling was mutual. What a contrast he was to our cricket coach, Reg Cain, who got the best out of everyone. Mr Morris had absolutely no man-management skills, so he got little out of his players. I would come up against Mr Morris in the classroom, too. He taught physics and was in charge of the Science Sixth Form, which did nothing for my motivation.

In 1949 we moved to a slightly bigger house in Purley Road. I'm not sure why. Mum and Dad were both working now, so perhaps they felt able to move up in the world. However, I suspect it had more to do with getting us away from The Bog and playing out in the street at all hours now that I was at the Grammar School. I was now several streets away from the friends I had made there and with whom I went to football matches etc. Over time I would see less of them and more of new friends, the closest being Colin Atkins, who went to City Boys Grammar School, catching the same bus as me each day into the city centre. He loved all the things I did, so we spent a lot of time together. We had first met at the regular Sunday morning football game on a nearby playing field where boys in the neighbourhood met up, formed themselves into two teams and played a full ninety minute match. It was great.

On the corner of Purley Road and almost opposite our house there was a grocery and greengrocery shop. It was run by Mr and Mrs Shaw, who had a daughter, slightly older than me, and a son, who was about my age. We became very friendly and they would often take me out at weekends in their car. The girl was a bit of a tomboy and loved playing cricket on a nearby playing field. Moreover, she had a full set of stumps, a bat and a ball. I can remember clearly one Sunday, a lovely summer's day, when Mr Shaw drove us all the way to Sherwood Forest, north of Nottingham, to have a picnic and play cricket for hours in an open glade until Mr Shaw was exhausted. They were very kind to me.

Mr Shaw was active in the local Conservative Association and took me to some of their public meetings during the 1951 General Election, when I was fifteen. This was before the age of television or other modern means of communication so these meetings were a very important means of getting your message across. I learned how these events were orchestrated to get the audience aroused. Our candidate entered the room from the rear and walked down a central aisle. We were placed at strategic points down the aisle and got a signal as to when to start clapping and cheering as he moved towards the platform. It did not bring him victory, though. The two seats in north Leicester were solid Labour and he had little hope of winning. However, the Tories did win the General Election and a tired Labour Government gave way to a rejuvenated Conservative administration under Winston Churchill. I went to see my Headmaster to get permission to help on the day of the election, but he said no. That was the end of my flirtation with the Conservative Party. When I started to think seriously about politics I became a Labour supporter – not unreservedly, and not all the time, but that is where my general sympathies lay.

In 1950, when I was fourteen, I fell in love with Wales. Dad's sister, Aunt Carrie, and Uncle John lived at Abersoch on the Lleyn Peninsular in North Wales and they invited me to spend the summer holiday there. John was an architect who worked for the County Council in Caernarvon. I went by train as far as Caernarvon where he collected me in his car and we drove through the lovely Welsh countryside to Abersoch, a small fishing and sailing village. I had never seen a proper castle before - the kind you see in books and films - or mountains or rivers running through deep valleys down to the sea and I lapped it up. Carrie and John lived with their son in a bungalow at the very end of a road leading down to the small harbour. A gate in the garden hedge led straight onto the beach and estuary, where the river Soch flowed into the sea. I would spend many hours here turning stones over quickly so as to catch eels before they scuttled way. We would give them to Aunt Carrie, who would throw them into boiling water and we would have them for supper along with lobsters and crabs, caught in pots placed amongst the rocks. The first time I heard the ear-piercing screaming noises coming from the boiling water, similar to a baby crying, it put me completely off eating my food. It was in fact just the hot air escaping under pressure, rather like the whistle on a boiling kettle, but it seemed much more sinister.

We played games with the local village boys, who decided to put me through an early initiation test. They would gather regularly near the harbour and jump off the lower rocks into the sea, which was crashing onto the cliffs. The swimming wasn't easy, but even more difficult was getting out of the water again. I was not a good swimmer, but I could not get out of the challenge without losing face, so in I went. I survived, of course, and was then accepted by the rest of the boys.

Over the next few weeks I was taken on long drives by Uncle John and Aunt Carrie to see the sights. The weather must have been unusually kind that year, because I cannot recall any wet days. Snowdonia was bathed in sunshine and the countryside was jaw-dropingly beautiful for this city boy. I marvelled at the Swallow Falls at Betws-y-Coed, the bleakness of the slate quarries at Blaenau Festinniog, the magnificent castles at Caernarvon, Conway and Harlech, and the many beautiful beaches fringed by cliffs and rock pools. All too quickly my lovely holiday came to an end and I came home at the end of August, catching the train again at Caernarvon. Two days later, on 26 August, there was a dreadful train crash at Penmaenmawr, just down the line from Caernarvon, killing six and injuring 34 passengers, mainly Irish, who had got the ferry to Holyhead before boarding this train – the same one I had got only two days earlier. That holiday sowed the seeds of a long love affair with Wales and I would return there many times, initially back to the Lleyn Peninsular, then to mid-Wales and later on to Pembrokeshire with our good friends John and Jean Sefton.

Prior to this glimpse of Wales I had only known England's flat east coast. Factories in Leicester, in common with other industrial towns in the Midlands, would all close for two weeks in the summer so that workers could go off on holiday. We didn't have a holiday every year, and certainly not when we were all very young, because we couldn't afford one. Mum would save up in her "Holiday Club", run by a local shopkeeper. Working class people in our area preferred to save this way rather than in a savings bank and it seemed to work. I have fond memories of some holidays. They were all in Lincolnshire, Suffolk or Norfolk on the east coast, not because they were the best places for a holiday, but because the London and North Eastern Railway (LNER) or local bus companies went there. Very few people had cars in the '40s and '50s and hardly any working class families, so practically everyone went by train or bus.

We stayed near to Skegness, Mablethorpe or Great Yarmouth and, one memorable year, at Snettisham, near Hunstanton, in Norfolk. Once there, it seemed as if the whole of Leicester and Nottingham had gone east. We generally stayed on vast caravan sites close to the beach, where we spent most of the day, but in Snettisham we had a huge ex-army bell tent on a field with just a few other holiday- makers. It was unlike other holiday resorts we had gone to, with far fewer people and open countryside on our doorstep. It was the one holiday that I can remember spending time with my dad, getting up early in the morning to go and pick mushrooms, which he would cook with egg and bacon for breakfast. I loved that. In January 1953 this stretch of coast was hit by devastating floods, which destroyed homes and killed many people. Snettisham was particularly badly damaged.

On holiday with Sheila and Terry (and my cricket bat)

Those east coast beaches were vast and I would spend all day playing endlessly on them with my brother and sister and anyone else who wanted to join in our games. There would be candy floss and ice cream for a treat and visits to the fun fair, until the money ran out. Returning there as an adult I can now see how charmless many of these places are, but as a young boy they were a bit of paradise. I was seventeen when we went on the last of these family holidays. It was arranged at the last minute, so the only cheap accommodation mum could get was one large room in a big house at Gorleston, next to Great Yarmouth. Dad did not come, having lost his job and sullied his reputation, but Mum was determined to get away for a few days. I can remember it for two things, in particular. The first was the row with the landlady, who took exception to us preparing and eating food in the bedroom which, she insisted, was meant only for sleeping in – she had a point. Had we been in a caravan it would not have been a problem. We always took huge quantities of food on these holidays. We never ate out. We would fill a large suitcase with tins and other packages of food and take it to the LNER depot in Leicester for delivery to our destination. It was a nightmare getting that case to the depot, because it was so heavy, but it always turned up at the other end intact. We placated the landlady in Gorleston and got through the week peaceably.

The second memory is of an evening of variety at the theatre on the pier at Gt. Yarmouth. I don't know how we afforded it, but I am so glad we did. A very young Max Bygraves was top of the bill. He was then a rising star and he threw everything into his performance. He sang, danced, told stories and jokes, acted the clown and had a wonderful rapport with the audience. For me, who would develop a love of the theatre in all its forms, it was pure magic.

Apart from these holidays I did not spend a great deal of time with my sister, Sheila, although I have always got on very well with her. She was five years my junior and a girl, so we had different interests. She was a bright girl, though, passed the 11 plus, and went to Alderman Newton's Girls Grammar School, which was only a few hundred yards from mine, so we went together in the early days. As he got older I spent more time with Terry and we got on well together. He helped me with my stamp collection and we went on long rides into the countryside, but he was not a very strong person and was often ill. As a result, he had no interest in sport, so could not share with me my interests in cricket and football, which was a great pity. As we got older we drifted apart.

Chapter 3

Leicester
Growing Pains

The dominant Master in the school was Bert (H.E.H.) Howard, Head of History. He was a large, rotund man who wore a waistcoat over his ample belly and was hardly ever seen without a pipe in his mouth, whether it was lit or not. He was a very good teacher and I enjoyed his lessons. I was sorry to have to drop history when I moved into the Science Sixth Form. Because of him history was a very popular subject and there was a constant stream of boys from the school taking up places at Christ's College, Cambridge to join old-boy Jack Plumb, Professor of History there, and later its Master.

Bert Howard would patrol the school playground scrutinising the boys at play and making his own assessments of them. He cultivated the cleverer boys and would invite them to join him in various after-school activities. My involvement started with visits to his house in Highfields, a short bus ride from the City centre. He would buy iced buns at the corner shop and we would eat these hungrily before playing various fun games, mainly aimed at sorting out the nimble-minded from the rest. We were only there for an hour or so, but we all enjoyed it.

The next step up was to be invited to go camping at weekends in the early summer months at a farm near Markfield in the Charnwood Forest area north of Leicester. On Friday afternoons we would get the bus to Field Head and collect tents and other gear from the farm. Whether it was fine or pouring with rain we had to put up the tents and help prepare the evening meal, which was quite a challenge at times. We went home after lunch on Sunday, so we only had Saturday and Sunday morning for play, but we made the most of it. I can recall one baking hot summer day when some of the older boys were acting the fool, one of which was Neil McKendrick, a tall, lithe blond who would become Head Boy. Some music was being played and he was prancing around, stark naked except for a saucepan covering his private parts. He would go on to read history at Christ's, before moving to Gonville and Caius College, where he became a Fellow, then Professor and finally it's Master.

The next step up was to be invited to go sailing, firstly on the river Cam and later on the Broads. However, you first had to prove that you could swim two lengths of the freezing cold pool where we had swimming lessons every week. Bert Howard acted as supervisor and he would watch my progress carefully before declaring that I was fit to go. On our first trip to Cambridge we were taken to meet Jack Plumb in his rooms at Christ's. I soaked up the atmosphere. The mellow stonework of the quadrangles, the well-tended grass, the trees, shrubs and other vegetation helped to create an ageless and tranquil scene, which had the effect of striking me temporarily dumbstruck, as I took it all in. It seemed wrong to speak too loudly in such a setting. We were introduced to Jack Plumb, who chatted to us and bizarrely offered us sherry to drink, which I accepted – I was only fourteen. We sailed up the Cam from Cambridge to Ely, via the Great Ouse, and on up to the wide Bedford Cut. We stopped overnight at Ely and had a look around the great Cathedral and Close. It was all a great experience and I enjoyed it.

The next year I went on the Broads. We were in much larger sailing boats and we were taught how to take the sails in quickly when the wind got up, and to lower the mast and sails equally quickly when we had to shoot under low bridges, such as at Acle. It was wonderfully quiet, floating silently along the rivers which joined the different Broads. In the evenings we would go ashore to a pub and drink cider, strictly illegal, of course, before staggering back to the boat in semi-darkness and somehow getting from the shore to the boat via a narrow plank.

In the summer of 1951 the school went by coach to London to see the Festival of Britain. It was the last act of the outgoing Labour Government in an attempt to lift the spirits of the British people and show the world that we were still a major world player. The original proposal was to emulate the Great Exhibition of 1851, which was a showcase for the British Empire at its peak. Now, virtually bankrupt after the war, it was decided that we could not afford to repeat that, but should concentrate instead on promoting better quality design in rebuilding our towns and cities, particularly London, much of which was still in ruins. The Festival was spread throughout the country, but the centrepiece was the newly built South Bank Exhibition site in London. Warehouses and working class houses beside the Thames had been replaced by a riverside walkway, a new Royal Festival Hall, the Dome of Discovery and the cigar-shaped Skylon – a steel tower, suspended in mid-air, which became the symbol of the Festival.

It was a big thrill going to London, a kind of Mecca, and being able to stand on the banks of the Thames opposite Big Ben and the Houses of Parliament. I could not have imagined then that I would spend a lot of my time in that place some years later. In 1952 the newly elected Prime Minister, Winston Churchill, had the whole Exhibition Site, except for the Royal Festival Hall, raised to the ground, apparently just to erase these reminders of the Labour Government. However, he had to live with more substantial manifestations of that Government's transformation of our stricken country, despite the odds being stacked against it, the shining example being the new National Health Service.

That summer a classmate asked me to join him on a long cycling holiday around southern England because his friend couldn't go. After the first day I wondered if I had bitten off more than I could chew. He had a very lightweight drop-handled racing bike with several gears, which was ideal for touring, and I had a very heavy, ordinary "sit up and beg" bike, which was not. The first leg was to Stow-on-the-Wold in the Cotswolds, travelling along the Fosse Way, the old Roman Road, a distance of about sixty miles, which was a killer, particularly that final gruelling climb up the hill into the village. My legs were like jelly and my backside was raw and very painful. I did not think I would be able to ride the next day, but the Warden at the hostel had encountered this problem before and gave me some cream to sooth the soreness, which brought some relief. I had a very disturbed first night, trying to sleep on uncomfortable straw palliasses on a narrow bunk-bed. I did my share of the preparation for the evening meal and the clearing up afterwards, because that was expected of everyone in those days. The hostels were certainly not hotels or even guest houses. Despite the pain I did manage to appreciate my first glimpse of a Cotswold village, which for many tourists, particularly Americans, is synonymous with England. There was a set of stocks in the market square, close to the hostel, where miscreants would be shackled as punishment and subject to the taunts of the local villagers.

We set off south the next day in beautiful weather and I gradually forgot the pain. Each of the hostels was different, but each one memorable in some way. At Winchester it was in a very old mill above the river Itchen and we climbed right down to the mill-race to see the great mill wheel in motion. It is still a hostel, but now owned by the National Trust. The hostel at Tanners Hatch, deep into a beautiful wood in Surrey, was like stepping back in time and I half expected to see a woodcutter emerge from the hostel to greet us. Despite the dodgy start we had a great time.

Paedophilia has been constantly in the news in recent years. Shocking evidence has been uncovered of the systematic sexual abuse of young children, whether by prominent celebrities, football coaches or politicians or in institutions, such as schools and care homes, or just within the community, particularly in northern towns with a large immigrant population. It is not a new phenomenon, of course. It was certainly around in the '40s and '50s when I was young. On any visit to the cinema or other crowded places you would have to be on your guard and learn to cope with dirty old men. We all had some unsettling experiences. The one which really upset me and left a permanent scar, blighting the rest of my time at school, was on one of our school camping weekends with Bert Howard. We were all engaged in a game on the field when I felt unwell and went to my tent to lie down. Bert Howard followed me, entered the tent and lay next to me. The next thing I knew he was clambering all over me, reeking of tobacco, trying to kiss me. I lashed out with my fists, pushed him away and shouted at him to get off and get out, which eventually he did. I was very upset and angry and left early the next morning.

On Monday I told him that I wanted nothing more to do with him – no camping weekends, sailing holidays or visits to his house. He didn't try to talk me out of it, but he must have been worried that I might talk to others, either teachers or boys or my parents, about what had happened. I should have done, but I didn't. The repercussions would have been enormous. In truth, nothing drastic had happened, but it was clear where it might lead. It left me despondent for weeks afterwards and I struggled to work through the implications. It was a huge change for me to come to terms with. From being one of the school's brightest sparks I went into my shell. I lost a lot of my zest for school life, including my interest in learning. I was disillusioned and saddened by what I saw as betrayal by a trusted figure of authority. It was a body blow. The end result was that I dropped out of the group of high-flyers, all of whom, except me, would go on to Cambridge.

The Bert Howard incident wasn't the only reason. The teenage years are a difficult time as the hormones take hold and the young try to find their identity. It helps if they have a stable family background and feel happy at school. Suddenly, I had neither. The Bert Howard episode had punctured my enthusiasm for school and, out of the blue, my dad revealed that he had a serious problem at work. He had been using the insurance premiums he collected to gamble on horse races and had lost heavily. He was in serious trouble. He had not recorded the payments in his large ledger and it was about to be audited. I stayed at home to help reinstate the missing entries and work out how much he owed the Prudential. It was a huge figure. He was distraught, but got lucky. The insurance company were very lenient and did not prosecute him, because Mum promised to pay them back out of the proceeds of the sale of our house, which she did. She moved fast and found a small and very cheap terraced house in Acorn Street, just round the corner from her old family home. She had come full circle and was back where she started as a girl in a back-to-back house with an outside toilet in the back yard and a minute garden. There was a brick wall in the back yard separating us from the house in the next street, which was so close you felt as if you could open the bedroom window and shake hands with the occupants of the house opposite.

71 Acorn Street (recent picture)

Dad was a broken man and started drinking heavily. He started having rows with Mum and shouting at me, Terry and Sheila. He had never done that before. It was very upsetting for us all. I think at that point Sheila and I resolved to leave home as soon as we could. Sheila, as the youngest, had the hardest time, particularly as she entered her teenage years, although she says it was Mum rather than Dad with whom she was regularly at loggerheads. She left the Grammar School early after taking her Ordinary Level exams, went to work in a shop and then escaped from home by joining the Wrens. She would meet her husband, Derrick Lawler, there.

Eventually Dad sorted himself out, with the help of his own family, particularly his younger brother, Alan, who seemed to be in our house a lot. Dad had difficulty finding a decent job, so he took a very menial job as a caretaker and odd-job man close to my school. One of his main tasks was to maintain the heating system by stoking the boiler throughout the day. I went to see him there after school and he gradually regained some self esteem and zest for life. He was an ebullient character and could not be kept down for ever. He would later work for the Rank Organisation in a large ten-pin bowling alley in the town centre and was the life and soul of the place when I went to see him with Ann, my girlfriend. My dad was a proud man and this experience must have been chastening and humiliating for him. Everyone in the neighbourhood knew him, so they would be fully aware of his misdeeds, yet he got himself back on track and was able to hold his head up high again. I admired him for that.

Mr Morris, the Head of the Science Sixth Form, did not believe my explanation as to why I had been absent whilst I had been helping Dad reconstruct his ledger, and I don't blame him. I did not tell him the real reason, but his hostility was not what I needed at that time. I was thoroughly disillusioned with school life and decided to leave and get a job without even taking my Ordinary Level GCEs. What persuaded me otherwise was the encouragement I got from The Rev. Tom Pickering, who was now my Senior Maths Master in the Sixth Form. He was a curate at the nearby St Mary de Castro Church, a lovely 11th century Norman church, built in the grounds of the old Norman castle. He was a delightful man – kind, thoughtful, encouraging and a great motivator. Only a handful of us took maths so the teaching was almost personal. He treated us in a very respectful way, not just lecturing to us but getting us to research a particular topic and discuss it. He would ask us to give lessons on these topics. I gave one, I recall, on Induction Theory, which impressed him so much that he implored me not to waver, but to stay on to take the Cambridge Entrance Exam. From then on I did resume working, passed all my Ordinary Level exams in 1952 and in the next year, when I was seventeen, the A Level exams in Pure Mathematics, Applied Mathematics and Physics, all with high marks. I owe that success to Tom Pickering. He even arranged for me to have access to a lovely old room in one of the cathedral buildings adjacent to the school so that I could study in peace and quiet.

I became a School Prefect and then a Senior School Prefect. Prefects shared a lot of duties designed to help in the smooth running of the school and in keeping order amongst the boys. Nobody could miss the fact that you were a Prefect because you had to wear a hideous green cap with bright yellow piping from the crown to the peak and lower edges. In addition, a Senior Prefect had a large yellow tassel hanging down from the crown. You had to wear this cap at all times outdoors when you were in school uniform, which meant on the bus to and from home and when walking in the streets of Belgrave. Very few boys there went to a Grammar School and you got the expected reaction from them. It was excruciatingly embarrassing at first, but you learned to live with it. You certainly stood out from the crowd.

One feature of our education that would have pleased old-boy C. P. Snow, who obsessed publicly about Britain becoming a society of two separate cultures, was that the Science Sixth Form had lessons on art history. A young, keen teacher gave us weekly lessons for a whole year on each of the great painters and on the various shifts in art movements over the centuries. It was riveting and all quite new to me. I soaked up the lessons like a sponge and still have the notebook in which I tried to capture what he said.

The Sixth Form had its own large Common Room, complete with piano, which my friend David Crawley would sometimes play after school when we had finished working on the material for the school playground's notice board. I did the reviews of plays and films. It was a much more difficult task than I first thought, trying to encapsulate the nub of a film or play in just a few sentences whilst capturing the reader's attention, but I enjoyed doing it and got better at it.

With the date of the Cambridge Entrance Exams approaching Bert Howard invited those sitting the exams to his house one Saturday evening in order to meet Prof. Jack Plumb. Most there would be hoping for a place at Christ's in order to read history, in which Jack Plumb would have a direct interest, but he asked me, too. I said I would think about it. I was reluctant to resume any kind of dialogue with him, but I decided in the end to accept. It turned out to be an interesting evening. I had quite a long conversation with Jack Plumb on my own as well as in group discussion with the others. He was very approachable and good company. Bert Howard kept nagging me to get my act together and do myself justice.

In the summer of 1953 we had the coronation of Queen Elizabeth, the first big event to be shown on television. The audience was massive and TV sales rocketed. Until that point very few people had a TV set or had watched television, but this was the catalyst for its subsequent growth in popularity. It also coincided with the first ascent of Everest by Edmund Hilary and, in the previous year, the maiden flight of the Comet, the world's first jet passenger airliner, and the testing of our own Atom Bomb. It seemed to herald a new era of optimism as England started to renew itself after the devastation caused by the war. We were all given a book on the history of Leicester to mark the coronation.

Leicester had a rich history. I have already recounted how Richard III's body was found recently just down the road from my school. There was another famous death in the town. I knew that there was an Abbey Park, having walked through it along the River Soar, but I now learned that this was where Cardinal Wolsey had died in 1530 when trying to avoid the wrath of Henry VIII. The Abbey was destroyed by Cromwell eight years later on Henry's orders and little remains of it now. Wolsey's name, however, lives on in modern Leicester when "Wolsey" became the very successful brand name of a clothing manufacturer and retailer.

Fifteen centuries earlier Leicester had been an important Roman settlement, visited by Emperor Hadrian in 121 A.D. on his way north to build his great wall to keep out the Scots. He laid down the foundations of a smaller wall around Leicester and of a great basilica and forum, some remains of which can still be seen today. The one Roman legacy that is still very much in evidence today are their wonderful straight roads to move their armies quickly - the Fosse Way ran straight through Leicester whilst Watling Street formed the county's western boundary.

One legacy of the Danes, who later occupied Leicester for about a hundred years from 877 A.D., is our county structure. The army commander based in Leicester collected taxes for the Danish king, dubbed Danegeld, from the surrounding area, which we now know as Leicestershire. Similarly, Nottingham, Derby, Northampton, Lincoln, York, Warwick and Stafford were the collecting centres for their counties. Over a century later the Normans left their mark on the town, building a castle and some fine churches, amongst them St Mary de Castro.

Two other men of Leicester left their mark on both the town and the country in quite different ways. Simon de Montfort, Earl of Leicester, was actually French, but he made an impact on England that survives to this day. He was the leader of a rebellion by Barons against Henry III, calling two parliaments to remove the King's power, in the second of which leading citizens from towns throughout England were included for the first time. It is regarded as the birth of our system of parliamentary democracy. He was killed a year later, in 1265. Parliament actually met in Leicester in 1414 and 1450. The De Montfort Hall stands as a reminder of his link to the city. Another Leicester man to make his mark was Thomas Cook, who ran the world's first day excursion by train from Leicester to Loughborough in 1841. He went on to create what is regarded as the first tour company, which was still going strong 175 years later.

Getting back to modern times I boarded a train in 1953 to Cambridge to take the Entrance Exam. I was given a room in Sidney Sussex College. The entrance from the busy street was inconspicuous enough, in comparison with those of most other colleges, but once over the threshold there was that same tranquillity and sense of timelessness that all the colleges possess. You feel as if you are entering a closed community insulated from the real world outside and, in a sense, you are. The weathered stonework looked as if it had been there forever.

We had supper in the dining room, seated at long, wide tables under a high roof and surrounded by walls covered in large oil paintings, all adding to that sense of time standing still. I liked it, but felt a bit out of place.

The next day we sat the first paper, again surrounded by huge oil paintings. I found this very distracting and, for the purpose of taking an exam, would have preferred a much starker room in a more mundane building. The questions were difficult, as I expected, but not impossible to answer, and I felt I had done reasonably well. On the last day I had an interview at Christ's, mainly about my background and what made me tick. It was very informal and relaxing. I said that I liked cricket, football, cycling, going to the cinema and the theatre and reading, so he asked what I was currently reading. He was surprised when I said that I liked reading plays and was currently working my way through George Bernard Shaw's works. Finally, he asked if there was anything I would like to ask him and I said "how do you manage to do a degree course whilst playing cricket for the university?" "Good question", he said.

I have no idea if I handled that interview well, but I learned soon afterwards that I would not be offered a place that year. The Headmaster, however, was very optimistic about my prospects for getting an offer if I sat the exams again, but whether that was as a result of what the university had said or just his own feelings was not clear. However, I said that I would not be taking them again, but would try to get a place at another university. He was disappointed and asked my parents to come and see him. Mum came and the Headmaster tried hard to persuade me to change my mind. He appealed to Mum, but she said "if he doesn't want to go then he isn't going" and that was that. Several others in my year went on to Cambridge. I was clever enough, but I know that being clever is not all you need: they had shown the application and commitment that I lacked. It might have turned out differently without the Bert Howard incident and my dad's problems. On the other hand perhaps I got what I deserved. It was not until I entered the world of work that I fully regained that drive and motivation to succeed.

I found plenty to do outside school. Whilst I was addicted to the cinema for the escapism and optimism it provided I also developed a love of the theatre from my middle teens onwards. Once I had tasted it I was hooked. The event that is most vivid in my mind is seeing "Oklahoma", the musical that set the standard for everything that followed. It had recently completed a sell-out run at Drury Lane, with Howard Keel as the leading man, and came to Leicester on a UK tour. I saw the billboards advertising it on my way to school. I got a ticket, but did not know what to expect. The word "memorable" hardly does it justice. It was electrifying. The audience had heard nothing like it before and was ecstatic. Song after song was applauded to the rafters and encore after encore was demanded. We left the theatre as if walking on air. I have had nothing since to compare to that theatrical experience. I was sold on musicals and saw "Kiss Me Kate" there soon afterwards.

I had started going to the Theatre Royal as part of my theatre critic duties at school. Ticket prices were then very cheap and not just the preserve of the well-heeled, as they are nowadays. A seat in the gallery was just 5p in today's money. The Saxon Players provided a repertory programme of modern and classic plays and Colin Atkins and I would go quite regularly on Saturday nights, alternating with motor-bike racing at the Leicester Speedway track – quite a contrast. Sadly, both the Royal Opera House and the Theatre Royal have now gone, the first in 1960 and the second in 1957. Both were old, classic buildings, of a size and architecturally on a par with the grandest theatres in London, and would still exist today had they been listed, as they should have been, but the '50s and '60s were a time of pulling down and rebuilding, not preserving. What a waste.

Yet another, The Palace Theatre, is also no longer with us. It was pulled down in 1959, 158 years after it was built. It was a spectacular but garish building, bringing a bit of Moorish Spain to the Midlands. Whilst it seemed out of place in Leicester, the local people loved it and it was a thriving place of entertainment in its day until television came along in the '50s and audiences dwindled: it had to close. It was an enormous place, the largest theatre outside London, seating 3,500. It specialised in variety, putting on two performances every evening, except Sundays, of course, because that day was supposedly reserved for worship. It was one of the first stops in the country for variety acts on tour outside London. All the big names performed here – Charlie Chaplin, Dan Leno, Marie Lloyd, Will Hay, Harry Lauder, Robb Wilton, Max Miller, Ted Ray, Jimmy James, Peter Sellers, Benny Hill, Terry Thomas, Michael Bentine, Jewel & Warriss and a very young Shirley Bassey. There would be some seven or eight acts per show. There would always be two comedy acts and usually one or more singers, acrobats, trapeze artists or gymnasts and a short sketch, often a Victorian melodrama. I only went a few times, because it was not really my cup of tea, but I enjoyed it when I did go. I laughed at Max Miller, with his outrageous costume and double-entendre patter and at Jimmy James. A seat in the gallery for juniors was even cheaper there than at the other two theatres – just over 1p in today's money.

I was very lucky to live in a city like Leicester, which had so many venues hosting top events. Over the years I saw some great artists at the Granby Halls and the De Montfort Hall. The one that gave me the greatest pleasure was Danny Kaye, the American entertainer. I had seen him in two recent films, "The Secret Life of Walter Mitty" and "White Christmas", with Bing Crosby and Rosemary Clooney, which are now classics, so to see this famous star in the flesh was a bit of magic. He was such an engaging character, telling stories and singing the songs that would make him a household name, such as "There once was an ugly duckling", "Inchworm" and "Wonderful, wonderful Copenhagen". He came down from the stage, singing as he walked along the aisles and had the audience spell-bound.

Having rejected the option of taking the Cambridge Entrance Exam again I decided to apply to Birmingham and Leeds Universities to read mathematics and went for interviews. They were quite different. Leeds was all grey stone and cold whilst Birmingham was red brick and warm. Leeds was the more physically impressive, but not very intimate. It was more like the headquarters of a great company or banking group. Birmingham, on the other hand, felt and looked like a lived-in place of learning, set in a very green and leafy part of Birmingham, and I warmed to it immediately. When Birmingham offered me a place to study mathematics (with physics) I accepted immediately. The clinching factor was the discovery that Bill Slater, my football and sporting hero, had been appointed their first Director of Physical Education and I would be able to join in football and other sports training. I couldn't wait. I took and passed my A-level exams again, although I did not need to because my earlier grades were good enough to secure my place. I applied for a grant from Leicester City Council and was awarded £195 per annum. That was to cover all accommodation and living expenses and other costs of being a student. It did not seem much but, when supplemented by earnings from holiday jobs, it was enough. I was lucky that I did not have to pay for any tuition fees, unlike today's generation. From the moment I went to Birmingham I became completely financially independent of my parents, which must have been a great relief to them.

With my place at Birmingham secured I could relax and enjoy the summer of 1954. Colin Atkins and I decided to go on a cycling and camping holiday around southern England. We didn't have a tent so we decided to make one using war surplus balloon cloth, which was being sold off very cheaply. It was tough and very light and ideal, therefore, for carrying on a bike. At least that was the theory. The problem we had was in making it watertight. Colin had decided against going to university and had started work at a firm which made chemical products, including a new waterproofing solution. It was not yet available commercially, but Colin said he could get sufficient to treat our new tent. We designed it to be small so as to keep down the bulk and weight – in practice it turned out to be far too small. Mum helped us to stitch it together with her sewing machine and Colin got it waterproofed. We went on a so-called "dry run", camping overnight in a farmer's field in East Leicestershire. It certainly wasn't dry. It rained and it was almost as wet inside the tent as outside. The waterproofing was a complete failure. It was either the product itself or the way we had applied it, but it didn't work. We ended up buying a proven waterproofing product, which did the trick.

We set off full of optimism, but the holiday proved far from restful. By the time we had got to Bude on the north Cornwall coast we had had enough of camping and found a cheap B&B for our first good night's sleep in days. We cut our losses and came home by the quickest route we could find. Two lovely memories, though, stayed with me. The first was riding along Dorset lanes with the outline of Dorchester in the distance though a sea of golden fields on a beautiful summer's evening. It was England at its best, the kind of scene that Hollywood films strive for and we had it for free. The second was the exhilaration of riding down Porlock Hill in Somerset and trusting that your brakes would be good enough to stop. They were.

I also spent several weeks that summer working in the gardens of Quenby Hall, a beautiful Jacobean country house in East Leicestershire, about seven miles from Leicester. It was a large country estate with extensive formal gardens and a walled kitchen garden. The school had been asked to supply a few boys to help the head gardener with basic maintenance work. I loved it, especially working in the vegetable and fruit gardens. I saw peaches for the first time growing in the greenhouse on one of the garden walls. I had no idea that such exotic fruits could be grown in England. It was here that Stilton cheese was first made commercially in the mid

18th century by the Hall's owner. It was transported the short journey to the Bell Inn at Stilton on the Great North Road, where coaches travelling north and south would stop to change horses and passengers would take refreshments. The fame of the cheese spread and it became known as Stilton.

Whilst we were quietly working in the gardens the owner of the house, Sir Anthony Nutting, Minister of State for Foreign Affairs in Harold MacMillan's government, was negotiating a treaty with President Nasser for the withdrawal of troops from the Suez Canal after the President announced his intention to nationalise the canal. Securing guaranteed access to the canal was vital for British shipping moving between Europe and the Far East and Nasser's move created a major international crisis, which Sir Anthony was trying to defuse. He succeeded and a treaty was signed. However, two years later he resigned from the government when he learned of British and French plans to invade Egypt, with which he strongly disagreed. That effectively ended Sir Anthony's political career, which had looked so promising. He had become MP for nearby Melton Mowbray, at only 25 years old, and the youngest member of Winston Churchill's Government after the war. He had a glittering future ahead and Harold MacMillan thought that he would lead the Conservative Party one day, but it all came to an abrupt end on a matter of principle.

I was oblivious to such momentous events happening so close to where I was working. I was enjoying the baking hot sun and the work itself. We had to start early. I had to cycle about two miles to Scraptoft where we transferred to a farm truck, which took us to Quenby Hall. I missed it one day and had to cycle a further five miles to the hall, and back again after work! We left our bikes by the roadside, quite sure that they would not be stolen or damaged, and they weren't. That part of Leicestershire is completely rural and unspoilt still. It is prime hunting country. Sir Anthony was Master of the famous Quorn Hunt. It is a very beautiful landscape of rolling hills, huge country estates, large and well managed farms and tiny villages. It bears comparison with more well-known and lauded landscapes in England. By the time I had finished my stint there I was completely relaxed and brown as a berry. The next stop was Birmingham.

Chapter 4

Birmingham Independence

I loved my time at Birmingham, right from the start. I was independent and free to make my own choices. I had my own bed to sleep in, which was such a joy after years of sharing with Terry. I did not have my own bedroom, though, sharing one with Gordon Mallows, a dour and unadventurous geography student from Tyneside with whom I had absolutely nothing in common. There were very few Halls of Residence then and I was placed in lodgings in a large early Victorian house in Edgbaston, the leafy and very attractive part of Birmingham. Close by was the Edgbaston County Cricket ground, home to Warwickshire C.C.C., where I would later watch England play, and the very popular Calthorpe and Canon Hill Parks. It was a welcome contrast to Belgrave's treeless, uniform streets.

There were six other lodgers. Derrick Swann was studying Zoology. He would become a close friend of mine and of my future wife for the rest of our lives. He came from rural Suffolk, which we would get to know very well over the coming years. Bryn Jones was a State

Scholar studying Chemistry. He had a green open-top Morgan sports car and was very proud of it. A large leather belt strapped round the bonnet keep it intact and the engine had to be sparked into life using the starting handle. Lifts in it to the university were always a bit of an adventure. It was also a passion-wagon, judging by Bryn's tales of conquests on a Saturday night – the Medical School and nurses' accommodation were handily placed next to the university. Some forty years later I heard his lilting Welsh voice ring out as I walked through my home town – "Hey you, stop. I know you". We met up and reminisced. He was still a great talker. Other lodgers included two medical students and Alan, an engineer, who had a powerful motorbike on which I would get occasional lifts. We all got on pretty well together.

There was the occasional burst of political argument between us during the run-up to the 1955 General Election, won by the Tories under Anthony Eden. I went to one hustings in the cobble-stoned Bull Ring in the town centre which drew a large and noisy crowd. The next big political issue to stir us up was the nationalisation of the Suez Canal by Colonel Nasser in 1956 and the botched attempt by France and Britain to stop him, which polarised opinion amongst the student population. I was against it. That episode ruined Prime Minister Anthony Eden, who was condemned by the rest of the world.

Getting to the university involved a walk to the Bristol Road and a tram ride down the tree-lined road. The city had a bad image. Its reputation was that of a place of industry and little else, dubbed variously as "the workplace of the world" and "the city of a thousand trades". Those who did not know it saw it as a pretty bleak place blackened by the smoke of hundreds of factories. There was certainly plenty of smoke, but it was now mainly from household fires. I can recall one evening when the combination of smoke and fog, or "smog", as it was known, was so bad that I could literally not see a hand in front of my face and walked straight into a lamppost. I got a lump the size of an egg on my head. This was before the Clean Air Act came into force, which banned coal fires and led to the cleaning up of public buildings. Much of Birmingham, though, even then was very attractive and Edgbaston was, to my mind, a lovely place to be, but then I was young and ready to be impressed. I was to discover that there was more to Birmingham than factories. It has undergone quite a transformation since my time there and has recently been voted one of the top tourist destinations in the world.

Freshers' Week gave us the chance to get to know our way around the university, attend a lot of introductory meetings, and find out about our courses and what you can do apart from study. We kicked off with a pep-talk from the Vice-Chancellor in The Great Hall. "Don't waste your time here" was his main message. "Get enthusiastic, even passionate, about something. This is the time of your life to energise yourself, so don't spend all your time working", he stressed. I don't know if I misinterpreted his talk, but I embraced that philosophy rather too enthusiastically, I think. Not that I regret it, but I certainly didn't get the balance right.

The Great Hall was entered via a flight of steps in the centre of the main campus buildings. The campus itself is dominated by "Old Joe", named after Joseph

Chamberlain, the university's first Chancellor, dubbed "the finest Prime Minister the country never had". This landmark, 361 ft. high, is the tallest clock tower in the world and visible across the whole city. It looks Italian, its design based on the Town Hall tower in Sienna and similar to the Campanile in St Marks Square in Venice, both of which I would visit some years later. It sits in the centre of Chancellor's Court, a large, circular expanse of grass and pathways surrounded by a continuous series of redbrick buildings, inset with large stone mullioned windows and terracotta friezes around the top of the walls. Although it does not have the honeyed mellowness of Oxbridge colleges the overall effect is impressive and eye-catching. I found a lot of things impressive in that first week.

We were given our timetable of lectures and practical course work. Although I was studying mathematics, the course also included quite a bit of physics, whilst about ten of us did a full mathematical physics course, effectively two degrees in one. That was hard, but the ones who took this course were both very bright and, more importantly, very focussed and hard working. Years later I learned that, after graduating, a number of them moved to the USA and Canada and became professors or held other senior academic positions, whilst others did well academically or otherwise in the UK. Birmingham's Physics Department had attracted a lot of very bright students because Prof. Peierls, its head, had a huge world-wide reputation. He had been one of the key members of the small team that worked at Los Alamos in the USA on the development of the world's first atomic bomb, which ended the 2nd World War. He gave the hydrodynamics lectures, which I thoroughly enjoyed. The head of the Mathematics Department was Prof. Rogers, an expert in number theory, which I found the most interesting of all the subjects we studied. It was the nearest we got to pure, abstract logic, which is what mathematics is fundamentally all about and what appeals most to me. I would have a brush with him later, which probably did not help my cause.

Dr Mulholland, a senior lecturer, was assigned to me as someone to turn to if I had any problems. He was very pleasant. We had cups of tea and cake from time to time in his room, but nothing of significance was aired, except one contentious request I made to him, which I will explain later. What I really needed, though, was someone to act as a tutor, keeping my nose to the grindstone and reminding me why I was there. There were too many distractions – sport, bridge, drinking, sex, entertainment, student activities – which left too little time for work.

I learnt very quickly that the focus of student life was the large Student Union building, which sat at the entrance to the university grounds and opposite the Barber Institute of Fine Arts. If you were at all sociable this was the place to be. It was here that Freshers signed up for different Societies or activities. Practically everyone doing mathematics joined the Mathematics Society. It was very active, holding regular meetings, with talks by visiting speakers, plus sporting and social events and an annual dinner. I decided to get involved in it. I was elected to the committee as its first year (Freshers') Representative, then its Secretary in the second year and Chairman in the third. Because we had a number of very sport-minded members I extended considerably both the range and number of sporting events, including a match against the University Ladies Lacrosse team, which was a nerve-racking experience as we tried to avoid getting whacked. We played hockey, basketball and a lot of soccer matches, amounting to about one fixture every week.

I also set up reciprocal visits with Mathematical Societies at nearby universities. This is where I came unstuck. Nottingham University invited us to visit them and to look around an industrial site (Boots or Raleigh). This had to be on a Wednesday when the afternoon was always free for university sporting activities and there were only a few, if any, lectures in the morning. I undertook to approach the lecturers affected to see if they were agreeable to rearranging their lectures. The first was Dr Mulholland, who saw no problem, so I was encouraged to go on. The others all agreed, too. We went ahead and the visit was a great success. However, there was a major rumpus the following day when I had an urgent summons to see Prof. Rogers. He was absolutely livid, almost spitting blood. "How dare you interfere with my timetable? What right have you to act unilaterally in this way?" I explained that the staff member on the committee had agreed to this visit and saw no difficulties, and neither did the lecturers affected, but it was to no avail. He would not be mollified and I left on bad terms, which may have not helped my cause sometime later.

Another bit of the committee's planning went awry, too. Each year the whole university throws itself into Rag Week to raise money for charities. Our contribution one year was an ambitious project to build a space rocket, mount it on a lorry and parade it through the town alongside other "floats". The end product was very impressive and we set off to wow the spectators lining the streets, only to find that it was too tall and fell foul of telephone wires stretched across the road, breaking two feet off the top. We limped on, but it had lost its impact and only got a few sympathy donations.

My final duty as Chairman of the Society was to act as host at its Annual Dinner and to propose the toast to the Department. This went well. Prof. Peierls, President of the Society, responded graciously and my duties came to an end. I got the autographs of everyone on the top table, including Prof. Rogers, who seemed to have got over our spat.

I also signed up for football, basketball and cricket. There was a large turnout for the first football training session where I met Bill Slater, who had been the deciding factor in my coming to Birmingham. It would have been terribly disillusioning to find that he did not come up to expectations, but he did. He was everything I hoped he would be. Not only was he a brilliant coach, but he had great personality and the time just flew by. I learned a lot of technical skills, which we all practised until we had mastered them, and a great deal more about how to read a game and use space creatively. I was an inside forward, preferably on the right, but I could play on the left, as well. In my first match, for the fifth team, I think, I scored four goals and was picked for the third team in the next game. I scored again and was moved up to the second team, where I stayed for the rest of that year and the next two. Much to my annoyance I was never once picked for the first team where I would then have joined my closest friend, Dave Angove, who played on the left wing and was absolutely brilliant. He had played for his county as a schoolboy and was good enough to turn professional, had he wanted to. The first team's inside right was a very skilful Welshman, who was never once injured in his three years there: good for him, but bad for me.

The pattern for both football and cricket teams was to play matches involving short journeys on Wednesday afternoons, but to travel further afield at weekends. Most of the cricket 1st X1's weekend matches were against the larger town clubs in the Midlands and these were good games, but the football team played other universities or colleges, involving some long journeys.

I decided to play basketball simply because Bill Slater was also the coach for that. It was a game that suited me because in those days I was fast and nimble and knew how to make space for the telling pass. I ended up playing for the university first team. In one game I was the only Englishman. The others were all from the USA and Canada plus one Pole. At six feet tall I was also the shortest.

In the summer I played my first cricket match for the university, against Loughborough College, which was not then a university, but had a reputation for being strong on sport. I had a good game, taking some wickets and being not out in our innings, and was promoted to the second team where I stayed for the rest of that year. I was moved up to the first team in the next year, where I stayed throughout my time at Birmingham, batting at number four and occasionally opening. I had changed from bowling off-spin to bowling fast, opening the bowling for the second team and being a change bowler for the first team. I got my top score of 84 against Tamworth Town, throwing away my chance of a century with my only careless shot – cricket is a cruel game.

I did not get my colours because I declined to go on the tour to other universities in the summer holidays. I could not afford to. I needed to work to get enough money to pay my way throughout the rest of the year.

My most enjoyable game was against Bournville. The club was right in the middle of the green and pleasant garden village built for its workers by Cadburys, the chocolate manufacturers, who were Quakers and socialists. The ground was like a mini County ground with tiered terraces and a fine pavilion: the playing area itself was immaculate. We played them on a sunny weekend, so there was a good sprinkling of spectators and a nice atmosphere. The club was very hospitable. It was a great advert for the game of cricket.

My most disappointing game was in my final year against Walsall Town, which was a very strong club. I was going out then with Ann Tame. She lived in Walsall, and her mother and father came down to see me perform and I desperately wanted to do well, but didn't. I opened the batting and was out lbw in the third over for only two runs. It was a long, slow trudge back to the pavilion.

As if all this activity wasn't enough of a distraction from my studies I took up playing contract bridge. We played in the Students Union Common Room and some fifty years later a fellow student reminded me how I had taught him Van Goren's Point Count System, which was in vogue at the time - I was the only one who had the book explaining it! That system would, in time, give way to the Culbertson System, which would itself be superseded by Acol. I had played a lot of cards at home, partnering mum sometimes at whist drives, so bridge was a natural progression. It would have been better, though, if I had waited until after completing my course before taking it up, because it was very time-consuming.

The first year raced by. I did just about enough work to pass the end of year exams and carry on into the second on the honours course, but many didn't. A large number were sent down whilst a few were given the option of taking a general degree. Perhaps they had simply not been good enough to do a degree course, but I suspect it was more to do with the way we were taught and the lack of tutoring. I went home for the Christmas break and, like many students, worked at the Post Office, sorting and delivering letters, which I enjoyed doing. It put me in the Christmas spirit and brought me into contact with some of my old school friends, most of whom were at Cambridge. After Christmas I worked as a porter on the London, Midland and Scottish Railway Station in the town centre. I would repeat this pattern in the next two Christmas holidays, but thereafter would spend only one Christmas at home.

I did not go home in the summer at the end of the first year, but stayed on and took a job in Birmingham at the City and Guilds Institute, which ran courses throughout the country on a wide range of practical and academic subjects, with the emphasis on the vocational. My job was to apply a statistical formula for adjusting the exam results where there were thought to be significant differences in the marking. It paid well, was easy to do and I was surrounded by a lot of attractive females, so the time passed very pleasantly.

I had become great friends with Dave Angove, who was also on my course, and we went on holiday that summer to Cornwall with a friend of his. Dave's father was a Methodist Minister and it was standard practice to move parishes every three years. He was then in Helston, but had been to many parts of the county over the years. Drinking alcohol was strictly prohibited by Methodists and Dave was paranoid about being recognised if we went into a pub and word got back to his father, so we had to avoid them, which cramped our style a bit. He relented, though, when we finished our holiday at Looe and we had a good evening to round off a good holiday.

In the second year Dave and I decided to share a room in lodgings in Kings Heath, a short bus ride and a walk from the university. Our landladies were two ex-Tiller Girls, the famous high-kicking dance company. They were absolute dears and looked after us very well. When they heard that it was my 21st birthday in March of my final year they laid on a lovely lunch for me. My sister, Sheila, and her friend Christine, came all the way from Leicester for the occasion. The table was set out beautifully and they even provided drinks. They were very kind.

The most significant event in the second year, and of my life, was at the Saturday night "hop" in the Students Union where I usually ended up after a football or cricket match. Ann Tame, who was doing Zoology with Derrick, was there, but on her own. She had been going out with a medical student, Tony Lavelle, for over a year, but was not with him that night. We knew each other initially through Derrick because she would come to our lodgings in Edgbaston in order to go to concerts with him. I noticed her and was attracted to her, but did nothing about it. I had seen her walking hand in hand with Tony across the playing fields when I was hurrying to a cricket match and I thought she was hooked up with him. We would often sit together with others in the university refectory and my liking for her grew. Later on we would chat on our way to the bus to Kings Heath, where she lodged with Janet Philips, a beautiful Elizabeth Taylor look-a-like. That night at the "hop" was when it all changed. There was no spare seat and I offered Ann my seat or my lap. She chose my lap and the rest is history. We started going out together and would eventually marry.

Ann belonged to The Wayfarers Society and we went sailing with them on the Norfolk Broads, starting at Wroxham. Our skipper learned his sailing on the Clyde, so we felt in good hands. On the first day the weather went from calm to gale force very quickly. We reached Malthouse Broad and immediately took in part of the mainsail, but saw that one of the boats in our party just ahead was in trouble. Some of its crew had gone off in the yacht's dinghy, which had capsized. The skipper of the yacht must have been reared on "Boys Own" and other adventure comics because he dived into the water and swam towards the dinghy, leaving just one totally inexperienced female to steer the yacht. She shouted desperately for help. Our skipper, who was also a bit of a "Boys Own" type, sailed close to her, telling her to let go of the sails, which would have caused the yacht to slow down and stop, but she was in a panic and insisted on keeping hold of the ropes, so it kept lurching forward at speed. He decided that the only option was to ram her into the reeds, which he did, but at the cost of causing a large hole in the hull of our own yacht. We managed to get on board and calm the young woman down and then turned our attention to the capsized dinghy and crew. The irony was that when we got to them we found them standing in just four feet of water, so our heroics weren't needed after all. The Broads had been created by digging out vast peat beds for use as fuel and were not at all deep. We limped back to Wroxham for repairs. It was all very exciting.

I got through the exams at the end of the second year successfully and decided to stay in Birmingham and work over the summer holidays, partly to earn money, but also because I could visit Ann in Walsall. I worked in the wages department of John Lewis, which was very boring, but paid well. The university had a short break in mid-February and a group of us, including Ann and Derrick, went to London for two nights, specifically to see "Salad Days", the Julian Slade/Dorothy Reynolds musical which captured beautifully the innocence and optimism of students as they contemplated life after university. It was a show that captured both our mood and the country's, and it went on to be the longest running musical until "Les Miserables" overtook it.

In my last year, with my Finals exams looming, I set about finding a job. There were plenty on offer. The number of graduates was small and the demand for them exceeded supply, so it was a buyers' market. Larger companies set out their stalls in a "Jobs Fair" on the university playing fields, whilst others posted vacancies on display boards. I chose three to explore further. The newly formed Nuclear Power Group was looking for a mathematician/phycisist to join a small research group based in Knutsford, Cheshire. I went for an interview and was offered a job, which I eventually turned down. I had two follow-up letters urging me to reconsider, arguing that I would be in at the start of a new industry and implying, more or less, that I would be mad not to accept.

I also applied to go on a teacher training course because I liked the idea of combining teaching and taking part in school sports activities. I was warmly welcomed, of course, but turned this down, too. Again, I got follow-up letters urging me to reconsider, but I had, by then, settled on my third option. This was as an aeroelastician working on a Ministry of Supply contract to design, build and test five model aircraft capable of flying above the speed of sound. It was part of the programme to develop the world's first supersonic airliner, which would later emerge as Concord. As soon as I walked into the Design Office of Armstrong Whitworth Aircraft Company at Coventry I knew that this was where I wanted to work. There was a buzz about the place. It exuded energy and endeavour. I also took a liking to Joe Staite, the Assistant Chief Designer (Development), who was responsible for New Projects Section, in which I would work. When I was offered the job I accepted immediately.

I learned later that, because I was to work on a government contract considered to be important to our national interest, the job carried with it exemption from doing two years National Service, which all men under twenty six had to do. By the time I reached that age National Service had been abolished, so I missed out on two years playing lots more sport and getting three square meals a day. I would not have minded doing it.

When the end of year results came out I was disappointed, but not that surprised, to get only a lower 2nd, but that was good enough to secure the job. In truth, it was no more than I deserved given the minimal effort I had put in. My hopes had been raised, however, when my elasticity course lecturer said after the exams that: "You will be alright. You did very well". I took that to mean that, against all the odds, I might get an upper 2nd or better. If all lecturers had approached their subjects as he did then I might have been alright. Only a handful of us had opted for his course, so his lectures were very interactive and almost personal and we developed a very close relationship with him. He would routinely set us questions and discuss our responses the following week. I imagine that is rather like the tutorial system practised at Oxbridge colleges, where you undergo a critical examination of your understanding of the course's subject matter on a routine basis. That way you really get to grips with the subject. I enjoyed studying elasticity and it had a direct bearing on my decision to go into the aircraft industry as an aeroelastician.

The other lecturers operated differently. They took the easy route, standing in front of the class and writing on the blackboard, relying on students to capture the pearls of wisdom whilst taking rapid notes. There was no follow-up, no testing of your understanding of the subject matter until the end of year exams. It was a poor way of imparting knowledge. The only way you could get to grips with the subject matter was to read the set books. We might just as easily have been given printed handouts of each lecture. Attending many of these lectures was almost a waste of time and I missed several, relying on my fellow students to fill me in afterwards about what was covered.

Surprisingly, I was still second out of those taking mathematics. There was one upper second, one other lower second and the others all got thirds. Those taking mathematical physics did much better, many getting firsts, so it was possible. My room-mate, Dave Angove, was ill with glandular fever for months leading up to the exams and could not take them, staying on for another year. Sadly, I lost track of him after I left, despite trying to keep in touch, but heard that he was given an aegrotat degree.

Mum and Dad came to see me graduate. The coloured gowns, the formal ceremony and the Great Hall setting, surrounded by huge stained glass windows, reminded mum of a coronation, she said. She was absolutely thrilled and very proud. I exhausted them showing them round the university and where I lodged, but it was a memorable day for them and for me.

Finally, Ann and I went to the Graduation Ball, which was the last time we would see most of those we had studied with. Fifty years later I went to a reunion to mark the 50th anniversary of our graduation, but only one other from my year came despite my contacting all of them by e-mail. I got a lot of interesting replies. Many of those who had taken mathematical physics had done very well indeed, mostly abroad. Sadly, two had already died. I could not trace Dave Angove, though, which was very disappointing. I hope he has had a good life, but I suspect he may not.

I was not sad to leave Birmingham. I had a great time there, but it was time to move on and do something useful and I was looking forward to the job in Coventry. What was desperately sad, though, was that Ann and I were going our separate ways. She had accepted a job in Huntingdon at an animal research centre. I wanted to get engaged, but she said no, quite rightly, because it was too soon to take that step. What I needed to do was to keep courting her, even though we were miles apart, and convince her that I was the one she should marry. That's what I did.

Chapter 5

Coventry

A Flying Start

So I moved to Coventry and stayed there for seven years. They were very good years. I enjoyed the work and my personal life just got better and better. Coventry had the feel of a vibrant and prosperous city. The UK car industry was born here and this was its golden age, before foreign competitors captured the market. It seemed that every other car on the roads was a Jaguar. An ambitious new theatre, The Belgrade, opened in 1958. There were successful sports clubs -Coventry Rugby Club and Coventry City Football Club; and some of the UK's leading car manufacturers – Jaguar, Armstrong-Siddeley, Triumph, Rover, Riley, Healey, Humber and Hillman; plus the world's leading motor bike manufacturers. The world's first man-made fibre, viscose rayon, was being manufactured at Courtaulds. Twenty five years later it would have collapsed into a place of high unemployment and rising crime, but in 1957 it was a good place to be.

Coventry was also an ancient city, its origins pre-dating the Romans. It thrived in the Middle Ages when it was the capital of England for a while. That historic past was wiped away in one barbaric night in November 1940 when the old medieval city centre was reduced to rubble by the German Luftwaffe. It was attacked again on other nights, leaving over 800 people killed and two thirds of the city's industrial sites badly damaged. It was a deliberate act by Hitler to destroy our morale and our manufacturing capability. Once the war was over it was rebuilt, but with the most unattractive, utilitarian buildings imaginable. Concrete was all the rage. Whereas the National Theatre in London showed how to make good use of this material in the hands of a great architect, the overall effect in Coventry was dreary and drab. Its sole virtue was that you could rebuild quickly and cheaply. The one good bit was the cathedral. It was decided to retain the ruins of the old building and to rebuild alongside it. What brought it to life was the tapestry of Jesus Christ by Graham Sutherland, which dominates one end. The statue of Lady Godiva survived the bombing. She had ridden naked through its streets in the 11th century in protest at the high taxes being levied by her husband, who ran the place. The term Peeping Tom derives from the one man who did not turn his head away when she passed by and was reputedly struck blind.

My lodgings, adjacent to Greyfriars Green and close to the town centre, were just a short bus ride to Whitley, on the outskirts of the city, and the Design Office of the Sir W.G. Armstrong-Whitworth Aircraft Company, to give it its full name, or AWA for short. It was an enormous open space, more like an aircraft hanger than an office, with desks placed end to end in rows facing each other. Most desks carried a Friden calculator on which staff would be busy tapping away. These were the desk-top computers of their day, enabling quite sophisticated calculations to be carried out quickly. They were expensive. The noise from these plus the chatter and the ringing of telephones was deafening at times, but it created an atmosphere of great activity and energy, which was infectious. You did not see people twiddling their thumbs or talking aimlessly.

At the far side of the office were ranks of draughtsmen, perched high up on their swivel chairs in front of enormous draughtsman's boards. Down one side glass-fronted offices housed the departmental heads. I was taken to see Joe Staite, Assistant Chief Designer (Development), who was responsible for New Projects Section. With his handlebar moustache and mop of tousled hair he could have been taken straight out of a boys' adventure storybook. He only needed a flying helmet to complete the picture. He introduced me to the two Section Heads, the hefty Arthur Cleaver (Structures) and the wafer thin Vic Page (Aerodynamics), to whom I reported.

New Projects Section was quite small - just twelve of us. We got on like a house on fire. Terry Carter and Geoff Nash, two brilliant Cambridge mathematicians, were the pick of the bunch academically, but together we brought a lot of brain-power and tremendous energy to our work. Our conditions of service made no concessions to the fact that we were graduates working in an office. We were treated in the same way as workers in the nearby production factory at Baginton. We were paid weekly in cash, queuing up on a Friday afternoon to receive and sign for our pay packets. I was paid twelve pounds and five shillings a week (£624 p.a.), but earned more by working overtime. Most of our Section worked overtime on Saturday morning. We had no pension provision. We had to "clock on" before 8.30 a.m. and "clock off" after 5.30 p.m. when a piercing siren would sound. Being late was frowned upon and your wages could be cut. We had short tea breaks in the morning and afternoon and a longer lunch break. The siren would mark the start and finish of all these breaks and we were expected to resume work immediately. Some days that was just enough time for Terry, Geoff, Tom Marsh and me to complete the Daily Telegraph crossword.

This regime sounds draconian, but we did not resent it. We did, however, have a rebellion on pay when we received derisory small annual pay rises. Instead of showing players' names on our football team sheet, which we regularly displayed outside Joe Staite's office, we put each player's weekly wage. Joe was not at all pleased, but took it in good humour. It did the trick and eventually we got a bigger increase.

Such was the camaraderie in the Design Office that it had its own cricket and football teams, which I played for. We played other parts of AWA, such as the draughtsmen and the guided missiles sections. In one of the football games I was playing against an ex-Derby County player, who was also in my lodgings, and he didn't like the way I was controlling the game, so he carried out what is known in the modern game as a professional foul, clattering into my right ankle with both feet. I could not stand and was carried off the field by our goalkeeper, Ken Johnston, one of the largest men I have ever known. My foot was not broken, but the ligaments were damaged and it was very swollen, turning spectacular colours of red, purple, black and yellow before eventually returning to normal. I was on crutches for over a week.

I enjoyed these games, apart from that one, but it was the cricket matches that I looked forward to most. Lawrie Raffle, Chief Performance Engineer, was our popular captain. I took on the job of arranging the cricket fixtures, including several matches against village teams in Northamptonshire. That is still one of my favourite counties and, like East Leicestershire, is relatively unknown to most people. Its rolling hills enclose small villages of honey-coloured stone houses and thatched roofs, and big country estates that have held back rural expansion and industrialisation. Among my favourites was Badby, easily reached by car after work on a Friday night in mid-summer. Phil Harding would often give me a lift in his big, open-topped Jaguar. Ann came with me to one match and loved the ride, but her hair was blown as straight as a die by the time we arrived. We would collect after the match in the village pub for food and drink and play their version of skittles until the landlord threw us out. The drink-drive laws would not allow us to do that now. Another favourite was the match in the grounds of Catesby Hall, where the opposition had to clear away the herd of cattle and take down the barbed wire surrounding the cricket square before we could start. The cattle left their mark on the outfield, so it was not just the ball you had to watch carefully when fielding.

I certainly made the right decision by choosing to go to AWA. Not only was the work interesting, challenging and rewarding, but my colleagues were a joy to work with. Knowing that I was single and on my own at weekends some of my married colleagues were very kind and invited me to supper and sometimes to stay the night. I learned that Geoff Nash was a very good chess player and Tom Marsh and his wife liked playing canasta.

Sir Frank Whittle, inventor of the jet engine, was born and worked in Coventry and his son worked in our Design Office. He often lamented the way the UK Government had allowed the patent for his father's world-beating invention to pass to the USA and so lost us our competitive advantage. It was, of course, the quid quo pro for their support in the war and for their help in rebuilding our shattered and near bankrupt country afterwards.

New Projects Section's mission was to develop new aircraft and I had been taken on specifically to work on a Ministry of Aviation research project with the aim of creating the world's first supersonic airliner. AWA's role was to investigate the possibility of designing an airliner to carry about 100 passengers at a cruising speed of Mach 1.2, where Mach 1 was the speed of sound. It would have M-shaped wings. The thinking behind this design was that its swept back wings, rather like a seagull's, would avoid wing wave drag. The key question was whether it would be aero-elastically stable and that is what I had to find out.

AWA's contract was to design, build and fire five scaled-down rocket-propelled replicas of the proposed full–scale airliner. The five models had kinks at different points of each wing's span. The models were small - the rocket body was only 100 inches long and the wings either side only measured 24 inches. The plan was to fire them at Larkhill on Salisbury Plain, close to the Royal Aircraft Establishment (RAE) at Farnborough and capture data on frequencies of vibration and wing distortions as the rocket model went up to and beyond the speed of sound. We had to submit a final report to RAE, Farnborough by 31st December, 1960, giving us three years and four months from when I joined. We just made it.

AWA had a superb Experimental Shop and the best guided missiles capability in the country, so making the models and fitting them out was not likely to be a problem. The most likely problem area was mine because of the length of time it would take to do the analyses and calculations for five separate models. After completing the theoretical work and tedious calculations for one model, I concluded that I could speed up the work by making use of the company's brand new Ferranti Pegasus computer. I had learned all about this new phenomenon when playing cricket with Phil Harding, who was one of the company's two computer programmers. It sounded like the answer to my prayers and I persuaded my bosses to let me turn all my calculations into computer programmes. To modern ears that may sound small beer, but in 1958 it was revolutionary. It turned out to be a great success, but it was not without its problems.

Computers in those days were huge, their serried ranks of seven foot high grey metal cabinets filling a large room. They were packed full of valves, which generated tremendous heat, so they were replaced on a routine basis before they failed. In the summer months, when the temperature rose, several buckets of dry ice were placed around the room to cool it down. Breakdowns were commonplace. The input process, involving paper tape and temperamental tape readers, was another source of breakdown and frustration, but eventually we got there.

I got little supervision or direct help. It was left to me to develop the theory and use it to predict the models' aeroelastic behaviour, which I did, with the help of advice from RAE. I was only twenty one and wet behind the ears as an aeroelastician, but I had the confidence of youth, which counts for a lot. Now that I am much older, and have many grandchildren, I am constantly astonished at what they can achieve when they are motivated.

For each of the five models I needed answers to three questions - what were its natural modes of vibration; would it become unstable and break up because of either flutter or divergence, or both; and at what speeds and frequency of vibration?

All aircraft and other structures, such as bridges, have natural frequencies of vibration. If you sprinkle fine sand onto a plane's wing and increase its frequency of vibration there will come a point at which lines of sand will form which are stationary whilst the structure either side will be oscillating. You will have reached one of its natural frequencies of vibration. As you increase the frequency you will find others. The lines of sand indicate the modes of vibration (i.e. how the structure will bend at that frequency).

Flutter occurs when these natural modes of vibration are activated by the flow of air over the structure and the amplitude of the vibrations increases uncontrollably as the structure takes in energy from the airflow, leading to instability and structural failure. There have been some spectacular examples of this, and perhaps the most famous, because it was captured graphically on film, was the collapse of the Tacoma Narrows Bridge in Washington State in 1940. It was spectacular. The great iron bridge, buffeted by exceptionally high winds, heaves up and down and twists violently from side to side before dramatically breaking up and falling into the sea. Nearer home, AWA's own revolutionary Flying Wing, the AWA 52, broke up in 1949 whilst on a flight to test its airworthiness. The pilot was the first in history to eject safely from an aircraft in flight. Ironically, my boss, Joe Staite, worked on that project and it did his career no harm. That experience was etched into the collective memory of AWA's management, making them particularly sensitive to the problem of flutter, which would surface again in a big way with their new Argosy aircraft, on which I would later work.

The Tacoma Bridge disaster had been caused by flutter and its revolutionary structure was to blame. Using very thin, lightweight metal and a very long span between the supporting towers resulted in an exceptionally flexible structure with low natural modes of vibration. These were easily activated by the strong winds. To avoid this, therefore, the metal structure had to be stiffened to raise its natural frequencies of vibration. This is what they did.

The same principle applies in aircraft design. If flutter or divergence is calculated to occur at low speeds one option to cure it is to make the component parts thicker. However, this extra weight will require larger engines, thus increasing the cost of the aircraft and making it harder to sell at a competitive price. The Design Office's walls at AWA were covered with posters imploring the design staff to "Keep the weight down". There is a difficult balance to be struck between safety and competitiveness. Aviation industry standards err firmly on the side of safety.

I completed the theoretical calculations for the model with its kink at the midpoint of the wing's span by May 1958 and concluded that it would neither flutter nor diverge over the speed range of the flight test. I used the new computer programme to complete the work on the other four models. By the end of the year I had finished, well ahead of schedule, leaving me waiting for the physical models to be built, so that we could test them in flight.

The first of the models was completed in 1959 so we could carry out vibration tests on it. To my great delight and relief the results were in complete agreement with my calculations. We found six modes of vibration, the first at 25.2 cycles per second (I calculated 24.9c.p.s.) and the sixth at 385c.p.s. (calculated frequency 384.7c.p.s.). I now felt more confident about my other calculations and predictions. My report was well received by my bosses, resulting in me being drafted in to work on the AWA 650 Argosy, which had serious aeroelastic problems.

The Argosy was designed to be a general-purpose transport aircraft aimed at breaking into both the civil and military markets. Its large, bulbous fuselage hung beneath twin booms enabling its cargo to be directly loaded from the rear. It was a great floppy beast, not at all elegant – a sort of work-horse of the sky. If it met the market's needs and sold well that was all that mattered.

John Watts was responsible for the Argosy's aeroelastic work. I joined him at nearby Bitteswell Aerodrome where he was carrying out vibration tests. Because the Argosy was such a flexible structure its natural frequencies of vibration were very low, potentially giving rise to flutter problems at low speeds, and so it proved. Early test flights revealed serious problems and I was asked to identify and resolve them. In the short time available I succeeded in recreating the circumstances and matching the speed at which the flutter had occurred, but I could not recommend with confidence what to change in order to cure it. This was my first setback at work and it bothered me. I recall vividly a meeting with the Chief Designer, Eddie Keen, and my boss, Joe Staite, at which Eddie Keen said how disappointed he was that I had not found the solution he was looking for. I was crestfallen and annoyed that my boss, the much more experienced Joe Staite, just sat there and said nothing to help or support me. I was 22 years old and working effectively on my own to find the answers. I was resolved not to be beaten.

At its maiden flight on 8 January 1959 the Chief Test Pilot, Eric Franklin, was given orders not to exceed a very low maximum speed, calculated by me, in order to avoid flutter problems and potential disaster. As usual with maiden flights, Pathe News and other media outlets were invited to witness the flight in order to get maximum publicity. Afterwards Eric gave a press conference extolling the Argosy's virtues and waxing lyrical about how beautifully it handled, which the media lapped up. He was lying through his teeth. When he gave his staff debriefing afterwards it was a very different story. He was far from relaxed or happy. It was a bloody mess, he said, and we had to sort it out quickly.

Proving that a new aircraft is free of flutter is a crucial requirement for gaining its airworthiness certificate. It has to undergo stringent flight tests to prove it. We made further changes to the aircraft, but it still had flutter problems. A year after that maiden flight I finally sorted out the cause and proposed a cure for it. Changes were made and the flight results were at last positive. I was a relieved young man and so were the company's management and the Chief Test Pilot.

During all this time I was often at Bitteswell Aerodrome and got a lift back to the Baginton factory in a two-seater light aircraft, riding in the co-pilot's seat. I soon realised how much fun flying was. The plane itself looked and felt as if it could fall apart at any moment. The fin at the rear was joined to the tailplane by two thin wire struts and it all twanged and rattled noisily if you gave it a push. The pilot flew it as casually as I would ride an old bike. If there was something worth seeing down below he would lift his foot on the rudder pedal and swoop down to have a look and then swoop back up again. When we approached the grass airstrip at Baginton he would just clear the large oak tree at the end of the airfield and plunge straight down to the ground before landing perfectly. He obviously enjoyed it and so did I. It was probably the highlight of the day for him (and me).

In the midst of all this activity I was enjoying my private and social life. It was the fashion in the 1950s for large companies to provide sports and social facilities for their workforce. By keeping the workers happy they would, hopefully, be better workers. It also fostered a degree of loyalty and commitment to the company, so workers were less likely to leave. Cadburys, at Bournville, and other Quaker firms, were amongst the first, but industrial giants such as Unilever, at Port Sunlight, and Imperial Chemical Industries (ICI) also set a high standard. AWA and Armstrong Siddeley, which made cars, combined to provide shared facilities in Coventry under the name of "Sphinx". This came from the distinctive emblem on the bonnet of Armstrong Siddeley cars, similar to the jaguar on Jaguar cars. Employees enjoyed the use of extensive sports facilities for their rugby, soccer and cricket clubs. There was financial support, too, for the Sphinx Drama Group and other clubs. During the war the Sphinx Light Orchestra was formed, giving lunchtime concerts at Baginton and Whitley in order to boost workers' morale.

Soon after joining I got involved in the company's football and rugby clubs and in the Drama Group. I started by playing soccer, but a friend persuaded me to switch to rugby. We played other works teams in the Midlands, including Dunlop from Birmingham. They had a reputation for being tough and dirty, and they were. I was playing fly-half against them for the first XV and having a good game, when their open-side wing forward decided to target me and, after several late tackles, I was taken off with a groin injury. The dark bruise developed into phlebitis, which was potentially dangerous in those days, and I was off work for nearly two weeks until it cleared up. The rugby club decided that it had had enough and cancelled future fixtures with Dunlop. I stopped playing rugby and changed back to soccer, first for the Sphinx Football Club, which I did not enjoy, and later for Coventry Technical College, which I did.

In the summer I joined Coventry & North Warwickshire Cricket Club, which was much the best club in the area and one of the best in the Midlands. The standard was very high and I could not get into the first team. It was a nursery for budding professional cricketers. In recent years Ian Bell started there before playing for Warwickshire and England. Just before my time there

Tom Cartwright, a fast-medium bowler and useful middle order batsman, did the same. Inadvertently, he played a key part in the events that would lead eventually to the fall of the apartheid regime in South Africa.

Basil D'Oliveira, a very good coloured cricketer, had moved to England from South Africa because he was barred from playing with whites there. He played for England in the first test match against the Australians in 1968 and scored 87, but was dropped for the next match because the selectors wanted to avoid having to pick him for the coming tour of South Africa. There was a public outcry and he was reinstated for the final test match, scoring a magnificent 158 to clinch the win for England which squared the Ashes series. Still he was not selected for the tour, a decision that was widely condemned by the Labour government and commentators, so when Tom Cartwright was injured and withdrew from the touring party, the selectors finally chose Basil to replace him. The South Africa government made it clear that he would not be allowed to play there and the MCC cancelled the tour. The International Cricket Council banned South Africa from international cricket and it would be 26 years before that ban was lifted.

A colleague at AWA, Brian Pudner, persuaded me to join the Sphinx Drama Group. In March 1958 it put on "My Three Angels", a comedy by Sam & Bella Spewack, and I was Assistant Stage Manager. It went down well with audiences and I learned a lot about the practicalities of staging a play and getting it to run smoothly on the night. Actors get all the attention and credit, but I became more aware of how important backstage staff are to a play's success and how little credit they get. That experience emboldened me to offer to produce and direct the next play. I proposed doing "I Am a Camera" by John Van Druten, based on Christopher Isherwood's stories about his time in Berlin before the war. It has since been made into a very successful film and musical, "Cabaret", but is a difficult play to get right.

I chose it partly because in Ann Lazenby, a vivacious redhead with bags of personality, I had the perfect actress to play the amoral Sally Bowles. I cast Brian Pudner as Christopher Isherwood. In real life Ann was trying to hook him as her husband, but he was not taking the bait – a bit like his character in the play. On one occasion, coming back from a night out with them, she suddenly wrapped herself around me and kissed me ferociously in an attempt to make the other Brian jealous and get him to react. He didn't, just as in the play itself. It should have been perfect casting, therefore, but it wasn't. Ann was great, but Brian was simply not up to the task. In fairness to him it was a very difficult part and I should have chosen a more experienced actor. The rest of the small cast did their best, but it was not a great success. The theatre critic's review in The Coventry Evening Standard was pretty harsh and it discouraged me from having a go at another play later.

The Sphinx Drama Group was a member of The Theatre Guild of Coventry, which brought together the large number of drama clubs in Coventry and nearby towns. I joined its committee as The Sphinx's representative and agreed to take over as Editor of its quarterly publication, Theatre Guild News. I enjoyed doing it and it all went well, but I had one early hiccup. I persuaded the newly opened Belgrade Theatre to put our publication on sale there to raise awareness of forthcoming productions by our member clubs. I ran into trouble after writing an editorial voicing some misgivings, expressed to me by member clubs, about transferring the Guild's Annual Drama Festival to the new Belgrade Theatre. They saw the task of building much larger and taller "flats" for the scenery a bit daunting, as well as expensive, and I said this. The local newspaper picked up on this story and made a meal of it, as newspapers do. The Belgrade's management were not pleased and I had to mend fences pretty quickly. Calm was eventually restored and the Festival went off well.

The opening of the Belgrade Theatre in 1958 was a significant event in the theatrical world. It was the first theatre to be built after the war and it attracted a lot of rising stars under Bryan Bailey, its first Director. Sir Ian McKellen, Joan Plowright, Michael Crawford, Frank Finlay and Leonard Rossiter were all company members in those early years. Trevor Nunn joined as Assistant Director in 1962. I can still recall his production of "The Caucasian Chalk Circle", which was mesmerising. He went on to be an acclaimed Director of The National Theatre and one of the most influential figures in the theatre world. The Belgrade was a great addition to the town. The tickets were cheap and I went as often as I could.

During all this time I was engaged in the long distance courtship of Ann, who was living over seventy miles away in Huntingdon. I wrote regularly and visited as often as I could, but it was an expensive process. Getting there was not straightforward either. It was a difficult cross-country journey involving three buses and two trains each way. I would race out of the office after work on a Friday and catch a bus into town, then a train to Rugby, race to change platform to catch another train to

Kettering, then a bus to Thrapston and yet another bus to Huntingdon. There were only minutes between all these connections, but amazingly I caught them. The couple who ran Ann's lodgings were not particularly friendly to me, so I stayed in a hotel in the town. Ann told me later that they had told her father that I was a bad influence on her, which simply confirmed my belief that they were narrow-minded bigots.

Ann and I would have just one whole day together on Saturday, which we would often spend walking along the river to Granchester, or in nearby Cambridge, trying unsuccessfully to punt on the Cam, or going to the Arts Theatre. For something completely different we went to the Dorothy Tearooms where they held a dance at teatime. The small string orchestra played mostly sedate waltzes, foxtrots and quicksteps and the atmosphere was very old-fashioned and genteel. I was not a good dancer, because I had never been taught how, but we managed to enjoy it. I would spend Sunday mornings with Ann wishing that I did not have to go back, but eventually I would have to set off on the return journey. It was much slower, because there were fewer buses and trains on Sundays, and I would not get back to my lodgings until well after midnight. It was all quite a trek, but worth the effort. As soon as I had got back I was looking forward to the next time. I kept asking myself how soon I could ask Ann to marry me with some prospect that she might say yes. The opportunity came after about a year.

Ann's work at the research centre involved injecting experimental drugs into rats and monitoring their effects. She got to like them and decided to show them to my parents one weekend when we visited Leicester.

Despite the rats being in a metal cage, with no prospect of escaping, my parents were petrified, particularly my dad. They couldn't sleep the whole weekend and could not wait for us to leave. Ann did not understand what the fuss was about.

Ann only stayed at Huntingdon for a year. She moved back to Walsall and decided to become a teacher, like her father, teaching general science at The T.P.Riley School from September 1958. She found it very hard, mainly because she was thrown in at the deep end without any training, particularly in how to control a class. She was also not teaching a subject that she was comfortable with. Had it been biology or zoology she would have fared much better. For me, however, it meant that I could see her much more often at her parents' house or in Birmingham, which was a halfway house for both of us. When she came with me to Leicester one weekend, where we had a genteel tea at Granny Smith's, I finally asked her to marry me and she said yes. I was overjoyed and we cut short our stay, returning to Walsall immediately, even though it was quite late, so that I could ask her father for his consent - that is the way it was done in 1958. He said yes, of course, and we became engaged. By implication I was also asking him to pay for the wedding and he duly offered us £130 to cover everything – dresses, church costs, reception, photographer etc. We had no savings of our own, so we decided to delay getting married until September 1959, which was good for tax reasons, and it allowed us time to save a deposit to buy a house.

We decided to have a holiday together, travelling by train through France to the Costa Brava in Spain. It was very beautiful. This was before Spain's coasts were ruined by commercialisation. We stayed in Blanes, a quiet fishing village at the southern end of the Costa Brava, a few miles south of Tossa and Lloret de Mar and north of Barcelona. The fishermen would spread their huge nets out to dry along the length of the beach. I doubt if there is a fisherman left there now. These old villages are now just tourist resorts, dominated by high rise hotels and gaudy shops. In 1958 they had a few tourists, mainly Germans, and were delightful places to stay. This was the first of many travels to foreign lands that we would make over the coming years.

I did a lot of overtime, working long hours on most weekdays and Saturday mornings, in order to save some money. I moved out of my lodgings to share a dismal flat with Doug Watts, which also saved me some money, but it was not good for my health. I missed having regular meals and would often have my evening meal just before midnight at the cheap and cheerful King Wa Chinese restaurant. I paid the price when a few months later I developed a peptic ulcer, which was both very painful and a nuisance. There were no magic pills available in those days and I had to go on a strict diet, consisting mostly of fish and milk products. It gradually improved.

Ann's last day of teaching in July 1959 came as a great relief to her, but there was one happy outcome to her time at T.P. Riley. She met a young history teacher there, Ray Rundle, and would take him to play tennis at her club, where he met Jill Mullins, Ann's old school friend. They would marry a couple of years later and have been our lifelong friends ever since.

Ann and I were married at Great Barr Church, Walsall on 5 September 1959. My old friend from Leicester, Colin Atkins, was my best man and the two bridesmaids were my sister, Sheila, and Ann's sister, Janet. They looked lovely in their pink dresses. My family nearly spoiled the occasion by not turning up at the appointed time. There was a large Leicester contingent and they had hired a coach, which got lost. Had I asked all or even most of my aunts and uncles they would have needed to hire a train. We invited several university and school friends as well as family. It was a lovely, sunny day and everyone seemed to enjoy the occasion. The unmarried ladies were keen to catch Ann's wedding bouquet, but the men were totally disinterested in Ann's garter: tradition says that whoever catches these will marry next. We left after the reception to catch a small plane to take us to Guernsey for our honeymoon and the start of over sixty years of happy married life together.

Who wants the garter?

We looked at flats to rent, but they were gruesome, and decided instead to use the money we had saved as a deposit on a small, end-of-terrace house on a fairly new estate at Finham on the southern edge of Coventry. It cost £2,250 and we took out a mortgage for £1,950, about three times my annual wage (ignoring overtime). These figures seem derisory by modern standards. We had a tiny garden at the front and a larger one at the rear, big enough for us to have a small lawn and to grow some vegetables and fruit. The house was built on prime farming land and the soil was extraordinarily fertile. Everything I grew turned out well. You could fool yourself into thinking that you were a good gardener with soil like this. Our neighbour at the other end of the terrace was Ernie Robinson, the Coventry and England hooker.

The house had just one through-room downstairs, which served as both lounge and dining room, and a narrow kitchen. We had saved enough money to buy furniture for the bedroom, a cooker and basic kitchen utensils. Aunt Alice and Uncle Jack had given us an Ercol coffee table as a wedding present and others had bought us glassware. That was it. We had no easy chairs or settee to sit on or even curtains for the lounge. All we had was an old carpet donated by Ann's granny and an old nine inch black and white TV, which we watched stretched out on the carpet. Unlike now, it was the norm at that time not to live on credit, so we decided not to buy other things for the house on "hire purchase", which preceded credit cards, but to save until we could afford them. Eventually, we bought other furniture, but it was some time before we got a 'fridge.

After a while Ann decided she needed to work again. Her first job was in the Children's Department at the

Council Offices in Coventry and the second as a dental assistant to a Polish dentist at nearby Tile Hill. They were a welcome relief from the stress of teaching. She also decided to learn how to cook and took the City & Guilds' Cordon Bleu cookery course, which she passed and has since become a very good cook. Then, two and a half years after marrying we would start a family.

Events were moving quickly on the work front, too. The five M-wing models were all ready for rocket-launched test flights by late 1960 and I travelled down to Larkhill on Salisbury Plain with two colleagues from the Test Laboratories. I met E. G. Broadbent from the Royal Aircraft Establishment, Farnborough, one of the top gurus in the world of flutter. I had exchanged a lot of letters with him and was curious to know what he was like. Boffin is the word that best described him, but very supportive and encouraging to this new entrant to his rarefied world. The test site was a pretty unimpressive and bleak place – a series of low level buildings that looked as if they were not meant to be there long, sitting in the midst of the vast expanse of Salisbury Plain.

Given all the hard work devoted to designing and building the models and calculating how they would perform in flight the actual launch was a bit of an anti-climax. It was over in a flash. The model with its kink at 0.5 broke up after just 1.86secs. Two models broke up before they reached the rocket's top speed and the other two reached the top speed unharmed. My calculations had predicted flutter at very high speeds, well above the rocket's top speed, and so it proved. If a full scale M-Wing airliner were to be built it would not be flutter, but divergence that its designers would have to deal with. I wrote a full report and sent it to the R.A.E.

I cannot recall any great celebration by AWA management when the M-wing contract was completed satisfactorily. Management's indifference, I think, was because it had lost interest in the M-wing as a possible aircraft of the future. A similar research project on a rival design, in the shape of a dart, known then as the "narrow delta", had shown it to be a viable solution. It would go on to be developed commercially and became Concord, the world's first supersonic airliner.

AWA management's focus was elsewhere, firmly fixed on sorting out the Argosy's problems and trying to make it a commercial success. Eventually they did get it to work satisfactorily, introducing changes identified in my report, and it gained its airworthiness certificate, but it was not a great commercial success. Only seventy four were built. It did not break into the civil aviation market, as it hoped, with only eighteen being sold to airline operators in the USA, New Zealand, Australia and the UK. The RAF took the other fifty six.

AWA was not alone in having problems. The whole aircraft industry was struggling to survive. The Defence White Paper of 1957 had sounded its death knell when Duncan Sandys declared that the future for our defence lay with guided missiles and not military aircraft. He cancelled most military projects and would have cancelled the English Electric's "Lightning" had its development not been so far advanced. What a mistake that would have been. Companies such as AWA now had to build for and sell solely to commercial airlines, but it was very difficult to win orders in countries which had their own aircraft industries and national airlines. The USA and France, in particular, but other countries, too, were highly protectionist and we didn't stand a chance.

The final blow for AWA was the decision by the Labour Government in 1965 to cancel the order for a replacement for the Beverley and Hastings aircraft. Production work at Baginton finished in that year with the loss of 4,600 jobs. The wider impact on the local economy and on suppliers was much greater. It was a sad end to a great pioneering company and the beginning of a downward spiral for Coventry.

Having delivered my report on The Argosy's problems and completed the M-wing contract, and with no prospect of further work on a supersonic airliner, my role as an aeroelastician had seemingly come to an end. I did not, however, feel under threat of being made redundant because I had developed a reputation for being an innovator and good problem solver.

My experience of using the Pegasus computer to speed up my M- wing and Argosy calculations convinced me that this was how other problems would be solved in future. I asked if I could learn to programme Pegasus. Joe Staite agreed and I went on a course in London, held near London Wall. It was a shock to see the utter devastation there caused by the wartime bombing. Soon afterwards that whole area was redeveloped and now houses the Barbican.

I settled into my new role and churned out technical solutions and computer programmes every few weeks for problems arising from The Argosy's construction and flight performance. I found writing the programmes quite a challenge because they were written in "machine code", a very basic language, and all the instructions had to be executed in a small number of fast "registers", into which data had to imported and then exported before and after each minute calculation. It called for a lot of patience and meticulous attention to detail, which suited my temperament.

By early 1961 I had reached the conclusion that I needed to move on. The aircraft industry was shrinking at an alarming rate as firms, originally about forty of them, either closed down or merged with others until there were only three large groups left. AWA merged first with Avro, then with Hawker Siddeley, then De Havilland, eventually forming British Aerospace. Then I got lucky. I noticed in the Coventry Evening Standard that Courtaulds, also in Coventry, were looking for someone to start a scientific computer programming service to its technical and production departments. It was ready-made for me. I got the job. AWA management tried to keep me, offering me promotion onto the monthly staff payroll, which carried with it entitlement to a pension, but I declined. They then asked if I would like to move, on promotion, to the De Havilland factory at Hatfield. I said that I had no intention of moving south. How ironic then that three years later I would end up living just four miles from that factory.

Chapter 6

Coventry
A Family Man

My move to Courtaulds proved to have far-reaching consequences, but there was no hint of that on the first day when I was taken to my workplace by my boss, Fred Musk, the Computer Manager. Whereas the Design Office and production factory at Armstrong Whitworth were in separate locations, here production, development and administration sat cheek by jowl and the pungent smell of chemical processes permeated the whole site. It was scruffy and noisy, but not with the buzz of enthusiastic young staff engaged in creative activity, as at AWA, but of scores of bored young women operating antiquated punch card and card sorting machines in a large openplan space, part office and part store. I was in the midst of all this. My heart sank and I wondered if I had made a bad decision. Thankfully, I hadn't. I was moved to a quieter area and was soon tackling some challenging problems.

The company's Elliott 405 computer was no more advanced than AWA's Pegasus so writing programmes posed similar problems, but it was much more exciting to look at with its large consol covered with dozens of flashing red, green and orange lights. It felt more like playing a gambling machine or flying a plane than operating a computer.

Courtaulds was one of the UK's biggest manufacturing companies with several factories in the UK and abroad. The one in Coventry was started in 1922 and was huge, employing about 5,000 people. It had the tallest chimney in the UK. The company was founded in Essex in 1794 to make silk, crepe and textiles, and by the time I joined it was the world's leading producer of man-made fibres. It was also a major producer of chemicals, employing a lot of top-rate chemists and chemical engineers. One of these, Trevor Bridges, was grappling with the design of multi-component distillation columns. These were very complex structures for extracting specific chemical compounds from liquids which were fed into a high tower and passed over a succession of heated metal plates. By calculating the number of plates required and the correct plate temperatures, and by regulating the amounts of the liquid fed in, you could siphon off just the chemical compounds you wanted. Getting all these numbers right is a complex problem involving chemistry, physics and mathematics. The key to finding a solution lies in the mathematics. That's where I came in.

My boss, Fred Musk, and Dr Eric Totman, a chemist who was now in the Operational Research Section, had just published a paper setting out a method of doing the calculations. It needed a computer to turn this into something useful and it also needed further work on the mathematics. I was asked to sort out the mathematics and to write a computer programme, which I did. The results were well received, both within the Management Services Group in which I worked and the wider company, and earned me a lot of Brownie points.

As a result, the Operational Research Section, also part of the Management Services Group, asked for my help on another production problem. Clarifoil, a clear film used for packaging, was cut into strips and rolled onto spools to match customer orders. They wanted to find ways of reducing the amount of waste generated and so reduce production costs at the Spondon Works, Derby. This is the classic "paper trim problem", a recognised problem in the Operational Research (OR) world, which can be expressed in mathematical terms as a "linear programme". Solving such a linear programming problem is not easy and a computer is essential. Even then it is difficult. There was no linear programming software package for me to use for the Elliott 405, so I wrote one quickly.

Using this software we showed that it was theoretically possible to save waste, but it took far too long to be used in practice. I devised a simpler solution and turned that into a computer programme. I went to Derby with the OR team to set up a trial run from the factory, transmitting customer orders to the computer at Coventry and sending the cutting schedule back to Derby. It took very little time and worked well. The estimated savings were significant.

It was on this assignment that I first came across Neil Jessop, the Head of OR. It was not an auspicious start. During our visit to Derby the OR team had taken me to have lunch at the county cricket ground. I was in their hands and went along with it. When I submitted my expenses claim for the trip Neil was not at all happy. We were apparently well over our allowance and he approved it very reluctantly. It was an insight into the high standards Neil set and expected others to keep to. I would get to know and respect him enormously over the next few years.

Neil and the Courtaulds management saw the potential for much greater savings if we could apply the same approach to the much larger British Cellophane factories at Bridgwater in Somerset and Barrow-in-Furness in the Lake District. This brought my own future into sharp focus. Should I remain in the Computer Section or transfer to OR? I wanted to move, but Fred Musk wanted me to stay with him.

Eventually Fred Musk relented and it was agreed that I should move. I was put in charge of the assignment at Bridgewater. It was a very significant change for me, which would open doors that would not have been possible had I remained a computer programmer.

However, to get things in perspective, there was another much more significant change for me and Ann at about this time – the birth of our daughter, Helen, on St Patrick's Day, 17th March 1962. It was supposed to be a home birth, as was the norm in those days, but the midwife took a late decision, when the birth was imminent, to move Ann into Warneford Hospital, Royal Leamington Spa. My worries obviously showed and the midwife told me not to look so scared because it would only make Ann anxious. It all went well, after which we were very happy, and relieved.

The following winter was one of the coldest ever and I can recall Helen's bedroom frequently having a layer of ice on the inside of the windows. Ann wrapped her up well and would take her for healthy walks in her iconic Silver Cross pram. Helen was a happy child and a fast learner. The grandparents and the rest of the family doted on her, but she did not get spoiled, because that is not Ann's style.

Mum and dad with Helen

I was now both a new father and a novice operational researcher, but with no training in how to do either! The first role I learned, like every other parent, by trial and error and in effect I did the same with OR. Having no formal OR training did not matter in practice, because that is in keeping with how it all started in the Second World War when groups of eminent scientists, such as Prof. Blackett, were brought together by the government to tackle some of the most difficult military problems facing the country. They became known as Blackett's Circus, introducing operational changes that would have a significant bearing on the outcome of the war. Two that are often cited are the battle against German

U-boats and the deployment of radar to detect enemy aircraft.

In the first they looked at the way depth charges were used to blow up U-boats and the way convoys of merchant ships were protected. The key, as in all OR projects, was an analysis of the key factors affecting the operational outcome and the creation of a mathematical model linking these factors. In this case they showed that the depth charges would have greater impact if they were set to explode at a different depth. The results were immediate and slowly the battle against the U-boats was won. They also changed the way merchant ships were protected, which led to fewer of them being sunk so that more food and other scarce supplies from the USA could successfully reach the UK. The results for the deployment of radar were equally spectacular.

This activity became known as operational research, essentially applying a scientific approach to the analysis of operational problems, and it was taken up after the war by the Ministry of Defence and the National Coal Board and by some large commercial companies, such as Shell. It gradually spread to most other large companies and in the '60s was being introduced into universities. Since then, as computer technology has become more sophisticated, the concept of "modelling" became a tool for other disciplines to use and no longer the preserve of OR.

It was far more congenial being part of the OR Section. I had been a lone wolf in the Computer Section with little contact and little in common with the others there, who were working on accounting, payroll and similar administrative functions. Now I had like-minded colleagues to interact with and bounce ideas off. I got on well with John Luckman, who was a statistician from Imperial College. All the others were Oxbridge graduates. In practice, however, I had limited contact with them over the next fifteen months because I spent so much time at British Cellophane.

I would travel to Bridgewater down the Fosse Way and through the gorgeous Cotswolds in my bouncy Morris 1000 Traveller. It was a lovely journey in good weather, but not much fun in bad. I had my favoured places to stop for refreshment – the tea rooms in Stowe on the Wold and the Hare & Hounds Hotel at Tetbury. If I started out in the late afternoon or early evening I would sometimes stay overnight in Wells, Glastonbury or Bath, and travel on to Bridgewater early the next morning. Neil Jessop would come with me at regular intervals for stock-taking meetings with Jim Sturge, British Cellophane's Chief Accountant, who was a very important figure in the company. Although my work was exclusively in the production department it was Jim who was the real client for this work. He wanted to save money. He was very easy to get on with but did not fit the usual image of an accountant. He was tall, fair haired and very popular with the many ladies who worked for him. He took to referring to me as "the professor".

On one trip Neil Jessop and I stayed at the Crown Hotel in Wells. At dinner I got another insight into Neil's insistence on high standards when he rejected the wine offered and sent back the steak. I was neither that discerning nor that sure of my ground. I was too embarrassed to go there again. I got to know Neil well and he invited Ann and me for lunch one Sunday at his home in Bishop Stortford.

The British Cellophane factory at Bridgewater was then the town's dominant employer. It was built in 1937 on the former Sydenham Manor Fields, had a nice feel about it and was a pleasant place to work. My first task was to get to know the processes for producing cellophane. A film of cellophane was created in chemical vats, several feet wide, and captured on large rolls from which smaller rolls of film were cut to meet customers' orders. The production control department would determine the width of the main roll and produce a schedule for cutting it into the smaller rolls. They had years of experience and were pretty good at avoiding waste, so any improvements that I might put forward would be hard to sell to them.

My task was to improve this cutting schedule in order to reduce the waste generated and so save money. I concluded that the mathematical solution I had proposed for the Spondon Works at Derby could be applied at Bridgewater. I suggested that we be allowed to prove it by undertaking our own scheduling in parallel with the factory's for a one month trial period and this was agreed.

Before embarking on this I spent some time at the company's other factory at Barrow-in-Furness to see if that required a different approach. After a month or so I concluded that it didn't. That was a relief. Whilst the journey through the Lake District was a joy, I did not fancy having to drive regularly along the nightmarish, three lane A6. I concentrated my efforts on the Bridgewater factory.

British Cellophane had recruited its own OR worker, Angus Reid, with whom I got on very well. We tackled the trial together, working long hours every day for four weeks, including weekends. Jim Sturge offered to pay for a chalet at nearby Burnham-on-Sea so that Ann, our newly born daughter, Helen, and I could be together, but we rejected that. It would have been impractical and very lonely for Ann. Instead she went to stay with her parents in Walsall. I stayed at the Royal Clarence Hotel, which had 29 rooms and I slept in nearly all of them over the fifteen months I was working on this project. It was hard work.

We got copies of all the customer orders as they arrived and we used my methodology to produce a cutting schedule in parallel with the production department's own decisions. We spent the weekends working out how much waste our method would generate and compared that to the actual results on the production shop floor. It was gruelling, painstaking work with no respite for four weeks and I was very tired by the end. In our final report we deliberately did not exaggerate the potential savings, but they were at least £0.5m per annum, worth over £10m p.a. at today's prices. The production department agreed with our estimates and everybody was delighted. There was general agreement that they should implement the methodology. The company had an ICT 1300 computer, which I learned to programme, and then set about the task of turning our methodology into computer programmes for routine use. It would take some weeks.

Given all the time I was working at Bridgewater it is surprising how little I saw of the town, mainly because I was working such long hours. What I did see, though, was very special. The highlight was their Guy Fawkes Carnival, a true spectacle which attracted over 150, 000 visitors in November every year. Over 100 motorised "floats", some of them over 100ft. long, paraded through the town in a three mile procession. There was a lively carnival atmosphere – cheerful, noisy and exhilarating. It was finished off with a spectacular fireworks display. The town itself was a busy one, as befits the leading industrial town in the county. It sat on the Parrett River and had been a leading port right into the 19th century, until Bristol became dominant. It had also had a thriving shipbuilding industry, but all that remains now are the quays where some cargo is loaded and unloaded.

My work at Bridgewater started in earnest in 1963 and carried on into 1964, but before that there were some other important family milestones. Ann's sister, Janet, got married in 1962. She was working as a house mother in the National Children's Home (NCH) at Evenly Hall, Brackley when she met Alan Meakin, one of the most remarkable, talented and likeable men I have ever known. He had been brought up at Brackley under the kindly oversight of its Director, Mr Clark. Alan went into the navy, where he was a frogman, amongst other things, and met Janet on his return. He was extremely intelligent and quick to learn. Mr Clark taught him to play golf and in next to no time he was playing off a single figure handicap. He swam like a fish and even at over seventy years of age he would still swim about two miles every morning before breakfast, followed by one or more rounds of golf. We would later go to see him run in the London Marathon, leading the field of non-club runners. Few people in the country were as fit as him at his age. He was quite a phenomenon. After marrying they moved into a flat in Coventry, so we saw a lot of them. Alan tried the police and prison services before deciding that he, too, would work in the NCH, where he eventually became Director of the Princess Alice NCH in Birmingham, the largest in the country. Having them close to us at Coventry was a bonus.

Helen with Janet and Alan

My sister, Sheila, also got married in 1962. Her husband, Derrick Lawler, was a solid and cheery Londoner. He had been in the Navy, where they met, but was now a fireman. She looked lovely on her wedding day and I hoped the marriage would turn out well. For a while it did and they had three children, but later Derrick went off with another woman, leaving Sheila devastated and heartbroken. She has never really recovered from that blow.

We had kept in touch with Derrick Swann, our old university friend. He came to live with us for a while when he was going through a period of depression. He was struggling to come to terms with his homosexuality, which you had to deny or hide in those days. The new Labour Government brought in legislation in 1965 to legalise it and Derrick's anxieties eased.

We went to stay with Derrick at his parent's home in deepest rural Suffolk, midway between Halesworth and Beccles. His parents lived at Church Cottage, a short walk from Sotherton Church and the very attractive sixteenth century Church Farm, where we slept on our first visit. There was no other habitation in sight, just an expanse of farmland, hedges filled with bullaces and blackberries, tall trees and big skies, captured for ever in John Constable's paintings. It was so quiet and utterly peaceful and pitch black at night.

Derrick's father was a farm labourer and Church Cottage came with the job. When he stopped working he and his wife would have to find somewhere else to live. Derrick solved that problem, some years later, by buying them a bungalow at nearby Halesworth. After his parents died, Ann and I and other friends would go there with him for restful breaks. For years Derrick's father had looked after the big Shire horses which pulled the plough, and he knew them all intimately, but they had now given way to a tractor. It must have been a sad day for him when they were taken away. If he came across a cast-off horseshoe in the fields he would know immediately which horse it belonged to. Wherever he was working on the farm during the day, come rain or shine, his wife would take him a bottle of tea and sandwiches at lunchtime and cake at teatime. It was a simple, repetitive life, so far removed from anything I would experience.

Our first car was second hand, but Ann had not reckoned on the one I got. It was a large 1936 six cylinder Wolsey Hornet with leather bench seats in front and back and a handle to start the engine. I paid just £14 for it. Steering was a joke, but Ann thought it no laughing matter. We set off to visit Ann's parents in Walsall, but after only half a mile or so and having negotiated a few bends with great difficulty, Ann sounded the alarm bells and asked me to turn back. We abandoned the trip and got rid of the car to our next door neighbour. He worked on it and eventually made it roadworthy.

Undeterred, I bought a black second hand Morris 1,000 Traveller and we ventured north for a weekend with our friends Jill and Ray Rundle in Lancashire. Misadventure stalked us again and we broke down on the newly opened M6 motorway. The engine's "big end" had gone. We had a young baby and lots of luggage on board. Fortunately, the AA responded brilliantly and we were taken to our friends in comfort. I vowed that my next car would be a new one. From then on I bought only new cars and replaced them every three or four years before they could become a liability.

Having a car enabled us to explore Warwickshire, particularly the nearby towns of Leamington Spa, Warwick, Kenilworth and Stratford-upon-Avon and further afield. We were so lucky to have these wonderful historical treasures on our doorstep. I have fond memories of a dreamy summer's day we spent with Alan and Janet and our gorgeous new daughter at Chedworth Roman Villa, the National Trust property near Cheltenham. Some years later I would revisit the great castle at Warwick, in its romantic setting on the banks of the river Avon, with a visiting Austrian family and they found it an awesome sight, as did I.

Ann and Helen at Chedworth Villa

Bruce, our first son, was born in October 1963. This time the birth was at home and I was present throughout. The experience made me glad I was not a woman. I now had someone I could eventually play football, tennis, cricket and badminton with. He would later have two brothers. We would all play a lot together over the coming years.

Sadly, Ann's father did not see his first grandson. He caught a kidney infection and died suddenly of nephritis. He was only 59. It was a terrible blow for Ann's mum, Ida, but she coped well with the loss. It was a great blessing that Ida's own mother, Nanna, was still alive and living nearby. Nigel, Ann's brother, was only fourteen and entering a crucial phase of his life without a father. Had his father still been alive, however, I think those teenage years would have been very challenging for both of them. His father was a hard taskmaster and a bit short on encouragement and praise.

We would spend a lot of time with Ida and Nigel over the coming years, taking them on holidays and having them to stay at our house for long periods. Ida would strike up a surprising friendship with my own mum. I had got on reasonably well with Ann's father, although we did not have a lot in common. He was talented, but quite vain. He played the violin and had his own Mercia String Quartet, which would practice on Sundays in the house, a sound that Ann remembers well. He was scornful of my love of jazz, pop songs and musicals. He was also a good painter and took great photographs, processing them at home himself. He taught at a secondary modern school and I imagine he was a good teacher. He was very conscientious, but a bit of a pedant. He claimed to have been a member of the Communist Party when young and was now a staunch Labour supporter. We talked about that sometimes and found some common ground. One evening we went to a local pub and he talked to me about his sex life, which I found excruciatingly embarrassing. He was a bit of an enigma.

The '60s was the decade when the country finally cast off the shadow of war and started to live again. Millions took cheap package holidays abroad and got a taste for more exotic foreign food and wine. There was a new energy and optimism in the land, especially amongst the young. Music and fashion led the way. Rock and Roll crossed the Atlantic and swept the country. The wonderful Beatles took Liverpool and then the whole country by storm and went on to become a sensation in America. Since then their music and songs have spread across the globe and, over fifty years later, can still be heard every day on radio, TV or in public places. In the fashion world blue denim jeans became ubiquitous. Mary Quant was the new queen of fashion and mini skirts were only just long enough to cover a girl's embarrassment. London was swinging. Carnaby Street became the in-place to shop. The country shook off its image of straight-laced respectability and began to let its hair down.

This desire for change extended to politics, too. Harold Wilson caught the mood brilliantly and led the Labour Party to a narrow victory in the 1964 General Election, promising to harness "the white heat of technology" to make Britain great again. The old-fashioned, fuddy-duddy Conservative leader, Lord Hulme, seemed like a relic from the past and the electorate rejected his party after 13 years in office.

This was the background then in early 1964 when Neil Jessop invited me to join him in setting up a new Institute for Operational Research in London, about which we had often spoken during the many car journeys we made to Bridgewater. It was a time of great change and expansion in the OR world following its successful use in war-time and its adoption by increasing numbers of leading firms and organisations. Universities were also getting in on the act by setting up OR Departments to produce the graduates needed to fill the new jobs being created. A number of leading lights in the OR world were jockeying to secure these new opportunities and Neil was very nervous that his hopes would be dashed, but he need not have worried. His rivals got their posts and Neil secured his. With the backing of the Operational Research Society and with Sir Charles Goodeve and Prof. Rus Ackoff, a leading American academic, acting as brokers, the Institute for Operational Research (IOR) was born. The Tavistock Institute of Human Relations agreed to provide it a home.

I readily agreed to Neil's invitation to move south and join him despite having two small children, Helen aged two and Bruce just a few months old. It was a leap in the dark for me and a big challenge for Ann, but we discussed it and agreed to give it a go. What captured my imagination was the chance to extend the use of OR to the public sector. I was becoming more and more interested in politics and public policy issues generally and wanted to get involved in a practical way. My chance would come with a two year project to do research on the way the hospital service adapted and changed.

My work at British Cellophane had come to a halt. I had made good progress on writing the computer programme needed for scheduling customer orders when Jim Sturge decided that they would buy a new computer from Honeywell, as Courtaulds itself had done a year earlier. I had agreed to stay on at Courtaulds for three months in order to leave the project at British Cellophane in a good state and to achieve an orderly handover to Angus Reid and to Dr Eric Totman, the Courtaulds colleague who would replace me, but this new development meant that I was now free to leave. Neil had hoped that Eric would join him at IOR, but Eric decided that his future lay at Courtaulds. This proved to be a tragic mistake. He took over my role at British Cellophane, travelling up and down the Fosse

Way to Bridgewater, as I had done. On one such journey he was involved in a collision with a large lorry transporting trees. It had failed to stop at the traffic lights at Northleach and Eric was killed instantly. It was a sobering thought that it might have been me.

Jim Sturge tried hard to get me to stay on and join them. He offered me the job of Chief Cost Accountant. When I protested that I knew nothing about cost accountancy he replied that I would master it within six months. I was flattered, but turned it down. Before I left Courtaulds and finished travelling to Bridgewater I agreed to give a talk to the Mid-Somerset Productivity Association on the origins and use of OR. It was well received by the large audience, mainly drawn from small and medium sized firms, plus a number from British Cellophane, including Jim Sturge. After the talk he asked me to call into the factory before I left the next day when he wanted to put another proposition to me. Once again I said no. I was firmly committed to joining IOR.

Ann and I had to decide where to live. It had to be north of London, so that we could get easily to the Midlands, and within one hours travelling time from home to office. We decided to have a look at Welwyn Garden City, 25 miles north of London in mid-Hertfordshire. I knew nothing then about its origins, but I had visited it one evening some years earlier and took an instant liking to the place. I was on a course in London when Derrick, our old university friend, who taught at the Grammar School there, invited me to play at his tennis club. The tennis wasn't memorable, but the town was and that memory stayed with me. It was so green and beautifully laid out, with grass verges, flower beds and hundreds of trees. It was like living in the country. Ann's first impressions were also good and we searched for a house.

We ended up buying a four bed-roomed mid-terrace house on the edge of the old part of the town, which looked over the golf course at the front and had a small spinney at the end of our back garden, so we had privacy. It was within easy walking distance of nursery, primary, junior and secondary schools and about twenty minutes fast walk to the station and town centre, so it fitted the bill. We sold our Coventry house easily for £3,100 and bought the new house for £5,800. Since my salary was to be £2,100 I had no problems with a mortgage. How times have changed - would that my children and grandchildren could move about with such ease. They would not be able to afford that house now. It was recently on the market for £580,000, exactly 100 times its price fifty years earlier.

I was given a good send-off by my colleagues at Courtaulds, who presented me with a metal filing cabinet, which I still use today. So Ann and I packed our belongings and became part of the "drift to the south east", which was gathering in pace.

Chapter 7

Welwyn Garden City Blossoming Out

Our move south did not get off to a good start. The house's previous owners had removed a hot water geezer, leaving water flowing freely into the sink, so we had to get it stopped on the day we arrived - not the best of starts with two small children and a van full of furniture to unload. Was this a bad omen? No, it wasn't. We went on to have over fifty happy years in the town, but it wasn't all sunshine and roses. We had a number of serious crises on the way, but have come through them intact.

Welwyn Garden City is a delightful town. It was started in 1920 as a new concept in town planning, but it was not the first garden city - that was Letchworth. Bill Griffin, the charismatic Managing Director of Welwyn Department Store, and the star performer at the town's annual Old Time Music Hall, trotted out the same joke each year that Letchworth might have been the first garden city, but Welwyn was the one they got right. That's unkind to Letchworth, but true about Welwyn.

The garden city movement was the brainchild of Ebenezer Howard, who wanted to create an antidote to the appalling slum conditions working class families had to endure in Victorian London. His answer was to offer them decent housing, with a garden, set amidst green, open spaces, flower beds and magnificent trees. It would be "a town designed for healthy living and industry, of a size that makes possible a full measure of social life, but not larger". The town's early planners did well in putting these aims into practice, striking just the right balance between the physical, social and working environments. The natural environment is what makes it particularly attractive and springtime is a very special time when its streets are transformed into a candyfloss world of trees heavy with blossom and air heady with scent. Autumn is pretty good, too, as thousands of trees undergo multiple changes of vibrant colours.

Although W.G.C. has doubled in size since we moved there, and had a target size of 42,000 inhabitants, it still feels more like living in a large village because of its clever design, creating a strong sense of community. This was fostered by creating small cul-de-sacs, some of them with tennis courts, where nearby residents formed their own tennis clubs. Some had allotments attached. We were active in the nearby Dellcott Family Club, which had a simple clubhouse, three tennis courts, swings, slides and other facilities for children. Ann and I ran the annual tennis competitions for both juniors and adults and the "tea and tennis" events on Sundays, which were hugely popular, especially Ann's teas. Dellcott was a great boon to our family. The children joined in all the competitions and played there for hours throughout the year and, in particular, during the long school holidays.

Dotted around the town are several local shopping parades. Although there were only a handful of shops it encouraged people to walk to get their groceries, newspapers etc (or to get their hair cut), which helped local people to interact and get to know each other. If they chose instead to go into the town centre for their shopping there was Welwyn Department Store's twenty one departments to cater for all their needs – an early "one stop shop". Its food hall was said to rival Harrods. John Lewis took over the store in 1983 and got rid of the food department, concentrating on household goods and clothing. With its colonnaded front it is an impressive building and a magnet for shoppers from far afield.

Industry in the town was dominated by ICI Plastics until it moved out in 1982, leaving a great hole to be filled. ICI employed a high proportion of graduates and highly qualified technicians, so it was a significant change for the town, but the transition to other forms of commercial activity has been managed very well. Tesco, the UK's largest retailer, later moved its headquarters onto the vacant site, as did other leading companies. The early planners did extraordinarily well in attracting a large and diverse number of other top quality firms to set up business here - Murphy Radio; Lincoln Electric; Crown Marconi; Roche; Smith, Kline & French; Norton Abrasives; Shredded Wheat; Cresta Silks and others.

There were creative industries, too - Welwyn Film Studios turned out some iconic films, including Graham Green's "Brighton Rock", starring Richard Attenborough. Amateur drama thrived in the town. It got its own permanent home in 1931 when old farm buildings from

Lower Handside Farm were converted into the much loved Barn Theatre. The famous film star, Dame Flora Robson, started her acting career there. It is now one of the leading amateur drama companies in the country, attracting talent from a wide area. The standard of some of its productions is very high indeed. Two of our younger granddaughters, Ines and Rosa, now perform there and I get enormous pleasure when I go to see them.

Another centre of artistic endeavour was Digswell House, a fine early 18th century mansion, fronted by four huge columns, sitting next to the town's cricket club and St John's church. From 1959 to 1986 it was home for up to sixteen artists, some internationally famous, who lived and worked there. It was not in a good state of repair, though, so the arts centre found a new home at the old forge in nearby Digswell.

The town's overall appearance was fundamental to the way it was planned. Wide boulevards in the centre, bedecked with flower beds and flanked by tall poplars and blossom trees, set the tone. A classic neo-Georgian style was adopted for its buildings. Householders had to conform to strict rules to maintain the standards laid down and those that flouted the rules would be required to make good their transgressions. As the town developed, however, these rules were relaxed and the east side of the town does not have the same overall neo-Georgian look, which is a pity, but probably inevitable. The standards on the west side, however, have generally been maintained and it still looks extremely attractive nearly one hundred years after its inception.

We settled in very quickly. Our immediate neighbours were Mrs Wilson and her son, Harry, on one side and

Molly and Hugh Martin on the other. Harry was one of the country's leading athletics coaches. Opening our bedroom curtains in the morning we would often look out onto a clothes line full of athletics kit drying next door. He became the UK's National Middle Distance Coach and his greatest achievement was to coach Steve Ovett to win the 800 metres gold medal in the 1980 Olympic Games. Ovett's great rival was Sebastian Coe, who lost out to Ovett in the 800 metres final, but beat him to take gold in the 1500 metres. The rivalry between them was intense and made compelling viewing for the watching public on TV, which did a great deal to raise the profile of athletics generally. Steve Ovett would visit Harry regularly and it was whilst staying next door on one of these visits that Harry had a sudden heart attack and died, aged 73. He was a very unassuming man and kept his achievements very much to himself.

Molly and Hugh Martin, on the other side, were a delightfully old-fashioned couple. We got on very well with them and our children found a good friend in their son, Richard. "Richard come over" was a regular chant from Helen and the boys, inviting him to come and play.

Across the road lived Dennis and Gill Lewis, who made early contact and took us to our first Old Time Music Hall. Gill's brother was the accomplished artist, John Bratby, and she was talented, too. Dennis had been Secretary of W.G.C. Cricket Club for many years and easily persuaded me to become a member. Within a year I had become Dennis' Assistant Secretary whereupon he announced that he would be "moving on to higher things", which turned out to be standing as a Tory candidate in the forthcoming Local Council elections. He was duly elected and over the last fifty years has been an outstanding Councillor and leading light in the town. I succeeded him as the club's Secretary and would later become Chairman of the General Committee and, much later, Fixtures Secretary. I put a lot of work into the Secretary's job and when I stepped down I was presented with a complete set of wine, champagne and other glassware – courtesy of Ian MacLaurin and Tesco, I think – by Dr Joe Tobin, the club's Chairman, who was fulsome in his thanks and praise. It was unexpected and I was very touched.

My time as Secretary coincided with Ian MacLaurin's as captain and it was a rich period for the club. He took over from Alistair Buchanan, whose Sunday 1st XI was unbeaten in 1966. I contributed to that record by sharing an unbeaten century stand with a very young Malcolm Bateman, turning what looked like certain defeat into an honourable draw. I played in about half of the 1st XI's fixtures that year, but annoyingly missed out on the team photograph which now hangs in the club's pavilion. We already had some talented cricketers, but under Ian MacLaurin we became the leading club in the county, attracting a lot of top class players. John Smith, a fine all-rounder, joined us from Hertford. He and I combined to good effect in one match, against Cockfosters, to get three batsmen out "c. B. Smith b. J. Smith" from three quite different positions in the field. The three Brown brothers all joined. They were all Young England players and the sons of Freddie Brown, the former England captain. Freddie would come to see them play, sitting in a chair on the boundary drinking tea on a tray supplied by Ian MacLaurin's wife, Ann. He was a large, ruddy-faced character, who would often be seen wearing a neckerchief in his playing days. I hoped he might get a bit more involved in the club, but he confined himself to occasional visits to watch the play. He was a very easy-going "old school" character. The 1st team became too strong for me to get into, except occasionally, and I played for the second XI, becoming its vice-captain and then captain for several years.

Ian was an accomplished opening bat and occasional spin bowler, playing regularly for Hertfordshire as well as captaining the MCC. His wife, Ann, could be a harsh critic, though. One afternoon, I was sitting on the boundary with her, watching Ian score yet another century and praising his skills, when she complained that he needed to do it against stronger opposition.

Ian and Ann made great efforts on behalf of the club. They lived close to the ground and held an "open house" day, inviting club members to drop in for some food and drink. Ian and I were chatting outside when he shouted out "no fornicating on my lawn, Mr Brown, thank you very much", having spotted Chris Brown getting a bit too deeply engrossed with a young lady. Chris was a larger than life character who tried to persuade me to invite nurses from the local hospital to come to the club for a drink after the games on a Saturday night, but I didn't bite. He was a real asset to the club, though, both on and off the field, bringing twenty six guests to our 50th anniversary dinner & dance, which I organised.

The club's main social event was its annual dinner & dance, which was always well attended, but we decided to have another supper each year solely for the club's cricketers and with the focus on the cricket season. We held it in the clubhouse and our ladies provided us with excellent meals. We got a succession of well known England cricketers as after-dinner speakers – Ian MacLaurin got Peter Parfitt in the first year and I got Fred Titmus in the second. I would start the after-dinner proceedings with a review of the year before announcing the season's awards, which our celebrity speaker would present. Ian would then entertain us for ages, reeling off a stream of very funny self-deprecating Jewish jokes. They were good evenings. It all helped to forge a strong club identity amongst the players and the results on the field bore that out.

Ian's wife, Ann, did her bit, too. They invited me and Ann to have a meal at their house so that they could sound us out on some of their ideas for running the club. Ian's Ann had ideas for improving the catering and my Ann was happy to help. They made a good pair. Trays of tea for spectators sitting on the boundary became very popular. Sadly, after Ian and Ann had moved from W.G.C., we learned that Ann had died suddenly, far too young.

The partnership between me and Ian lasted just three years and it was a very fruitful one for the club, but then I had to give up the Secretary's job and Ian, who was on the way up in Tesco, moved away. He went right to the top, first becoming its Chief Executive and then Chairman, for which he was knighted, before going one better and becoming Lord MacLaurin. He rose to the top in the cricketing world, too, becoming Chairman of the England and Wales Cricket Board, introducing many reforms to make English cricket more competitive and successful. He succeeded in that, but it was a bumpy ride for him. The old-fashioned cricket establishment were not too keen on change. We had a brief chat recently whilst I was on a walk through nearby

Brocket Park and Ian was playing golf there. "I'm on my second hip", he announced cheerfully, but looked as fit as a fiddle. He was as positive in outlook as ever.

I would go on to play for the club until I was fifty, by which time it was fielding five teams on a Saturday, had a thriving juniors section and very successful youth teams, for which my youngest son, Graham, would play. In fact all my children would play a part in the club. Helen was my scorer when I captained the 2nd XI, Bruce was a brilliant scorer for the 1st XI under Malcolm Bateman and Benjamin helped with the scoring, too. The credit for the growth of the club must go to John Adams, though, who pressed for starting a 3rd XI when he was 1st XI captain and I captained the 2nd XI. I was doubtful if we had the players to make it work, but he was quite right and it was the making of the club. John went on to become President some years later. I never really got on with him, though. He was too full of his own certainties for my liking and we were constantly at loggerheads. Because I was never made a Life Member, despite 22 years service, on and off the field, I have lost touch with the club in recent years.

Ann and I soon made other friends, mainly as a result of Ann meeting other mothers with small children living nearby. They formed a play group, which met in each other's houses and gardens. Catherine and Len Hall, Jean and John Sefton, Elizabeth and Ron Thomas, Mary and Michael Jackson, Sue and Pete Ackroyd, Joan and Bob Taylor, and later Bev and 'Stew' Stewart all became particularly close friends. These friendships were a great help to Ann, who had to cope with bringing up four children aged seven or under at one point. Whilst I helped as much as I could the main burden fell on her. This would put a great emotional strain on her at times, but she has got over many hurdles and successfully reared four children she can be proud of, and they would produce ten lovely grandchildren.

As the children grew up Ann had time to do other things. She and Bev Stewart, and later Joan Taylor, started doing garden maintenance for a few elderly neighbours. She reckoned that the regular contact with these customers was more important than the actual gardening work – a kind of social service.

Ann also joined the local Citizens Advice Bureau (CAB) as a volunteer adviser and would work there for over 25 years, for which she got a national award. She would often come home with harrowing tales of the plight of some clients who she would want to help out of her own pocket or give them shelter, but volunteers were instructed not to do that, so she didn't, but very reluctantly. Later, she would persuade me to become the CAB's Chairman. Her friend Elizabeth Thomas was also a volunteer adviser. She and her husband, Ron, both qualified librarians, put their expertise to work to develop a sophisticated subject referencing system for the CAB. It was such a good system that it was adopted nationally by other bureaux. Tragically, Elizabeth and Ron would both die very young.

Ann has always enjoyed her tennis, but decided to move on to join W.G.C. golf club, which was only just round the corner from our house - ideal for her because she did not drive a car. I would later play there, too. This was where England's most successful golfer, Nick Faldo, started. His application to improve his game was legendary. The club's pro tells how he would teach Nick, then a young teenager, how to do something early in the morning and tell him to go away and practice. Nick would come back several hours later and announce "I've got it" – he had been practicing non-stop. That's how you become the world's best golfer.

The town has other claims to sporting fame. Its Gosling Sports Stadium was built out of a disused gravel pit, which had been created when the town was built. It was a great asset for the town, providing tennis, squash, badminton, football and other sports facilities as well as a home for one of the largest bridge clubs in the country. I played squash and bridge there as well as forming my own small badminton club with friends, appropriately named The Goslings – it should have been The Ganders. A unique feature of the stadium was its cycling track, home to Welwyn Wheelers, whose most famous member was Laura Trott, winner of no less than four Olympic gold medals.

The opening of a direct electrified railway line into Moorgate brought significant changes to the town. It has become a commuter town for highly paid workers in the City. Property prices have soared. There is much more money around, many more restaurants and pubs, and expensive cars are everywhere. Newcomers with lots of money and very little taste have been allowed to extend or alter their neo-Georgian houses in ways which would not have been tolerated when we first came to the Garden City, so its unique charm is gradually being eroded. Several of the small cul-de-sacs with local tennis courts and play areas have given way to housing developments, so the opportunities for getting to know and socialise with your neighbours are fewer. Whilst it still remains a good place to live, something precious is slowly being lost.

However, back in 1964 I was full of enthusiasm for my new life in my new town. My walk to the station each morning along tree lined roads, passed well kept, colourful gardens and down the wide boulevards of Parkway and Howardsgate, framed by lines of massive poplars and other trees, was pure pleasure. I used to look forward to the walk back in the evening, not just because it was the end of a day's work, but to soak up the atmosphere and enjoy the sights of nature all around. By the time I got home I was relaxed and had generally forgotten whatever problem I had been grappling with at work. Ebenezer Howard's vision had certainly worked for me.

Chapter 8

Marylebone Health Matters

So I became one of the 3 million workers commuting into London each day. I got quite a buzz out of it. Provided you got a seat on the train it could be relaxing, too. I would generally read a newspaper or a book or something to do with my work. After a while you got to know other passengers and would chat to them instead. Bob Taylor was one of these. He and his wife, Joan, lived close by and we became good friends. They were Americans, who had lived in Australia and had now settled in the UK. He was a lively character with a sharp, enquiring mind and a ready laugh. He worked at the School of Oriental and African Studies (SOAS) and was a specialist on Burma. He would often feature in BBC news items when they wanted expert comment on some event in that country. He was a member of the Travellers' Club, in London, where Ann and I had a very enjoyable dinner with him and Joan. A low point for me was when they invited us to lunch on Boxing Day with someone from the Burmese Embassy. At the very last minute I told Joan that I could not go. I was exhausted and did not feel well, partly physical, but largely psychological, and just could not face being sociable. It is the only time I have ever done such a thing, but I have never forgiven myself since for letting them and Ann down.

Some years later Bob had hopes of becoming SOAS' Director, but the job went to Tim Lankester, whom I happened to know through playing cricket. Bob was bitterly disappointed, so he left SOAS to become Vice Chancellor of Buckingham University, the private university. Its Chancellor was the Prime Minister, Margaret Thatcher. The thought of having to provide dinner and entertain her filled his wife, Joan, with dread, and she opted to stay in Welwyn Garden City. The two of them eventually split up, which was very sad.

Another fellow commuter was Tony Freeman. He worked for the Prudential, the insurance company, and would become its Chief Executive. Years later, when I worked in the City, I would have some dealings with him. Waiting for the train one day I introduced him to Margaret Novelli, whom I knew because I played squash each week with her husband, Rick Novelli, an Italian. Over the coming weeks Tony and Margaret would often sit together on the train. A friendship blossomed and turned into an affair. They each left their spouses and settled down together. It was devastating for Rick. I was sorry that I may have been instrumental in starting it off, but perhaps it would have happened anyway.

My journey was a simple one – a 20 minute walk to the station, a train to Kings Cross, then a short tube journey to Gt. Portland Street and a short walk to the IOR's offices – just over one hour in total. In the early days I chose to go just after the morning rush hour and return after the evening one. I would leave home before 8.30am and be back home by 7pm, just about in time for the children's bedtime stories. It was very civilised. Dennis Lewis called these "gentleman's hours", and they were, but it would not always be like that.

The IOR's offices were in Hallam Street and our parent body, the Tavistock Institute, was just up the road, which made for easy communication between us. I liked this part of London and enjoyed exploring it. It had a bit of everything. We were within easy walking distance of Soho, Regents Park, Marylebone High St. and Oxford St. People here worked mainly in retail or service jobs or in medical practices, but some in small clothing workshops. People still lived around here, too, from the very rich in the roads adjoining Regents Park to well-off middle class types, including medics, around Harley St., and the less well-off, but upwardly-mobile, in bed-sits around Soho. London is an amazing melting pot.

I enjoyed walking through Portland Place, just two streets away, its buildings faced in Portland stone. The majestically curved Nash terraces were at the end of that street, the Royal Institute of British Architects' Art Deco HQ halfway down, and BBC Broadcasting House at the bottom, with its Eric Gill sculpture of Prospero and Ariel on its front. On the opposite side was the Chinese Embassy, which was a constant source of entertainment. China was going through political turmoil and demonstrations outside it were commonplace. For a while it was occupied by flag-waving dissident Chinese activists and we weren't allowed to go near.

It was good to be reunited with Neil Jessop, who was as enthusiastic as ever about the Institute's mission. When our former colleague, Eric Totman, decided to stay at Courtaulds Neil thought I, too, might have changed my mind, so he was relieved to see me. He introduced me to the rest of the IOR staff. John Stringer, a bright and likeable ex-Cambridge engineer, was Neil's deputy and the leader of the hospital research project on which I would work for the next two years with Mike Luck, an ex- Cambridge mathematician. Mike was my age and very easy to get on with. I already knew John Luckman, a statistician and keen bridge player, who had followed Neil and me from Courtaulds. There were two other researchers and two secretaries in the London office and that was all. IOR did have another small office in Coventry where John Friend led the local government project, but contact between us was fairly minimal. From this modest beginning IOR would go on to make significant contributions in the fields in which it worked.

After the noise, energy and technical challenges of Armstrong Whitworth, followed by the pressures and high expectations of Courtaulds, the atmosphere at the Institute was positively serene. There was time to think, time to study the works of others in the field, and time to join in research seminars and discussions at the Tavistock Institute. Whilst this was all very stimulating I was itching to get my teeth into something more concrete and demanding. We started the hospital project.

John Stringer had negotiated a two year project, funded by the Ministry of Health, looking into the processes by which hospitals adapt and change. John Cornish, our main contact at the Ministry, wanted to find out if a research outfit such as ours could make a real contribution to understanding and resolving problems in the Hospital Service. Unusually for an OR team, our primary role was to analyse and observe, rather than solve problems, and we found it difficult at times to stand back when the hospitals in which we worked were grappling with difficult issues.

We tackled the project by carrying out four case studies in different parts of the country. I took the lead on the commissioning of a new Central Out-Patient Department (COPD) which served two hospitals in Stoke-on-Trent; and on the allocation of minor capital funds at Kings College Hospital in London. Mike Luck took the lead on the setting up of an Intensive Care Unit, as it later became known, at Whipps Cross Hospital in N.E. London and on the development of manpower policies in the Wessex Regional Hospital Board. We worked largely, but not entirely separately, sharing our thinking and making some occasional joint visits. John Stringer took the lead role at the end of the project in drawing together our general conclusions and recommendations for the final report.

I got acquainted with Stoke-on-Trent. It is a sprawling and unlovely city, created in 1910 by amalgamating the five towns of Burslem, Hanley, Longton, Fenton and Tunstall - made famous by Arnold Bennett in his Five Towns novels. This is the potteries, home to the famous Wedgewood and Minton factories. The bottle-kiln ovens of these and many other factories once belched out their thick smoke into the night sky until foreign competitors put most of them out of business. I decided not to stay in Stoke, but at Stone, a pretty village about seven miles south and a ten minute drive to the hospitals.

The two hospitals for which the new Central Outpatient Department (COPD) was being created were about a mile apart with the COPD midway between them. There was intense rivalry between them, despite being part of the same Hospital Group since the formation of the NHS in 1948. They had very different histories. The North Staffs Royal Infirmary (NSRI), founded in 1815, was a former voluntary hospital. The City General Hospital (CGH), formed in 1945, had started its life in 1832 as the Stoke Parish Hospital and Workhouse. They were both large, acute hospitals, each with their own outpatient, X-ray and records departments and pathology laboratories. Neither of them wanted the COPD, campaigning instead to improve their own rundown facilities. Their highest priorities were a maternity hospital, operating theatre suites and an accident unit.

So, why was a COPD being built here? The medical staff had not pressed for it. On the contrary, the Medical Staff Committee was adamantly opposed and voted against it. It was essentially a Regional Hospital Board concept, strongly supported by the retiring Hospital Group Secretary, with the aim of bringing the two uncooperative hospitals closer together. Despite the medical staff's opposition the RHB announced that it would still go ahead and submit the plans for the COPD to the Ministry of Health, which eventually approved them. There was an immediate public outcry and a demand from the Town Council for an urgent meeting to clarify what was going on. Some GPs wrote in to say that a COPD was not needed. The Hospital Group Secretary tried to diffuse this delicate situation by holding informal meetings with the Town Clerk and others and eventually the disquiet was quelled, after which the Medical Staff Committee did a U-turn and said it was now prepared to accept the COPD.

However, it was still the focus of many contentious issues. For example, a ward of 20 beds and two operating theatres had been included in the COPD's design. These had not been asked for by the medical staff, but put forward by the Ministry itself with the aim of treating patients in a single day and so avoiding some inpatient hospital admissions – an early "day hospital".

The building of the COPD was completed in April 1965, about the time we first became involved. A Steering Committee, comprised of senior medical staff and officers, was set up to oversee our research. It was extremely helpful to me throughout, providing complete access to all records and giving me free reign to talk to anyone I liked. The fact that we were doing this for the Ministry gave us great leverage.

With the COPD nearing completion attention turned to its commissioning. This required the cooperation of the two hospitals, which had historically always been a problem. This manifested itself immediately when the Radiologists of hospital A put forward proposals for reorganising the handling of their X-ray films and patient records. The Radiologists of hospital B would not accept them, simply because they were largely those operated by hospital A. There was a similar reaction from hospital A when the Radiologists of hospital B put forward their proposals, resulting in a complete stalemate. Eventually, with time running out, the Group Medical Records Officer (GMRO) exercised his authority and laid down the procedures to be followed.

Resolving issues in this way, however, was the exception rather than the rule because there was usually no single person with the authority to push through a solution. In the complex hospital environment resolving difficult issues required medical staff, nurses, administrators and others to cooperate to find workable solutions, but the mechanisms for doing this simply did not exist. In an industrial or commercial setting there would be a dedicated planning team tasked with getting such a new venture operating efficiently and on time, but not here. The Hospital Service's complex organisational structure did not produce the unified approach needed to get such a new venture off the ground. It fell largely to the medical staff to find sufficient time to address the problems of how best to use the COPD efficiently. Their first priority, however, was the treatment of sick patients, not management and organisational issues. To understand these problems better I got involved in a number of specific issues.

How would the medical staff make use of the unwanted 20 bedded "day hospital"? With the help of two doctors I explored the number and type of patients that might be treated in it, but identified only 98 cases per month, or about four per day, so there was plenty of room to spare. It was clearly far too large. What to do with the spare capacity? The medical staff proposed using just one of the two operating theatres for booked day cases and the other in conjunction with outpatient clinics. This would still leave most of the 20 beds unused. It was a bit of a white elephant.

The process of getting to see a doctor was a frustrating one for patients. Not only was the waiting time to get an appointment inordinately long, typically seven to ten weeks, but they would then have a long wait once they arrived for an appointment. The first problem was resolved by adding more consultant sessions. I turned my attention to the second problem. In today's world patients are given a specific appointment time to see their GP or hospital doctor and expect to be seen more or less at that time, but in 1965 there was no such provision. Patients were told to turn up at the start of a doctor's session and were then seen on a first come, first served basis. The opening of the COPD provided an opportunity to do better, provided the doctors agreed. One did. The consultant dermatologist was a willing volunteer and we introduced a more sophisticated allocation of appointment times. It was a great success and others copied this approach.

The timetable for the outpatient clinic sessions was another potentially contentious area. The way it was organised would clearly have significant implications for the workload on various hospital support functions, such as the X-ray department and pathology laboratories. These dealt with work for both inpatients and outpatients, resulting in large workload fluctuations within the day and from day to day. How do you decide what level of staffing and equipment should be provided? Since the difference between the peak workload and the lowest is about a factor of three, this makes a huge difference to both hospital costs and patient care. I was able to show that these high peaks and troughs could be avoided by reorganising the clinic session timetable and smoothing out the impacts on these departments. Armed with this information the consultants were then able to make informed decisions.

There was another useful outcome from this exercise. I had collected detailed data from a 30% sample of all outpatient and inpatient cases for one month so that I could measure the impact of different types of patient on the hospital system. There were huge variations. For example, a General Medical emergency in-patient needed an average of 20.8 bed-days and 1.9 X-ray examinations, whereas a General Surgical emergency inpatient needed only 8.2 bed-days and 0.85 X-ray examinations. Other patient categories displayed a similar pattern. I developed a way of using such data for hospital planning and commissioning purposes by creating what I dubbed the Hospital Activity Matrix, or HAM. It would enable planners to quantify the impact of different types of patient on all parts of the hospital system and to make plans accordingly. The Medical Staff Committee were genuinely excited by this concept and thought it had great potential.

I helped resolve several other commissioning problems before my time there came to an end. I was genuinely sorry to leave. I had learned a great deal about how hospitals really function and deal with change. This would all feed into our general conclusions at the end of the project.

About this time our second son, Benjamin, was born, so Ann now had three children aged three or younger to look after. It was quite a challenge for her, not helped by me being away a lot. It helped that Benjamin, or Benj as we would later call him, was such a happy child. Helen was a great older sister and all the children got on very well with each other. That harmony would continue throughout the rest of their lives.

The first of the two case studies on which Mike Luck took the lead provided IOR with the opportunity to be involved in one of the most significant developments in the treatment of critically ill patients in the NHS. Mike gave a very good lecture to colleagues in the Tavistock Institute on the work at Whipps Cross Hospital to create an Intensive Therapy Unit, later known as an Intensive Care Unit (ICU).

Essentially, in OR terms, the ICU was a queuing problem - a stream of very ill patients arise from various sources and need a bed and intensive care. How many beds, doctors, nurses and other support services were needed to meet the demand? Mike developed a mathematical model that captured the interrelationship between patient arrivals and bed occupancy for different numbers of beds. Developing such a model, however, was often the easy bit – getting reliable data and persuading the key decision-makers to act was generally the greater problem, and so it proved in this case.

Historically, the most seriously ill patients would be placed at the end of a 30-bedded 'Nightingale' ward, nearest to the Ward Sister's desk. Then, in 1961, three years before our study started, the Chairman of the Medical Staff Committee (MSC) at Whipps Cross, himself a surgeon, suggested that lives could be saved by providing special care for particular types of post-operative medical cases by creating a separate, dedicated "intensive therapy" facility. What he had in mind at that stage was simply an enhanced recovery room. Provision to build one was put into the capital works programme, but nothing happened until 1963 when the Ministry of Health said it would consider funding some patient care experiments. The hospital quickly put together a bid for a twelve bedded unit, but the bid was too late and the funds had run out. Disappointed, but undaunted, the hospital applied for a grant from the Kings Fund, which supported innovations in hospital practices, but was again unsuccessful.

However, the Regional Hospital Board, was now keen for the work to go ahead and offered to find £12,000 towards the capital cost. The hospital would have to find savings to meet the additional running costs. It was a common theme of our work that hospitals paid too little attention to the revenue consequences of capital schemes. It became clear that the only realistic option was to create space by reorganising the wards, but that proved to be far from straightforward, even though about 200 of the hospital's 978 beds were empty when counted at midnight each day. A Working Party was set up, supported by a research team in which IOR played the leading role in the search for solutions. To the dismay of the medical staff, who saw it as an unnecessary delay, the research team proposed a six month survey of patients to identify those needing intensive care.

Using data from the first eight weeks of this survey Mike Luck was able to use his mathematical model to predict the number of beds needed at any one time. His results agreed very closely with the survey's findings, thus establishing confidence in the model's ability to produce realistic and reliable predictions. Eight beds was the figure settled on for planning purposes.

Where to locate it? Funding for a new standalone building was not an option and finding a workable reorganisation to free up space proved far from simple, since all proposals involved extremely complicated chains of moves on which agreement could not be reached with the medical staff. They seemed to lose interest and were loathe to take the initiative. They left it to the Working Party and the research team to put forward further suggestions, which it did, but each of them was resisted by one or more of the interested parties: consultants were reluctant to give up beds, even though they had far more than the Ministry's recommended norms, and Matron was loathe to give up space needed for her sick nurses, and there were other obstacles. Complete stalemate.

This was eventually broken when the Medical Staff Committee agreed to discuss further proposals prepared by Mike Luck and the research team. This proved more fruitful because their findings genuinely surprised the medical staff. The emphasis of the consultant surgeon who first proposed "an intensive therapy" facility had been on saving his post-operative patients, but the survey showed that only 22.2% came via the operating theatre (11.1% of whom died). The vast majority of patients needing intensive care would come from elsewhere - 65.6% via casualty/emergency (34% died) and 12.2% via the wards (30% died). Having these concrete figures and proposals to focus on proved to be the catalyst in the search for solutions. Compromises were made and it was eventually agreed to make changes that would free up two wards, one of which would be for the ICU and the other for a Public Health Laboratory, which the RHB was now also keen to see built.

This agreement did not last long. The consultant surgeons changed their minds. They had long waiting lists and were reluctant to give up beds. Eventually, however, four physicians agreed to give up 28 beds, so freeing up a whole ward, but paradoxically this was now to be used for the Public Health Laboratory, which was deemed to have higher priority. It was back to square one for the ICU. The RHB then stepped in to provide funds for additional accommodation for sick nurses, which freed up a ward for creating an ICU. It was finally brought into operation in 1967, just after IOR completed its work. We did not quite witness its launch, but we had provided the evidence for creating it and were the catalyst for bringing it about. Its creation had provided us with invaluable insights into the ways in which decisions are made, or not made, and into the realities of bringing about change in these complex institutions. ICUs are now a standard feature of modern hospitals

We submitted our final report to the Ministry in September 1966. It was a weighty 500 page tome. Part 1 set out our conclusions about how hospitals adapt and decide to make changes. The four case studies in Part 2 provided the evidence. One of the conclusions that goes to the heart of our findings was: "The initiation of a change is not the result of a single decision taken at a point in time or in one place but occurs under a gradually changing climate of opinion. The rejection of a possible change is even less decisive. An implemented change that has not undergone this gradual process of acclimatisation will not be easily accepted." The hospital environment is very different from an industrial or other commercial setting. Decision-makers with clear authority do not flourish here. Overlapping lines of responsibility almost guarantee indecision. The term "Hospital Management Committee" was also a misnomer, we found. We saw no evidence they played any meaningful part in the actual management of their hospitals. Other conclusions were equally damning.

The Ministry was very pleased with our work and keen to support us in promulgating its findings. It provided funds for us to give lectures to hospital administrators, medical staff, nurses and others and looked for other ways of supporting further work, which continued until 1975, long after I had left. Over the next two years I gave scores of lectures throughout the country, either explaining the results of our work or showing how to apply some of the techniques we used. They were all very well received and I found it extremely rewarding working with such positively motivated people. This would have a bearing on how I chose my next job.

Birmingham RHB was keen to employ us on further work. Under the new Labour Government there was a significant programme of new hospital building, including a maternity hospital for the United Birmingham Hospital and a large District Hospital at Walsgave, Coventry. We were invited to work on both of these. They offered great opportunities for us to help get them off to a good start. Drawing on my experience of using Critical Path Networks at Courtaulds I drew up very large networks for the planning and commissioning of these two hospitals, capturing the sequence of activities that had to be completed before they were ready for opening.

For the commissioning of Walsgrave Hospital I drew up thirteen separate networks, each one dealing with a distinct hospital unit or sphere of responsibility, plus a general one which pulled it all together. Meetings with key staff forced them to focus their minds on what precisely needed to be done, by whom and in what sequence, and how long it might take. Every three or four weeks I met the key persons responsible, presenting them with a short report highlighting those activities that should be started within the next four weeks and any which were now critical (i.e. any delay would put back the whole project's completion date). This process continued until the hospital opened. It was bang on time. I like to think that my work contributed to this.

I enjoyed these meetings and I think the hospital staff did, too, despite the pressures on their time. My networks were the only tangible expression of the whole new building project and it enabled staff in different areas to get a feel for how it was all progressing and how their part fitted into the whole. They also helped Mike Luck prioritise his work on the development of operational policies for the hospital, which he was carrying out in parallel with mine.

I had become a bit of a guru on networks and other OR techniques and over the next two years gave lectures on them to university courses throughout the country, including setting and marking an examination paper for the Diploma in Management Studies at Aston University. I found lecturing very easy, but the thought of doing that repeatedly year after year did not appeal to me. I realised that I was a doer rather than a talker.

Other hospital-related work followed, but by the beginning of 1968 I was becoming very unsettled. IOR had grown significantly as a result of Neil Jessop's and John Stringer's efforts to attract new work and new recruits, who were of a very high calibre. Many would go on to achieve significant success in their later careers. I did not find the work uninteresting, far from it, but I was not at all stretched compared to my time at A.W.A. or Courtaulds. I also had far less personal responsibility. Then, by chance, one of my contacts in the Hospital Service pointed out to me an advertisement for a Computer Manager at St Thomas Hospital. I decided to apply.

Chapter 9

Lambeth & Kennington
The South Bank Show

By 1968, after nearly four years at IOR, I had become restless. The intake of new researchers had changed the working atmosphere and I found it unsettling. I had less responsibility for managing my own projects than I had at either Armstrong Whitworth or Courtaulds. I felt the need to run my own show rather than be under the wing of Neil Jessop and John Stringer, admirable though they both were. When St. Thomas' Hospital advertised for a computer manager for the newly formed Hospitals Computer Centre for London (HCCL) I decided to apply. It offered the prospect of being able to bring together my computer knowledge and my interest in developing their use in some of the most famous hospitals in the country. My application was seconded by the Secretary to the Birmingham Regional Hospital Board and his endorsement would have been key to me being one of the four chosen for interview. At 32 years of age I was the youngest, by far. The favourite, I thought, was the man from Shell.

It was no ordinary selection process. It was spread over two days with a hotel stay in London overnight. We assembled at St. Thomas' on the first day for an early lunch with senior hospital staff. Bryan McSwiney, Clerk to the Governors, and Peter Lumsden, St Thomas' Board member and Chairman of the Computer Centre Committee, welcomed us. I felt a tingle of excitement on entering St Thomas', which was founded in Southwark in 1173 and named after St Thomas a Becket. It is a very impressive landmark building. Its long northern front opened directly onto the river Thames, immediately opposite the Houses of Parliament, whilst its southern front was alongside Lambeth Palace. You felt immediately that you were in an important place in a historic setting. We walked the famous long corridor, which ran the length of the hospital, met some key people and admired the St Thomas' nurses, with their distinctive caps, who were the crème de la crème of the nursing profession. It was here that Florence Nightingale had established the first School for Nurses.

Most of the afternoon was spent at the Computer Centre, located in a large old house a short distance from the hospital. We spoke to staff there, who explained the systems they were operating or developing. The HCCL was a big undertaking by any standards and particularly in the late '60s. It was to serve all the London Teaching Hospitals and all hospital authorities in the North East and South East Metropolitan Regional Hospital Boards. This represented about one quarter of the Hospital Service. It was planned to move in the following year into a brand new building in the grounds of Lambeth Hospital, which we visited.

The idea of a computer centre to serve a large number of London hospitals went back to the mid-sixties. The Ministry of Health set up the embryo Computer Centre in October 1967 with St Thomas' undertaking its administration. As I was to discover later there was a lot of in-fighting amongst the teaching hospitals about who was best placed to have this lead role. Although the Ministry provided the money to set up the Computer Centre its remit thereafter was to operate as a commercially viable unit in its own right, charging for its services and carrying no hidden subsidies to enable it to balance its accounts.

Throughout the day we were shadowed by Les Carter, a former Hospital Treasurer and acting computer manager, and by Peter Foot, Deputy Clerk to the Governors, asking us questions, probing our knowledge and generally sizing us up. This continued in the evening over a sumptuous dinner in Bryan McSwiney's beautiful residence, overlooking the Thames, in a separate house at the southern end of the St Thomas' site. We had drinks on arrival, more drinks with each of the four courses, which included venison, a first for me, and still more after the meal when we retired to Bryan's comfortable lounge. It was late and I thought that was it for the day, but it wasn't. Bryan proposed that we had a debate about the future of the Hospital Service and asked me to start it off. I had no forewarning, but plunged straight in, half drunk. I've no idea what I said, but I learned later that it went down well enough. I got to bed, very tired, but also exhilarated, just before midnight, but had to be up early next morning for the interview before the Computer Centre Committee.

I woke with a thumping headache and felt decidedly thick when I walked into the Boardroom. I was the first. It was not easy to think quickly and clearly and I declined to give an answer to one question on the grounds that I would rather give no answer than the wrong one. I was surprised, therefore, when two days later I got a call from Bryan McSwiney offering me the job. I suspect that I was not the first choice and that the Shell man, vastly more experienced than me, had turned it down: perhaps he had seen the problems ahead rather better than I had. Undaunted, I accepted and stepped into a new world.

The premises from which the Computer Centre currently operated were quite inadequate for its task, but nevertheless for over a year it had provided accounting services to eleven hospitals and was about to operate comprehensive payroll services, too. There was a development team of fifteen systems analysts and programmers and some twenty five data control and data preparation staff. The computing itself, however, was done using various bureaux, which all added to the timing and logistics problems. My immediate tasks were to manage the transition to the new Computer Centre, recruit additional staff needed and, crucially, deal with the diverse needs of the large customer base we were there to serve.

However, sorting out the operational problems of the new payroll service had to take precedence. It was very fraught for several weeks. The problems arose mainly with the weekly payroll. Timing was crucial. Data from as far afield as the south coast and the Essex coast had to be delivered to us, converted into machine-readable punched cards, taken to a computer bureaux for processing, returned to the Computer Centre for checking and, finally, delivered back to each hospital in good time for staff there to make up pay packets and give them out to the staff at the end of their shifts. If this process failed there would be serious repercussions, not only for the local Hospital Treasurer, but also for us as a credible service provider. Courier services were used extensively for collection and delivery and it was touch and go at times whether the timetables would be met, but amazingly they were.

We got through these teething problems and by the time the new Computer Centre opened in July 1969 we were dealing with 22,000 monthly and weekly staff and had firm plans to increase this to 125, 000 by March 1971. The advantages for Hospital Treasurers were not just in providing pay slips, of course, but in all the other comprehensive payroll accounting services built into the system and in the administrative back-up provided. I would visit hospitals to explain these advantages to the staff there and to deal with their questions and concerns. I recall a particularly pleasant visit to Hastings where the Hospital Treasurer and other senior staff gave me a very enjoyable lunch, after which I addressed a large staff gathering and tried to reassure them that the transition would be relatively painless. These meetings went well and I enjoyed getting out of the office and seeing those who would benefit from what we were doing.

During this difficult period I had to deal with any users who doubted our ability to cope. This was made much more difficult when one of my senior systems analysts left to work for Kings College Hospital, a rival teaching hospital group that was about to take our services. He started spreading tales about how unprepared we were and raising alarms in our user community. He had a point. We were. I had yet to appoint several key staff - a Chief Systems Analyst, an Operations Manager and a Computer Room Supervisor. I was summoned to a meeting to answer these charges. It was a very uncomfortable moment, facing considerable hostility from those round the table, but I managed to avert a crisis, and there were no further repercussions.

At about the same time I had another uncomfortable encounter. In trying to put my own stamp on how we ran the Computer Centre I fell foul of Jim Pearson, St Thomas' Treasurer. He handled all our accounts, making payments on our behalf and receiving payments from our users. He needed data from us in order to charge our users. Before he sent out the next invoices I wanted to meet him and get agreement on how we apportioned the costs and determined the unit charges to levy. He was furious when Les Carter told him, on my instructions, that he could not have the data yet. We had a row on the 'phone and he told me in no uncertain terms to provide the data immediately or there would be trouble. I had to agree, but on condition that we met and settled on a better way of charging our users, on which I had done a lot of work. It was a matter of principle for me. Although Jim Pearson handled our accounts, it was my responsibility to make the Computer Centre cost-effective and self-financing, so I had the right to set the charges for our services. We met and reached an amicable agreement, but the affair left a dent in our relations, which was unfortunate because he was a very important player on the various committees which oversaw our work.

Having our own computer, a large ICL 1904E, in the new Computer Centre, rather than using a bureau, would clearly remove one source of uncertainty and delay in the process. I then turned my attention to the data preparation process. A new method of data input, using magnetic tape encoders, made by Mohawk in Canada and marketed in the UK by NCR, was coming on the market. Les Carter and I met NCR salesmen and were soon convinced that they were what we needed. This was cemented over a boozy lunch at which I experienced for the first time the delights of Gevrey Chambertin, the renowned French burgundy.

NCR were very eager to get the business. We would be their first customer for these encoders in the UK. They were very pushy, but I explained that I had to get the agreement of the Computer Centre Committee first and then the Ministry of Health, who would be paying for them. This took a while because the MoH, quite rightly, were sceptical about whether spending £125,000 represented value for money – a very large sum some fifty years ago. Also, if they allowed us to have them and they proved a success, then the rest of the Hospital Service would want them, too. It was a very big investment in 1968, but I made a strong case that it would prove a good one. I had a good meeting with MoH officials, following an exchange of letters and several telephone conversations, and I went off on my summer holiday, confident that they would agree.

A sheepish Les Carter greeted me on my return and produced an NCR contract note, signed "L.J.Carter", ordering the equipment we wanted. He insisted that it was not his signature, but it was as perfect a forgery as I will ever see: too good, in my opinion. I alerted the key people in St Thomas' and the MoH and had an angry exchange with the senior NCR salesman, insisting that they deal with his junior colleague, who had signed the contract. It transpired that he had won the top salesman award in previous years, which carried with it a big bonus and a luxury holiday for two in the Caribbean, and he needed this order to win it again. NCR did not sack him, but took him off front-line sales duties. I never saw him again. The Ministry agreed to us buying the equipment, which proved invaluable when the new Computer Centre came into being. My relations with Les Carter were never the same after that incident. We got on well enough together, but my doubts remained and my respect for and trust in him were irreparably damaged.

I recruited the three key senior posts and several supporting staff. John Steadman, from Vauxhall in Luton, became Chief Systems Analyst; Len Whitrod, our Operations Manager; and Harry Baker, our Computer Room Supervisor. Harry was a delightful, cheery, optimistic character and a good acquisition. John and Len were more difficult personalities and there were tensions between them and Les Carter, in particular. Len was ex-Royal Navy and not very flexible in his views. He complained when I authorised Les Carter to go ahead with his proposal to engage a company to supply and maintain potted plants for the reception area in the new building. Len thought it wasteful and said he could find better uses for the expenditure. He found an ally in John, who turned out to be rather a brooding introvert, and they asked that, in future, minutes should be taken of our weekly management meetings. I did not want to operate in such a formal, bureaucratic way and refused.

It did not make them happy team members, but I was determined to run things my way.

Although our working conditions in the old building were quite inadequate we continued to take on more users onto our current systems, as well as developing the new ones and preparing to move into the new building. It was quite a challenge. Although the current systems were quite sophisticated and comprehensive, they needed now to cater for the needs of a much larger user base. However, I was not my own master in deciding how to set about this task. The Computer Centre Committee led the way. It chose to oversee and drive through the development of these services by setting up technical committees drawn from the two Regional Hospital Boards and of the Teaching Hospitals Association. There was one for accounting services plus three others. Their work was overseen by the Computer Centre Committee, chaired by Peter Lumsden, and by the Advisory Committee of Officers, chaired by Bryan McSwiney. So, there were committees at four levels. I served on or attended all of these, plus others. It was a bureaucratic nightmare. Trying to reconcile the conflicting demands of this disparate group of potential users was not easy.

The Computer Centre was already providing some other non-accounting services and I planned to offer a lot more, drawing on my research work in hospitals. These included a system for the ordering and control of hospital supplies, which was a significant administrative and logistical problem for hospital staff; a system to help manage the scheduling and supply of equipment for new hospital developments; and a network analysis service to project manage the commissioning of such developments.

Of particular interest to me was our Hospital Activity Analysis service, which collected data on the admission, treatment and discharge of patients, providing reports to consultants and hospital managers on waiting and treatment times plus various diagnostic analyses. We planned to extend this to help planners at hospital, regional and Ministry levels by reporting on the use of beds, operating theatres and other hospital resources, and on waiting times for different treatments and medical conditions. We already provided services to one orthopaedic surgeon, recording and maintaining data on patients suffering from Scoliosis. We planned to provide similar services to consultants operating hypertension clinics, maintaining detailed clinical records for each patient, and similarly for obstetric patients. Cancer registrations would be taken on in 1971. I felt that we were really starting to make progress.

With the opening of the new building imminent I wrote a brochure explaining the background to the Computer Centre and setting out how we would provide all these services and what help users could expect from us. Peter Lumsden wrote a brief foreword which captured very well the challenge we faced in trying to satisfy the large number and variety of authorities served. The modern generation, for whom the use of computers is commonplace and accepted, may not be able to appreciate quite how difficult it was in the 1960s to convince people that their use was a good thing. In the Introduction I wrote: "the future may well see each of the authorities served linked directly to the Computer Centre through remote terminals and able to use the computer facilities at the touch of the telephone dial".

All of which is now commonplace, of course, but a bold prophecy at that time, over fifty years ago.

The new building was vast in comparison with our current premises. It was very much a product of the '60s, all plate glass and functional, but a huge improvement as a working environment. The room housing the computer was very large, because computers were in those days. So, too, was the data preparation room, in which the mini-skirted operators of the splendid, new magnetic tape encoders were perched neatly in rows on their swivel chairs. There had been a scare shortly before the official opening when a van driver, making a delivery, walked straight through the large, newly cleaned glass plate window in the reception area. He was not badly hurt, but we had to get an urgent replacement window in very short time.

The Rt. Hon. Richard Crossman, Secretary of State for Social Services, officially opened the HCCL on 18th July 1969. It was a great day for us. I showed him round the building, introduced him to the staff and explained what services we planned to provide. He was a good listener and extremely easy to get on with, unlike some other Ministers I would have dealings with in later jobs. He asked a lot of questions, was interested in what the staff had to say, and left everyone feeling buoyed up by the occasion. It was a very good day, but not sufficiently memorable or important to warrant a mention in the published Crossman diaries.

Talking computers to the Rt. Hon. Richard Crossman

With the opening of the new computer centre I changed my journey slightly. I now walked from the Elephant & Castle instead of Lambeth North tube station. I much preferred the old walk. That part of Lambeth was popular with Members of Parliament. I would recognise some, including Richard (later Lord) Marsh, the Labour Government's maverick Minister of Transport, whose contribution was pivotal in starting the transformation of British Rail, following the body blow of the short-sighted Beeching Report and its drastic cuts to the rail network and services, which severed towns from the rest of the country and led to many of them suffering a slow death. We witnessed this in Alford, Lincolnshire where our friends, Jill and Ray Rundle, lived: it never recovered. Richard Mash was a rising star in the Labour Government, but Harold Wilson unexpectedly sacked him for opposing Barbara Castle's "In Place of Strife" Bill. He was subsequently appointed Chairman of British Rail. Until Richard Marsh came on the scene the consensus was that the railway age was over, just as the railways had replaced the canals, and the development of motorways would see cars and lorries take all the traffic. We now know how important it is to have a thriving railway system, but that was not obvious fifty years ago, and we have a lot to thank Richard Marsh for.

That part of Lambeth comprised streets of residential terraced housing, a bit reminiscent of Leicester, but higher quality, catering for a mix of working class and middle class families. It had a few "squares", not as grand as those for the upper middle classes in Bloomsbury and elsewhere, but smaller, triangular shaped "gardens". I enjoyed walking through them. The area was heavily bombed in the war. I would sometimes have a pub lunch with Les Carter, but would more often go for a short walk on my own at lunchtime to clear my head and get some fresh air. I discovered the old church of St Mary-at-Lambeth, next to Lambeth Palace, which has since been converted into the Museum of Garden History, following the discovery there of the tombs of John Tradescant, father and son, renowned 17th century royal gardeners and plant hunters. Their names live on in the plants in my garden.

My new walk, from the Elephant & Castle, was very different and less enjoyable. The starting point, the hideous shopping centre there, must be the ugliest in the country and quite a threatening place. Kennington itself is a more up-market area than Lambeth. The houses are generally taller and more imposing, often with gardens, front and back. It feels less cosy and friendly than Lambeth. The Imperial War Museum is close by, but I didn't find time to visit it. The Oval cricket ground was also within walking distance. It's not my favourite Test Match venue. Although it had perhaps the best playing area, which was vast, its seating was bleak and soulless. It was tolerable on a fine summer day, but dreadful when it turned cold and windy.

Throughout my time at the HCCL I was also heavily involved in the running of the town's cricket club and in local Labour Party politics, which added to the pressures on my time and Ann's patience. Throughout the year, as cricket club secretary, I had various committees to run, plus the AGM. For these I had to produce and distribute numerous papers, all of which had to be typed and copied. This was done using an old-fashioned, clunky Imperial Typewriter to produce stencils which could be run off on Gestetner copying machines, using lots of messy black ink and muscle power. The era of word processors, electronic devices and photocopiers was a long way off. My secretary at the HCCL, Lynda, was an absolute treasure. She offered to do the typing and to help me run off the copies, after working hours, on the HCCL's equipment – strictly illegal. I offered to reward her for her efforts, but she would take nothing. Her husband, becoming suspicious of hanky-panky, I think, came along as chaperone towards the end of my time there, but ended up helping me collate the papers.

W.G.C. Cricket Club's Annual Dinner. Ann and I are on the left.

For the local Labour Party I helped with canvassing and other tasks at local and national elections as well as collecting contributions from members every Friday evening for a fund-raising scheme. Ron Thomas, a friend of ours, was chairman of the Handside Ward committee and I was secretary. At the time there was a strong Labour Party presence in our ward and we were very active. However, since the electrification of the railway line into Moorgate, the make-up of the town generally and our area, in particular, has changed and it is now overwhelmingly Conservative or Liberal Democrat. In 1968 the town's Council was run by Labour and local politics was quite lively. I attended the party's General Management Committee meetings, but found them tedious and a waste of my time, so I stopped going. I detest petty party politics.

In my experience it is not generally just one event or factor that causes you to think seriously about moving on, but a variety of circumstances that together conspire to give you itchy feet and then propel you to take action. With the official opening of the HCCL successfully accomplished I took stock. I was fed up with the bureaucratic nightmare of the committees, panels and working parties through which we had to work and the political infighting that went with them. I was not happy with some of my key senior staff - Les Carter, John Steadman and Len Whitrod – on whom I relied in order to get anything done. Nor did I like Jim Pearson, the St Thomas' Treasurer, with whom I had to work closely on the Computer Centre's costs and its charges to customers. Finally, Ann was pregnant for the fourth time and was struggling. This was not helped by my long hours of work, leaving home at 7.15am and getting back after 8pm, with a journey time of nearly one and a half hours each way to and from Lambeth Hospital. I decided to leave and applied for the post of Management Services Manager for ITT Components Group (Europe), based at Harlow, about 30 minutes drive by car from home. I got the job and started in mid-September 1969.

As the 1969 cricket season came to an end I said my farewells to staff at the HCCL and St Thomas'. They were shocked by my decision, and disappointed, but I was convinced it was the right one. Although I had only been in the job for just under two years I felt I had achieved a great deal. It was my first management job and I had done it reasonably well, I thought. I had steered the Computer Centre through a very difficult transition and seen it successfully launched. Whoever succeeded me would have a good base on which to develop the Computer Centre's services.

Chapter 10

Harlow

Now We Are Four

So, I was now ITT's Management Services Manager at Harlow. Dennis Wragg, my new boss, asked me to join him for a drink in a local pub where I would meet the three staff who would report directly to me. We got on well. At that stage of my life this move suited me perfectly. I did not have to leave home until about 7.45 a.m. and got home by about 6.30pm on most days, so I saw more of Ann and the children. In my last job I would often not have left work by that time and would have left home earlier in the morning. I also got more money and did not have the expense of a railway season ticket, so it was a win-win situation. Providing the job turned out to be OK this would go down as a very good move. It did. I settled into the new routine, which was much more relaxing.

I enjoyed my new journey to work, which was delightfully simple. There were no long walks, trains and tubes. I simply got in my car and drove to Harlow. It was also a pleasant route, through the tiny villages of Cole Green, Birch Green, Staines Green and Hertingfordbury before reaching Hertford and then on to Harlow. It wasn't the quickest of journeys, but I didn't mind that. It's much quicker now after a new dual carriageway was built to bypass the villages, swallowing up yet more of our fast diminishing countryside.

ITT's factories and my office were on the outskirts of Harlow and I never really got to know the town itself. The original town is now known as Old Harlow. It had one of the oldest cricket clubs in the country, founded in the late eighteenth century. I liked what I saw of it, including many fine 16th - 18th century listed buildings. I had no need to go into the new town and what I saw did not encourage me to go again. It was founded in 1947, following The New Towns Act of 1946, which was the Labour Government's response to London's chronic housing problem as a result of the bombing in the war. The people who moved there from London would have found it a breath of fresh air, but it does not come up to the standards set by the first New Towns, including Welwyn Garden City.

I was given a royal welcome on my first day. The Chief Executive, Doug Stevenson, and all the other Divisional Managers were there to meet me and wish me well. It was such a surprise. I still do not know if they were just there for my benefit or had assembled for a meeting that just happened to coincide with my arrival, but I was impressed and it got me off to a good start. Ken Walton, the Comptroller for the whole European operation, based in Brussels, and a very powerful operator in the company, was also there. It was a bit of a comedown, therefore, to be taken afterwards to my new office, which was in a corner of a large open plan area, with screens to provide some privacy. I had forgotten that this was how manufacturing companies operated. Separate offices, with walls and a door, were reserved for a handful of the company's most senior managers, and I wasn't quite in that category.

My responsibilities included providing computing services to the company, based on an ICL 1904E, with which I was familiar, plus O&M and Work Study services. In practice, I devoted most of my time and energies to computing. In Dan Lynch, my Systems Manager, I had a real star. Together we would tackle the company's lack of an overall systems strategy - separate systems had grown up, like Topsy, under my predecessors. There was also an Operational Research capability in the company, but curiously it did not report to me, but directly to Doug Stevenson, the Chief Executive. The only time I had any serious contact with them was when Doug Stevenson asked them to give an opinion on the strategy that I would put forward for rationalising and improving the company's computing services, which they endorsed.

ITT – International Telephone and Telegraph – was an enormous company, comparable in size to IBM. It was founded in 1920 with headquarters in New York. It had become a very diverse manufacturing enterprise, having taken over several key technology companies, and now operated in 32 countries. In the UK it had acquired Standard Telephone and Cables, which was now part of ITT Components Group Europe. In the UK there were factories in Harlow, where I worked, and in Paignton, Devon, where I also had some of my staff.

The company was organised as a number of separate Divisions responsible for manufacturing specific electrical and electronic components. These Divisions were all customers of my Group and we provided completely separate systems for each of them, even though the basic requirements were largely the same, which seemed crazy to me. Their sales promise to their retail and wholesale customers was to satisfy orders very quickly. They needed systems, therefore, which captured and kept track of customer orders and kept close control of the stocks in the factories to supply these orders. These then fed into the production and scheduling systems for replenishing the stocks. We ran systems for each of these stages for each Division. There were also the usual systems for payroll, accounting etc, but it was the systems which supported the sales and manufacturing processes which took most of our effort, mainly because of the need to run and maintain so many different systems and to deal with regular requests for changes to them.

I set about rationalising these old systems, identifying a common set of requirements which a common set of new systems would meet. Dan Lynch and I developed our ideas and held a series of seminars with each Division to try to win them over, and gradually we did. The final step was to get the approval of Doug Stevenson, Chief Executive, to both the new strategy and its cost implications. He turned to his Divisional Managers and his Operational Research Officer for their views. They all gave it the thumbs up and we were up and running. The programming team then took over and the new systems were developed.

I liked that part of my job, dealing with people in order to bring about change. I liked the challenge and then the reward when it all came good. Other aspects of my job were a bit more frustrating at times. Being part of an American company and of a European Group brought with it a number of obligations. The Chief Executive

Officer of ITT, Harold Geneen, was a legendary micromanager. He ruled his empire from New York through an elaborate planning process, requiring all parts to set out in great detail what they planned to do, what it would cost, what it would achieve and how you would measure the outcomes. He set ambitious annual sales growth targets, which he expected companies to meet, and would hold regular meetings with each part of his empire to review progress against the plan.

We went through this elaborate planning process once a year. The plans could not be in prose. It was no use writing an essay on what you aimed to achieve. You had to produce hard figures, agreed with the Heads of Divisions that were using our systems, which wasn't easy. Since I was new to this game, Ken Walton, the Comptroller for the European Group, asked my opposite number in Germany to guide me through the process. He came over to see me and I would then visit him in order to finalise the figures. It was approaching Christmas and I spent a lovely evening with him roaming round Nuremberg's famous Kris Kringle Fair, beneath the towering sandstone city walls. There was thick snow on the ground and it was all quite magical. I was less enchanted by the driving of my host at over 100mph on the largely empty autobahn.

As Comptroller, Ken Walton took a particular interest in the computing activities across the Group. Every year he brought together all the European Management Services Managers for a two day conference in Brussels. I flew over with him and we talked through the change of strategy I had in mind for the UK's operations. Before we had got off the plane he had persuaded me to give the keynote talk to the conference the next day. As a new boy I thought I would be sitting back and listening to what others had to say. Instead I was closeted in my hotel room frantically trying to put together a talk which would not bore the audience to tears. Ken seemed pleased enough with the result.

Whilst I was working out how to deliver this talk, Ann was about to deliver something much more important. Our third son, Graham, was born in late October and we then had four children aged seven or under, which was a huge burden for Ann, especially as she did not drive a car. I look back on the years that followed with amazement at how well she coped. She was helped by some exceptionally good friends – Catherine Hall, Bev Stewart, Elizabeth Thomas, Sue Ackroyd, Jean Sefton, Mary Jackson, Joan Taylor and others. When their children were very young they collaborated in running an informal play-group for their pre-nursery school children, taking it in turns to look after them. Catherine and Sue, in particular, gave Ann a lot of support and encouragement when she most needed it.

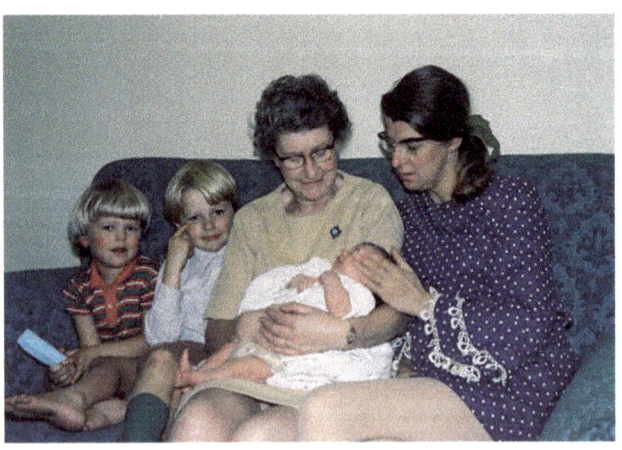

Ida and Ann with baby Graham and the boys

Helen was also a great older sister and particularly good at entertaining Graham. The children had happy childhoods and grew up to enjoy each other's company, which they still do.

Bruce, Helen with baby Graham, and Benj

The saddest event of 1969 was the death of my father. Although he had finally given up smoking, following warnings from doctors and entreaties from me, it was too late to reverse the damage to his lungs, which eventually stopped working. It was a pitiful sight to see him struggling for breath after only a short walk. In December, just before Christmas, I got a call from mum. Dad had been taken into hospital and wanted to see me. I drove up to Leicester and spoke to the doctors, who said that his lungs were like tissue paper and he would not recover. I said my good byes. He died the next day, aged 61.

I had never been particularly close to my dad. We simply did not do enough things together in the same way that I did later with my own children and they do now with theirs. We had also gone through the difficult period in my late 'teens that I described earlier. Nevertheless, I was fond of him and very sad when he died. I have two abiding memories of him. The first is of him deep down in a hole he had dug in the ground to repair a broken water pipe for a neighbour. He would do this and similar favours for nothing. He was a very kind and generous man. The other is of him walking down the street on Sundays dressed in his best suit, immaculate white shirt and red tie, with a neat white handkerchief in his breast pocket. His hair would be plastered down with Brylcream, neatly parted, and he would always have a cigarette in his left hand. As he walked he would greet and be greeted by almost everyone he passed, always ready with a witty comment and a broad smile. He liked to be liked and he was.

It was a difficult time for mum, but she had my brother, Terry, living just a few doors away in Acorn Street and my sister, Sheila, close by, too. She spent increasing periods of time staying with us and going on holidays with us, particularly to the Lleyn Peninsular in Wales in spring. It was often very wet and windy. One year the children and I braved Hell's Mouth beach in a howling gale which bent us double and threatened to blow us all over, the wind whipping up the sand into a sandstorm and stinging our legs painfully. Another year it rained so heavily every day that we decided to come back a day earlier, having run out of ideas as to what to do with the children. Some years it was sunny, though, and when the sun shone it was a magical place. There are few better places to be with young children on a fine day than Abersoch and Llanbedrog beaches. Alan and

Janet (Ann's sister) and their children came with us one year and we had a good time together.

Ann's mum, Ida, would often come and stay with us at the same time as my mum and the two of them got on surprisingly well, despite their very different backgrounds. After a while mum decide to sell her house so that my brother, Terry, could move into it. It was typical of her generosity that she gave £1000 each to me, Sheila and Terry, leaving herself very little. I tried to talk her out of it, but she would not change her mind. She then moved in with Sheila's family, which was probably not a good thing. Sheila's husband, Derrick, later left Sheila for another woman, leaving Sheila devastated. She never really recovered from that blow. Sheila found mum a very good flat in a brand new sheltered housing scheme nearby and mum had several happy years there.

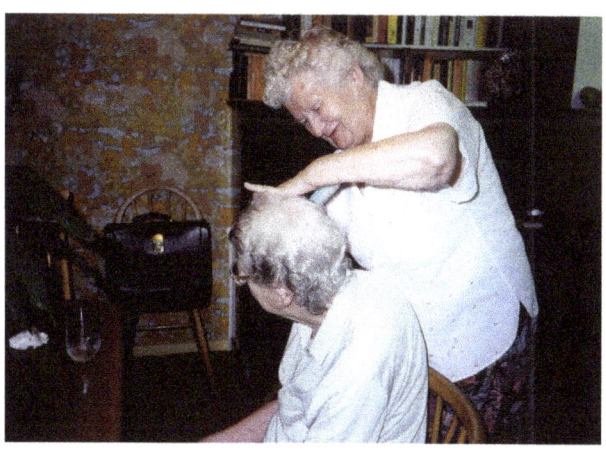

Mum does Ida's hair

In April 1969 Neil Jessop, IOR Director and my old boss, died suddenly of a heart attack. He had suffered from high blood pressure for some years. I went to his Memorial Service held in the Royal College of Physicians building, which fronted Regents Park. It is a striking building, but not universally liked. It was designed by Denys Lasdun, a controversial architect, who was also responsible for the National Theatre, which broke new ground in its use of bare concrete and narrow slits for its windows. The Physicians' building was equally unusual. The main structure echoed the National Theatre in its style, but attached to it was a large dome-like building, which housed the conference halls and lecture rooms, made of dark blue and black bricks, giving it an austere appearance. Some thought it was quite out of keeping with John Nash's elegant and ornate Cumberland Terrace that defines this road. Its saving grace, just like the National Theatre, however, is that it works wonderfully well from the inside. It also has tall narrow slits for its windows, but inside it seems light and spacious. I loved it, but it had a lot of detractors. It is now a Grade 1 listed building.

The Service was very well attended, a tribute to the affection and respect in which Neil was held. There were several glowing tributes. I talked to ex-IOR colleagues afterwards, including John Stringer, who was now IOR's Director. He wondered if I would be interested in coming back to the Institute. They had just been asked to undertake a very high profile project for the Civil Service, reviewing the scope for relocating Central Government from London, and he needed someone capable of leading it. He also revealed that he, Mike Luck and John Luckman had been writing a book, "Hospitals, Patients and Operational Research", about IOR's research work in hospitals. It was about to be published. Some of it was work that I had been involved in and he realised that it would be appropriate to add my name, which he did. It was too late, however, for me to change the content, but I did read it before it went off for printing. I could have argued for some changes, but I let it pass.

John Stringer wrote to me about the work I might undertake, should I return to IOR. He was keen to have me back. The more I thought about his offer the more attractive it became, despite having to resume commuting into London again. I found the prospect of working inside Whitehall irresistible and told John that I would rejoin in the autumn. He was delighted. Dennis Wragg, Dan Lynch and others at ITT were not so pleased, but I left them in a stronger and more satisfactory position than when I joined.

And so I became a commuter again.

Chapter 11

Whitehall
Your Move, Sir Humphrey

So I resumed my old journey to IOR's offices in Hallam Street. It was good to be working with John Stringer again, but there were now many new staff that I had to get to know. I would soon engage nearly all of them on a major assignment that IOR had secured and that John had asked me to lead. This was the Government's Review into the potential for dispersing government departments from London. The Machinery of Government Division of the Civil Service Department (CSD) had the task of conducting this Review under the overall direction of Sir Henry Hardman. They had engaged CSD's Management Services (Operational Research) Division to do the investigative work. MS(OR) had, in turn, subcontracted the bulk of that work to IOR. Our main contribution was to design and carry out a study of the pattern of face to face communications within and between Government Departments in London and to build a model that would analyse the data and measure the implications of moving some of the work of those departments out of London.

The driving force behind the work was Clive Priestley, who was then only a Principle, but had the bearing of someone several grades higher, which he soon would be. Clive was an absolute delight to work with. Unlike most of his senior colleagues he was not a product of Oxbridge, but of Nottingham University, where he was President of the Students Union. He was the epitome of an English civil servant and would not look out of place in "Yes, Minister". He was very slim, thin faced, bespectacled and immaculately dressed with not a hair on his head out of place. He would stride out to meetings across Whitehall, with a furled umbrella on his arm, wearing a tailored overcoat with an astrakhan collar and a bowler hat. He spoke very precisely in a clipped voice, but had a great sense of humour. When he was agitated he would smoke furiously. This assignment was both a big challenge and a big opportunity for him. Get it right and his promotion to Assistant Secretary would be assured. He did.

Sir Henry Hardman had made his name as the first Permanent Secretary (i.e. head) of the modern unified Ministry of Defence (MoD) after the separate departments for the Armed Services (Army, Navy and RAF) were all brought together under one Ministry. He was very easy to work with and was comfortable using an operational research team to do the work. He will have been familiar with the use OR in his MoD days, where it had a major operational role.

This was my first experience of Whitehall and I was fascinated by it. Our meetings with Sir Henry, Clive and his senior colleagues were in the Old Admiralty Building, one side of which fronted onto Horse Guards Parade. The rooms, windows and doors were all unusually large and the ceilings high. Its long, wide corridors had attractive, marble tiled floors. This gave it a somewhat clinical atmosphere in which every footstep set off a series of echoes. It would have made a good hospital. Our meetings were around large, rectangular oak tables. When Tom Caulcott, Clive's Under Secretary held a meeting he would often conduct it lying down on his chaise-longe, because he had a heart ailment. It was a bit bizarre, but it worked. I got to understand how the Civil Service pecking order worked, the best example of which was when Clive submitted a memo - dubbed a 'minute' in Civil Service parlance - which went to five more senior colleagues, in turn, with the Head of the Civil Service as the final recipient, if those below agreed to forward it.

Clive and I got the Review underway with visits to the 31 Government Departments and 34 other government bodies which were candidates for dispersal. It was a bit of a marathon, having to keep repeating the same messages at each meeting, but it was important to get it right and secure the credibility of the review process from the start. We would first meet the Permanent Secretary (i.e. department head) to explain the process and what we wanted from them. Sir Henry would take the lead on visits to the very largest departments, such as the Ministry of Defence, but Clive and I would do most of the talking. The possibility of being dispersed was clearly an emotive issue and we held several large departmental meetings to explain to staff what we were doing, how we would do it and why. Because we had prepared well these meetings went much better than I might have expected.

I explained how we planned to carry out the communications study. Staff would complete a questionnaire about their pattern of face to face contacts within the department or with other departments or with others outside government. Each department appointed a small team to carry out the study and we provided a "linkman" to support them. These "linkmen" were largely IOR staff, whose attitude to the project was very mixed. They enjoyed the insight they got into the work of government departments, but their roles were not very demanding and a long way from what they considered to be 'proper' operational research. Keeping them motivated was an important issue for me.

We classified the bodies under review into 1,500 different blocks of work, which were deemed indivisible, and identified some 6,000 others with whom they had contact. On completion of the questionnaires we presented reports to the head of each block of work showing its pattern of communications. This data was then incorporated into a computer model, developed by my IOR colleague, Dr Hadley Hunter, which calculated the "communications damage" that would be done if a block was dispersed to particular locations and staff had to travel to maintain these face to face meetings. Various options were explored in Sir Henry's final published report, but his preferred recommendation was to disperse 31,427 (about 36%) of the 86,000 posts under review, to 19 locations scattered throughout the UK. These ranged from Plymouth in the south west to Teesside in the north east, Cardiff in Wales and Glasgow in Scotland.

The review went to great lengths to allow for the effect on the efficiency of departmental operations, the attractiveness to staff of different locations and the capacity of these locations to accommodate the work. There was also a very good study by colleagues in the

Tavistock Institute on the "human aspects of dispersal", flagging up the measures needed to make dispersal a success, which were very well received when Sir Henry's report was published.

The final report was published in June 1973 and Kenneth Baker, then Minister for the Civil Service, presented it to Parliament. Sir Henry and I sat high up in the gallery in the House of Commons looking down on the proceedings. Clive and his colleagues sat down below in the special boxed area reserved for Civil Servants, which is to the right of the Speaker's Chair and sufficiently close to the front bench where Ministers sit to allow for messages to be passed. I would soon become familiar with that practice myself.

Kenneth Baker handled the debate and the many questions from MPs with great assurance and skill. He was a good operator. Sir Henry and I listened with a certain amount of trepidation, anxious to see how MPs would react to our work. It was soon apparent that the only issue which really concerned them was the choice of locations and, in particular, why nothing was coming to their constituency - Scottish MPs were particularly vocal. How we carried out the review and arrived at the numbers recommended was not challenged. Neither was it challenged by the departments affected or by Civil Service staff representatives. I think that speaks volumes for the way the review was planned and carried out. Clive Priestley thoroughly deserved his promotion to Assistant Secretary that would soon follow.

This assignment cemented the reputation of operational research as an effective tool for tackling difficult policy issues and we got a lot of accolades. More work for IOR followed. Clive became Head of Special

Assignments Division, which was carrying out a programme of Management Reviews of Government Departments. Buoyed by the Dispersal Review experience he asked MS (OR) for assistance and it, in turn, turned to IOR, so I got involved in these reviews.

I spent the best part of the next year travelling to and from Edinburgh to work on the Management Review of the Scottish Office. Staying in Edinburgh was a real bonus. I loved it. I stayed in just about every hotel in the city centre and got to know all the nooks and crannies of its dark granite streets. On a cold, wet evening with the wind howling from the east it can be a forbidding place, but when the sun shines it is very attractive.

I happened to be there when the Edinburgh Festival was on – in those days it was held in the late autumn as a way of extending the tourist season, but is now a late summer event. After supper I decided to go to a Fringe event and was walking down The Royal Mile when I saw a large blackboard propped up outside a church hall with the words "O.U.P. 7.45pm" on it. It was advertising an Oxford University Players show, so I went in. There were only a few other people there, so I sat near the front of an open stage. A young man came in with a very large rag doll, which he proceeded to talk to and play with for the next hour or so. By the end I was begging him to stop because he was so funny and we were all laughing so much that it positively hurt. I told Ann about him when I got home. About two years later I saw him again on TV and he was just as funny. It was Rowan Atkinson, who has since gone on to be one of our most successful and clever comedians.

Back in London I had lunch with the Head of MS (OR), Ken James, at The Athenaeum, one of the more imposing gentlemen's clubs that can be found in the area between Piccadilly and St James Park. He wanted to persuade me to leave IOR and become a Senior Principal Scientific Officer (SPSO) in MS(OR) Division. Given the positive experience I had had of working with the Civil Service I was very tempted and promised to think about it. I was a believer in the value of public service generally, so I was seriously thinking of accepting when I had a counter offer from John Stringer at IOR. He wanted me to become his Deputy Director. That was a big surprise, as I told John, and I was very flattered. I was torn as to which way to go. I felt a strong allegiance to IOR, having taken the considerable risk of following Neil Jessop down to London ten years earlier, and wanted it to be a success. That counted a lot for me and I knew that I could work well with John, so I accepted his invitation.

However, nothing was ever quite that simple at IOR. Before the growth of the Institute such a decision would have been taken quickly and acted upon, but it was now a much bigger and more democratic organisation, so there was internal discussion about this change. Dr Robert Harris expressed some misgivings, for unexplained reasons, and tried to get others to join him. I suspect that their experience of the Civil Service Dispersal project might have led them to see me as a managerial, controlling figure rather than an innovator, which was spectacularly wrong. They were largely unaware of my creative contributions during the first four years of IOR and elsewhere. This reaction threw me and I told John that I did not want to be appointed against this background. I went back to Ken James and told him that I would accept the MS(OR) post.

So, in 1974 I became a Civil Servant. It would prove to be a very good decision and lead to opportunities that I could not have foreseen at the time. I continued to work with IOR for a while, employing them as contractors on specific projects. When I moved on to other posts within the Civil Service, however, I lost touch with them, except for occasional reunions. John Stringer himself left some years later to become a Professor in Sydney, Australia. Many other talented colleagues also moved on and became very successful.

John Friend, an old IOR colleague, had worked from the Institute's Coventry base and had made a name for himself and IOR on local government planning and decision-making. He tried valiantly to keep the old IOR flame alive, but the Institute eventually ceased to exist. More recently he invited me to open a gathering at the London School of Economics to mark the 50th anniversary of IOR's birth and to consider where OR was now heading. A few old IOR colleagues were there, including Dr Robert Harris. I found it a sad affair, but the general consensus was that the Institute had made a significant contribution to the development of Operational Research thinking, widening its scope and ambition, but the future direction of OR was far from clear.

Later, in 2007, on a visit to my old Mathematics Department at Birmingham University I learned that the department now regarded OR as an integral part of its curriculum rather than a separate discipline. The focus there was on learning straightforward modelling techniques that OR employed, which was a long way from its contribution in the early '40s to tackling anti-submarine warfare or, later on, trying to solve messy public sector problems with multiple decision-makers and fuzzy boundaries, which was IOR's raison d'etre. OR was not dead, but it was now regarded simply as a set of techniques.

Would it have made a difference had I stayed at IOR as Deputy Director? It would probably not have gone downhill quite so fast, because John and I would have found ways of keeping it viable and relevant, but the longer term outcome may have been the same. IOR may just have been a product of its time: the vibrant sixties and seventies were a time for social change and new thinking, but the eighties and beyond brought a harder edge.

More immediately I set about trying to make a success of using OR from within the Civil Service.

Chapter 12

Whitehall From the Inside

Yet another change for me to come to terms with. I was now a civil servant with a permanent office in the Old Admiralty Building in Whitehall rather than just a pied-a-terre. I liked both the office and the location. I had a spacious, high ceilinged room, complete with large oak table for holding meetings. I was within a short walk of Trafalgar Square, the National Gallery and the National Portrait Gallery in one direction and of St James Park in the other, all close enough to spend a few minutes there at lunchtime, if I could find the time.

Most of the time, however, I would not be in my office, but elsewhere carrying out a departmental Management Review. We first reviewed the Welsh Office where the Principle Finance Officer, Dan Griffith Jones, wanted to explore different approaches to distributing the Rate Support Grant (RSG) to local authorities in Wales. We developed mathematical models which captured the main determinants of local authorities' expenditure and collected the data we needed to use them. This enabled us to generate alternative RSG scenarios from which the Welsh Office could choose its preferred approach.

This review was a pleasure to work on. At the personal level I got on well with Dan Griffith Jones, enjoying a lovely dinner with him and his wife one evening. I also relished this chance to go back to Wales, which I had fallen in love with as a schoolboy and continued to enjoy on family holidays. I had been to nearby Swansea and the Gower Peninsula, but Cardiff was new to me. It is certainly not as obviously a capital city as Edinburgh, but it has its features. The Welsh Office itself is both grand and stylish. Its gleaming white buildings stand out in the lush green parkland of Cathays Park, but for Welshmen the real powerbase is Cardiff Arms Park, the home of Welsh rugby and a shrine to its fervent supporters. It sits right in the centre of the city and towers over the surrounding buildings. There is a great atmosphere on match days with lots of singing and good humour as brightly coloured supporters flocked in from the valleys and elsewhere to cheer their heroes.

We moved on to review the Home Office's Immigration and Nationality Department (IND). It proved to be a minor triumph, to the delight of my new boss, Ken James, the Head of MS (OR). The IND was based at Lunar House, a hideous grey tower block in the centre of Croydon, which is itself a grey, bleak and soulless place, with long queues of would-be immigrants waiting patiently outside Lunar House to be seen.

Our first task was to understand IND's operations and the decisions they made. We analysed records to determine the numbers allowed to stay in the country, or not, for a variety of reasons, from which we created a mathematical model to simulate the streams of applications over three years. It was a painstaking job. There were row upon row of huge metal filing cabinets filled with cards, one for each person, created when they entered the country and updated when their status changed. We collated and analysed these by category for three years (1973-75) - e.g. work permit holders; students; visitors allowed to stay on various conditions; etc. The results were most unexpected. For example, of the 10,200 work permits issued in 1974 less than a quarter went to applicants newly admitted into the country. That was a big surprise to everyone. The largest number (28.5%) went to those who already had work permits and now wished to extend them; whilst another 25% went to applicants who had entered the UK earlier as students and now wanted to stay and work; and another 25% had entered previously as visitors and now wanted to stay and work. The results for other categories threw up similar surprises. The biggest surprise to me was that such analyses were not being carried out routinely. It was crying out for computerisation and we said so.

By OR standards it was a very simple bit of work, because it involved no complicated mathematics or optimisation, but it made a big impression on the managements of IND and CSD. The head of the Immigration and Nationality Department was absolutely delighted and wrote to me, praising the work fulsomely. It was an Olympics year and he wrote "if gold medals were in my gift I would award you plenty". It does not get much better than this.

I copied the letter to Ken James, who passed it on to Sir John Herbecq, the Head of CSD, and to Sir Ian Bancroft, Head of the Civil Service. Ken was particularly keen to have this opportunity to blow the trumpet of OR because in an earlier meeting Sir John had declared that he had not bothered to read the report "because it was only OR". There was clearly some past history there of which I was not aware.

Soon afterwards, following the UK's entry into the Common Market and the adoption of free movement for EU nationals, IND discontinued the completion of embarkation cards and the UK lost control of its borders.

After this review Ken James made a point of asking me to lunch at his club, the Atheneum, ostensibly to talk about current work and about the OR world more generally, but I realised later that he was sizing me up as his possible successor. Those plans, however, were quickly overtaken by events because I was offered a transfer to the Administrative Class and promotion to Assistant Secretary. This would be a very significant change which I needed to think carefully about, so I did not accept immediately. Ken James worked furiously to persuade me not to accept but to stay in OR, holding out the prospect of eventually succeeding him. He was the de facto Head of OR in Government. I was torn between the two, but eventually decided to accept the transfer and the promotion. My work on the dispersal project and the Management Review programme had given me insights into how the government machine worked and I was excited by the prospect of becoming a part of that machinery. Assistant Secretary is the first significant grade in the hierarchy of senior civil servants. I transferred in November 1978.

I was a bit apprehensive at first. Nearly all the others I knew at this grade and above were ex- Oxbridge and privately educated. How would I fit in? I need not have worried. I soon settled in. My new boss, Clive Priestley, who was also a grammar school boy and a graduate of Nottingham University, was a great help. He would regularly take me off to his club for lunch or "rest and recreation", as he would call it. He was keen to find out whether, as a new boy, I had any problems. I hadn't, but it was very reassuring to know that he was there if I needed any help. He was a good man-manager.

The first Management Review I was in charge of was of the Department of the Environment (DoE). There was a blueprint for doing them, the key to success being to make the department feel that it was in the driving seat. The department's Permanent Secretary chaired a Steering Committee of senior staff from his department plus senior CSD and Treasury representatives. The review team was led by an Under Secretary from the department with me as co-leader. We did a trawl of possible subjects for review and chose about ten. On completion the Steering Committee decided whether, and how, to implement the review's findings. The Treasury's clout generally ensured that they were implemented.

One of the projects in the DOE review proved to be plain sailing because it coincided with Michael Heseltine becoming Secretary of State. He wanted to introduce a reporting system which would show, for each activity and policy in his department, how much effort was being expended, at what cost and with what outcome. We developed this with some simple models and dubbed it the Ministerial Information System (MINIS). It was implemented and became a permanent feature. Michael Heseltine was very proud of this innovation and tried to sell the idea to ministerial colleagues, but I don't think there were any takers.

We moved on to other departments before the Management Review Programme was brought to a close. Whilst it had resulted in significant changes I suspect the Treasury were hoping for something more hard-edged and cost-saving, but that was not the remit I was asked to work to.

What would happen now to Special Assignments Division? It was decided to merge it with another Division to create a new Management Development Division. I was put in charge, but what on earth was its role, I asked? I had been handed a blank sheet. I asked my boss, Brian Pearce, Head of the Management Services Group, "What am I supposed to be doing?" Although he had been instrumental in creating the new Division, he did not seem to know either. He left soon afterwards to become a clergyman.

Finding interesting and hopefully useful things for my staff to do was not a problem, but I thought those above me had a more considered vision and plan, but apparently not, so I created my own. I first proposed trying to introduce Accountable Management into the Civil Service, because it was in vogue at the time in the private sector, but the Head of MS (Accounting) Division, completely missing the point, thought that he should do that, seemingly equating the word "accounting" with "accountable".

Undaunted, I proposed that we should embark on a programme to overhaul the forms used by government departments in their dealings with the public (e.g. Inland Revenue's tax forms or DVLC's vehicle licensing forms). I had long thought that they were in serious need of improvement because they left such a poor impression in the public's mind, so when I came across an article by the Plain English Society I invited them to Whitehall to discuss my ideas and seek their help. It was a good meeting and we worked out how we might take it forward. However, my plans were quickly overtaken by events.

I had continued having occasional lunches with Clive Priestley. He had been promoted to Under Secretary, which he thoroughly deserved, and made Head of an Efficiency Unit in the Cabinet Office to support Sir Derek Rayner, the former Managing Director of Marks & Spencer. He had been brought in by Mrs Thatcher to root out inefficiency in government, which really meant looking for cost savings. I had mentioned my plans to overhaul government forms to Clive and he had told Sir Derek. I was asked to meet Sir Derek and explain my ideas. We met in his beautiful room overlooking Horse Guards Parade. It was a very brisk, short meeting with no small talk or polite exchanges. He was demonstrating how successful businessmen worked, I think. He proposed taking over the work and wanted to give a presentation to Mrs Thatcher. "Would I give such a presentation?" he asked? I could hardly say no, could I?

I set up a comprehensive display of government forms in the Old Admiralty Building and waited patiently for Mrs Thatcher to arrive. Clive was very nervous as the appointed time approached. I was too busy rehearsing what I was going to say to be nervous. Then we got a message to say that she was terribly sorry, but she could not come, after all. I was deflated, but not at all surprised. I thought it was pretty small beer for a P.M. to spend time on, but it was also a complete waste of my time and effort. Clive and Sir Derek took over the work and the results can be seen in the much improved forms we all now use.

Soon afterwards I was invited by Robin Butler to transfer to the Treasury and take over as Head of Projects Division in the Central Computer and Telecommunications Agency (CCTA). Should I accept it? It was a different kind of job. For most of my working life I had been responsible for carrying out projects, but my role now would be to approve them (or not). I thought my past experience, both outside and inside government fitted me well for the job, so I accepted it.

It was yet another change of role. I was now an administrator, pure and simple, responsible for the approval of all computing and telecommunications developments throughout government, worth many millions of pounds annually. I had taken off my creative hat and donned my policeman's helmet. I had 55 staff to help me, twelve at Senior Principle or Principle level, who monitored closely each department's computing and telecommunications activities and dealt with proposals for new developments which needed approval. We set a cost level for each department below which they could approve their own developments, but needed our approval for anything above that. We were an arm of the Treasury and I was responsible for ensuring that the huge sums of public money involved were well spent. In particular, I had to try to avoid new developments ending up as expensive failures. There had been a number of these in the past and our track record was not good.

My new place of work was Riverwalk House, an ugly modern tower block on the Embankment by Vauxhall

Bridge, just a short walk from Pimlico tube station. Its only redeeming feature was that it afforded wonderful views along the river Thames from my office high up on the top floor. It was also only a few minutes walk to the Tate Gallery, which was a bonus, and close to MI5, where I would have many meetings.

The Director of the CCTA was Gerald Watson, a tall, gangly individual with a thick mop of tousled, black, wavy hair. I had been told he had a short fuse and did not suffer fools gladly, so I was on my guard. I only witnessed that once, soon after joining, when he reacted furiously on learning that one of the Inland Revenue's most expensive and high-profile computer developments was in difficulty. I thought he would explode. "Why hadn't I or my staff spotted this sooner", he asked? "Were we all asleep on the job"? I learned from that episode and made sure it did not happen again. Otherwise, we got on extremely well. He recognised in me, I think, someone who could get the job done and make his life easier.

We gelled, too, at a personal level. Gerald lived in a flat in Greenwich in the week and went home at the weekends to a lovely old farmhouse in Suffolk where his wife kept horses. Ann and I were invited there one weekend and enjoyed their very generous hospitality.

On returning to the office one afternoon Gerald excitedly ushered me into his office. "Look at this", he said, pointing to the TV screen where England were just finishing off the Australian's second innings to secure an improbable victory where defeat had seemed most likely at the start of the day. It was the Headingly Test Match of 1981 in which Ian Botham scored a stunning 149 not out and then Bob Willis bowled like a man possessed to take 8 wickets for 43 runs and snatch victory by 18 runs. What a match.

Before becoming Director Gerald had carried out a review of the way CCTA carried out its functions. There had been a number of highly embarrassing and expensive computing failures which Gerald concluded had been due to a combination of poor project management, inadequate procedures for systems design and development, and a lack of effective oversight by departmental management. In future each department would have to set up a senior level Steering Committee to produce a strategy for the department's computing and telecommunications developments and oversee its implementation. Specific methodologies would in future be used for the design and development of new departmental systems and also for their project management. Gerald was told to get on and implement these changes. In practice that meant that I would have to make it all work.

I attended the newly created departmental Steering Committees to make sure they were working effectively, which generally they were. It all went swimmingly. Departments took to it like a duck to water and there was no dissent. I was surprised, but soon realised that being arm of the Treasury gave us tremendous clout. However, it also meant that relations between us and departments were somewhat distant. I took steps to change that.

The catalyst was the twice yearly meeting in London of all departmental computer managers. The format had been set by my predecessors. It was a very large gathering. They all sat in serried ranks in the Civil Service College's long, narrow conference room whilst Gerald Watson and I sat on a raised platform at one end and delivered the Epistle according to CCTA. We were essentially lecturing to them on what we expected them to do. They listened in more or less stony silence, had lunch, listened some more and then left. It was mind-blowingly boring and I said so afterwards to Gerald. We could not go on like this, I said. We had to engage them and get some reaction.

I proposed instead holding these meetings at the Civil Service College at Sunningdale and to stay overnight. We would have two lunches together and dinner in the evening, allowing those present to interact, get to know each other and start conversations about their work and what they had heard during our meetings. It worked. The atmosphere was so much better and more productive. The programme, too, was more interesting. I arranged for some external speakers, which went down well. These events became ones for participants to look forward to rather than endure and our working relationships generally improved.

In 1981 I was faced with a major crisis when we learned that ICL was in serious financial difficulty. The UK government had become heavily dependent on ICL to supply its computing needs as a result of successive governments' "ICL preference" policy. It really was a case of putting all our eggs in one basket, but the basket now had a gaping hole in it. The UK was not alone in following this policy. It was common practice throughout the world for governments to support their own flagship companies. ICL could not be allowed to fail and Mrs Thatcher approved an injection of £200m to keep it afloat, but on condition that there was a complete change of senior management.

Robb Wilmot, who was currently running Texas Instruments in the USA, was persuaded to move back to the UK and take over as Managing Director. At 36 he was very young for such a challenge and he looked even younger, but he was up to the task. He did a magnificent job, averting the crisis and setting ICL on the road to recovery. We all breathed a big sigh of relief. Failure would have been a disaster for UK government computing.

There was another crisis at about that time, but one which I had to sort out. DHSS was engaged in developing CAMELOT, an ambitious project for handling transactions with applicants in local DHSS offices, where benefit claims were handled and payments made to the public. Its development was projected to cost about £10m (at 1981 prices), but my staff were convinced it was failing. I had an urgent meeting with the Deputy Secretary responsible and set out our concerns. I warned that I would have no alternative other than to order the project to be abandoned. He undertook to carry out his own enquiries and report back. He did. He agreed with our assessment and the project was halted. Better to have done it at that point than to have an even bigger and more costly public embarrassment later.

Soon after joining CCTA Gerald suggested that I should go on a fact-finding study tour to the USA run by the excellent Butler Cox Foundation. It was an absolute revelation. They say that travel broadens the mind. Well, this trip certainly did for this traveller, brought up in ICL-dominated environments. We were a large party, including a few wives. All of them held senior positions in their companies and the disparity between my meagre Civil Service expense allowances and their private sector ones became more and more apparent as the trip unfolded. On the flight out I travelled in "steerage" class in the middle of a row whilst they were all in business or first class, so I was knackered on arrival in Boston, whereas they were refreshed. Over the next two weeks, however, some of them realised that I was struggling to keep up with their spending power and would often offer to pay for a meal or buy drinks, which I gratefully accepted. I made several good friends on this trip and kept in touch with them over the next few years.

I liked what I saw of Boston. It had more of a provincial, British feel to it than other east coast cities. It was greener, its buildings were modest in size and height and Harvard University had a distinctly Cambridge feel to it – the district it is in is actually called Cambridge. My hotel was in one of the few tower blocks in the city. Jet-lagged and waking very early on the first morning I gazed out of my window, high up on the 10th floor, and looked down on the Charles River where a constant stream of men and women were already jogging along the river bank as the sun rose.

We visited the Wang factory on the first day. In those days it was the world's leading supplier of word processors. After the presentations they laid on an elaborate clambake with mountains of seafood sizzling in huge pans. At the time it was a great treat, which we all tucked into. The reckoning came a few hours later when about half the party went down with mild food poisoning. Not a good start to our trip.

That night the TV weather presenter urged everyone who wanted to see "the Fall" to get out in the next 36 hours because very cold weather was sweeping south from Canada and the trees would lose their leaves. The trees, in their autumnal New England colours, were spectacular, but very familiar to anyone from the UK who visits a wooded area in October. We left the next day and headed west to California and Silicon Valley where the weather was very warm.

We were treated royally by all the firms we visited, with the exception of IBM, who kept their cards very close to their chest. The others revealed where they were going quite openly because our party represented a huge slice of the potential IT market in the UK and they wanted to position themselves to get some of it. Intel's vision for microprocessors of the future surprised us all, but it all seems commonplace now.

We had time to ourselves at the weekend, so some of us explored the California coast. On the Saturday we spent time in San Francisco, visiting the famous Pier 39 in the old harbour area and watching sharks swim in the Bay around the island prison of Alcatraz. On Sunday I joined two others in a drive down the coast to Monterey and Carmel, where we drank Watney's Red Barrel beer in an English pub that had been transported from England and reconstructed brick by brick - it could only happen in America. We reached Big Sur and watched massive waves breaking on the shore, but did not see any whales. It was a good weekend.

We rounded off the trip in Los Angeles, staying two nights on the old Queen Mary liner, which was moored in Long Beach harbour. My cabin, with its polished mahogany furnishings and brass fittings, had a lovely warm feel to it. We finished off the tour in typical Butler Cox style with a mini banquet on the last night and then headed back to the UK and a mountain of work.

I had thoroughly enjoyed the whole experience and learned a lot. It had broadened my mind and provided insights into where IT was heading. It was a timely reminder to look beyond ICL for our computer solutions.

That thought process became a reality in 1982 when the European Union brought in laws forbidding countries giving preference to their own national flag bearers – not that this made any difference to the way the French behaved. In the UK's case that was primarily ICL. IBM had courted CCTA assiduously in order to be given an opportunity to bid for specific contracts, but hitherto had been up against the government's policy of supporting ICL. Now they saw and seized their opportunity. They wanted the contract to replace DVLC's computers and had developed a solution which would enable a smooth transition to be made from DVLC's current computer systems to theirs. Since the replacement cost would be greater than DVLC's delegated authority level, the final decision would lie with me. IBM set about trying to convince me.

Dr Paul Freeman had just taken over from Gerald Watson as CCTA's Director. He and I were invited to visit one of IBM's factories in the south of France and to stay overnight at one of their lodges. It meant a very early flight, which very nearly did not happen for me because I had stupidly come without my passport. This was before the days when the world was petrified about terrorist plots, so I was able to plead with the Customs Officers to let me through, vouched for by my two colleagues. I had to do the same when we landed in Paris and again when we took off for Montpelier and on arrival there. After much haggling I was allowed into France, but would I get back two days later? Fortunately,

I did, but it was a tortuous process. I have never forgotten my passport since then.

The visit convinced us that IBM had a viable solution and we could not rule them out. I told DVLC that IBM had to be considered. I was immediately summoned to a meeting with Lynda Chalker, the Minister of State with responsibility for DVLC. She greeted me cheerily on entering the room. "Come in, Brian, thank you for coming". She was every inch the ex-Head Girl at Roedean and I liked her immediately. We went over all the pros and cons, including the legal position. There is no doubt that IBM would have taken us to court if we ruled them out. I finished by confirming our conclusion, which the Minister accepted. ICL were not pleased and ICL's Ninian Eadie tried hard to convince me that theirs was the only viable solution, but to no avail. Because it was a test case and might receive publicity when the decision was announced I decided to get the approval of my peers in the Treasury and of the Chief Secretary, Leon Brittan. The meeting with him to discuss my recommendation took all of five minutes. "It's an open and shut case", he said, and I got my approval. IBM won the contract.

With the end of ICL preference other overseas suppliers put in a lot of effort to try to get government contracts and I was courted relentlessly by them. The two most persistent firms were Sperry Univac and Honeywell. I was offered hospitality at sporting events and invited to visit their factories in the USA and talk to firms over there which used their systems. I accepted some of this hospitality and went to the USA with both firms. As a senior civil servant I had to be very careful about accepting hospitality, lest it clouded my judgement when it came to deciding who gets what contracts. I can honestly say that it did not. Decisions were always based on whether a firm met the technical requirements and then on price. What my USA visits did give me was a better appreciation of their systems and how they might meet some of our requirements.

Huw Davies at Sperry Univac tried the hardest. Ann and I were taken to Henley where we spent practically the whole time in a field, which served as a car park, consuming a sumptuous feast and drinking wine without watching a single race. Another weekend we went to his house and played tennis and on another we played golf at Sunningdale. He was a charming man, who tried so hard to get a contract, but did not get a single one. His systems were simply not what we needed in the UK. They were a major player in the USA, as I found out when I went out there. We went to three cities, visiting their factories and some client installations. The most memorable was our stay in Salt Lake City where we learned how the Mormons had made a heroic trek westward across the Rockies and had decided to settle on the flat salt plain below, declaring that "This must be the place". They erected a memorial at that spot. They planted crops with grain they had brought with them, but their first harvest failed and many starved. It was a cruel beginning to their new life there.

Huw had planned an energetic weekend. It was very hot so we got up early for a short game of tennis, followed by breakfast and then a long trip up through the Rockies to a fantastic golf course, surrounded by mountain peaks, encircled by eagles, where we played a round of golf. It was exhausting, but a wonderful experience.

Jim Marsden of Honeywell was very different. He was a very good operator, totally focussed on getting some government business. They did get some, on merit, because they had a highly suitable product range which fitted the needs of the Ministry of Defence, in particular. I played golf with Jim at Wentworth and went to a number of Test matches at Lords where we had lunch with Ted Dexter, the ex-England captain, on one occasion and with Jim Laker, probably England's greatest off-spin bowler, on another. My son, Benjamin, came with me to the Ted Dexter lunch and got his autograph, which made his day. When we met Jim Laker he was also commentating on TV. He suddenly realised he had spent too long with us and dashed back to the commentary box. One minute he was with us and the next we were watching him on TV spouting away as if he had never been away.

Jim Marsden and I had a very good trip to the USA, visiting several Honeywell factories and customer sites. I was very impressed with their products. Over the weekend we were staying in Phoenix, Arizona, and Jim had planned to take me on a flight in a small plane over the Grand Canyon, which was some 150 miles away, but all flights had been cancelled because there had been a crash in one of the planes the day before and the cause was being investigated. I look upon that as a narrow escape. With a day to fill Jim asked if I would like to go on a drive through the desert to Las Vegas, 200 miles away. He was trying to be a good host and keep me entertained. That did not really appeal to me, so I said I was happy to relax and stay closer to our hotel. A look of enormous relief came over his face. He had been dreading having to go on that journey because he was very agoraphobic. He would have done it, though, if needed, just to keep a client happy. Instead, we went to an Indian reservation in the hills just outside Phoenix and I bought Ann a coloured necklace.

In early 1983 Robin Butler, the Principle Establishment Officer at the Treasury, who would go on to become Cabinet Secretary and later Lord Butler, invited me to move, on secondment, to Information Technology (IT) Division at the Department of Trade and Industry (DTI). I would have responsibility for developing and delivering the government's policies for the UK's IT industry. I decided to have a meeting first with Dr John Thynne, the current incumbent. He explained that the work on drafting a Bill to introduce cable into the UK had just been completed. It would now need to be taken through Parliament before becoming law and enable cable franchises to be awarded. I was reassured and agreed to the move.

Just before I moved I received a very gratifying personal letter from Richard Wilding, who had been head of Management Services and was now a Deputy Secretary in the Treasury. He wished me good luck in the new job, adding "you have come a long way over the period of our association so far and have a good prospect of going further". I found that very reassuring as I embarked on yet another leap into the unknown.

Chapter 13

Whitehall
Making Government Policy

This was a significant change of role for me. I was no longer just an administrator, but now working closely with Ministers to make government policy and put it into practice. I had a varied and demanding brief. I had to learn quickly how to deal with the pressures of parliamentary business, the most urgent being getting the new cable legislation through the House of Commons, whilst at the same time supporting Ministers on other debates in the House and dealing with a steady stream of Parliamentary Questions. But my main role was to be the 'sponsor' department for the IT industry. We implemented Ministerial initiatives to foster the IT industry which involved constant interaction with firms and pressure groups. I would go abroad, too, to regular European Community and OECD meetings and on trade missions to Japan and Canada.

This was a step change in responsibility and one of the most pressured jobs I would do in my whole working life. Gone was the option at lunchtime to take sandwiches and walk in a nearby park or pop into an art gallery for a few minutes. There was absolutely no time to spare on anything other than work. It meant long days at work, often continuing when I got home. I did not mind that too much. In some ways I thrived on it, because I am at my best when I am stretched, but it was hard on Ann, who struggled at times. It was not without its problems for me, too. Frequently, soon after starting a holiday or on a short break, I would collapse with bad migraines as I relaxed and the tensions eased. I would retire into a darkened room until my head cleared. Civil Servants make a virtue of soaking up all the work that is thrown at them, without complaint, particularly those who are near the top of the tree, and I was constantly amazed at more senior colleagues' capacity to cope. I doubt if Ministers fully appreciate their degree of commitment and level of effort.

Ministers and most of DTI's senior staff were based in Victoria Street, just down the road from Parliament and Whitehall. My office was close to Victoria Station and within walking distance of Ministers' offices. I had four Principles reporting to me, three of them covering specific sectors and one, Charles Blundell, covering general policy, the Cable Bill and much else. He was a great asset and I relied on him heavily in the first few months.

Although I was at DTI for only three years I served no less than three Secretaries of State, two Ministers of State and one Parliamentary Secretary of State. I was thrown in at the deep end. On only my second morning I had to accompany the Secretary of State to a meeting. I had no time to brief myself on the people we were meeting or what this visit was all about. What would I say if he turned to me for advice or asked a question I could not answer? Fortunately, I got through unscathed, thanks to my background knowledge from CCTA and my private sector experience, but it was an uncomfortable start.

Kenneth Baker was a rewarding Minister to work for because he knew exactly what he wanted to achieve and was totally focussed on getting it done. My job was to deliver what he wanted, which was a lot, but with the help of my excellent team we did deliver. He was the UK's first Minister of Information Technology. He was full of energy and commitment and brimming with ideas.

I had seen in the USA, whilst at CCTA, how advances in microchip technology and the merging of computing and telecommunications, as digital technology replaced analogue, would spawn new products and transform our capability for delivering information. Later on, the advent of the Internet, mobile phones and other devices would make that a reality. Information would be king. Technology was merely a means of delivering it. Global businesses selling access to information in all its forms have made huge fortunes. Kenneth Baker was alert to the urgent need for the UK to get its act together. He mounted a series of initiatives to get the UK in a better place to seize these business opportunities and to raise awareness of the potential for using IT productively.

He had plenty of advice from industry experts, several of whom I knew already. He had a small panel of IT Advisers. Officially they formed a Cabinet Committee and met in the Cabinet Office. They would also meet informally for occasional suppers at a restaurant in Henrietta Street, and I would often join them. I had already had direct dealings, whilst at CCTA, with Colin Southgate, CEO of Thorn-EMI, and Mike Aldrich, Chairman of Rediffusion, and got on well with them both. Mike was a leading advocate for developing interactive cable systems and one of the author's of 'Cable Systems', the government sponsored report published in 1982, which led to the cable legislation on which I was now working. He was also a major figure in the development of videotext and a pioneer of on-line information and shopping systems. His contribution to the development of IT in the '80s and to Kenneth Baker's thinking was very significant. He was a real eager-beaver and very likeable, his boyish smile and round, open face radiating optimism and energy - a winning combination. I discovered, too, that he was born at nearby Brocket Hall, which I passed on walks through Brocket Park. I thoroughly enjoyed these suppers and learned a lot simply by listening.

Kenneth Baker had launched a number of his initiatives before I moved to DTI. There was a nationwide campaign, dubbed IT82, to raise awareness of the significance of IT, aimed at getting different business sectors to raise their game. He was also adamant that the UK's future success lay in educating the younger generation in the use of IT, so he introduced microcomputers into every school coupled with lessons to teach children how to make use of them. He also felt particularly strongly about helping the disabled, so he funded the development of new IT products aimed at them. A very able Principle in my Division ran this programme, which was extremely effective.

When I joined in 1983 Kenneth Baker's first priority was to get the Cable and Broadcasting Bill through

Parliament. Although there was a strong Home Office interest, because it created a new medium for broadcasting, it was the emergence of a new form of technology that was the driving force, so DTI was in the lead. There were still one or two details in the Bill to sort out, one of which proved tricky because I had to disagree with a colleague in our British Telecom Division and take the side of my opposite number in the Home Office, Jon Davey. Jon and I would have meetings with a very laid-back Douglas Hurd, Minister of State at the Home Office, who would literally be laid back in an easy chair in his office, feet up on the table in front, every inch the creative novelist, which was his other career. He was happy with the final Cable and Broadcasting Bill and it started its passage through the House.

It passed its First Reading debate without mishap and reached the Committee stage, where the Bill is scrutinised by a committee of MPs and debated line by line. This took place in a separate debating chamber deep inside the House. Government and Opposition members sat opposite each other on tiered rows of benches similar to the House's main debating chamber, but less colourful and less comfortable– no green padded seats here. It was much smaller and more intimate than the main Chamber, which made for a more productive debate without the political point-scoring and grandstanding that you get in the main House. Another big difference was that Charles Blundell and I could sit immediately behind Kenneth Baker ready to provide advice and respond to any questions he threw at us. There were hardly any. He knew his subject matter inside out and backwards and dealt effortlessly with the points raised as each line of the Bill was dealt with. Members on the Committee were well versed in the subject matter, so it was a good debate.

The Bill went back to the House for Second Reading and then became law, after which Lord (Willie) Whitelaw invited me and Charles to his very grand rooms in the House of Lords for a celebratory drink. He was his usual cheery self, bubbling with delight at the outcome. He was a great favourite of Mrs. Thatcher and I could see why.

The stage was now set to invite applications from companies wishing to lay cable and offer cable services throughout the country. This lengthy franchising process was passed to another colleague to handle, to my great relief. Those bidding for franchises would often lobby Ministers. This led to meetings in the Minister's office or over lunch or dinner, at which I would support the Minister, who by this time was Geoffrey Pattie. The bidders seemed to think that plying Ministers and civil servants with food and drink would buy them favours, but it did not, of course. What it did do was enable us to get a better feel for whether the bidder was likely to be a suitable holder of a franchise.

It all went very smoothly. Bids were made and franchises awarded. Cable companies laid their cable and signed up customers for their services. I became one of these. I can get over 700 channels on my TV, some via a satellite link, and the same cable delivers interactive services to my computer. That early vision had very quickly become a reality.

When Norman Tebbitt took over as Secretary of State for Trade and Industry we gave him a presentation on the Cable and Broadcasting Bill. We set out the provisions in the Bill, explained how the cable franchises would be awarded and what the implications were for UK business and the general public. He listened intently, raised a number of questions and then thanked us for "a most useful and interesting morning. What a fascinating job you have. You must find it very rewarding". He was right. We had and we did.

Soon after this presentation I had to accompany the Secretary of State on a day's visit to Paris for a meeting with Laurent Fabius, his counterpart in the French government. I had to be at the airfield in Essex by 7.30 am. Norman Tebbitt had been a pilot before entering parliament and our small private plane was being piloted by one of his friends. There were just four passengers. The other two were the Secretary of State's private secretary and another DTI official. I anticipated a bumpy ride in such a small plane, but it was surprisingly comfortable.

I spent the journey briefing Norman Tebbitt on the issues that might be raised by the French and the ones we might want to raise. I was sure they would want to press their preferred choice of communications protocol for Direct Broadcasting by Satellite (DBS) because it was a constant refrain of the French delegation in the EU committee on which I served in Brussels. I hoped we could press on them the merits of System X, the new digital telephone system being developed jointly by GEC and Plessey, but without much hope that it would lead anywhere: the French have only their own self-interest at heart, for all that they claim to be ardent Europeans.

We met in a gem of a building in central Paris and sat at a long table, the four of us on one side and over twice that number of French on the other. They agreed to speak in English, which was a relief. The contrast between the two Ministers was marked - Norman Tebbitt, the right wing Conservative, dressed in a smart, dark suit and white shirt sitting opposite Laurent Fabius, the young left wing socialist, dressed in a jacket and casual shirt. They raised DBS, as expected, and pressed their preferred solution. I brought a smile to both Ministers' faces when I said that the UK was consciously pursuing a European solution, as advocated by the European Broadcasting Union.

We adjourned for an excellent lunch in equally palatial surroundings and the talk became more informal. Before we knew it, we had run out of time and had to leave in a hurry to enable the Secretary of State to attend a meeting at the Cabinet Office. Laurent Fabius sprang into action and summoned the French driver to "Alez, vite". He certainly did. It was the most hair-raising ride I have had in my life. He attached a flashing blue light to the car's roof and drove at a ridiculous speed in the outside lane virtually pushing other vehicles off the road. Thankfully, we got back safely and in good time for Norman Tebbitt's meeting.

I was back in my office at 8.30 am the next morning and found a note from Norman Tebbitt's Private Secretary saying that the Secretary of State would like to thank me for the valuable contribution I had made to yesterday's meeting. There was no need for him to have sent that. I was only doing my job, but it was much appreciated. It marked him out as a gentleman in my eyes.

A few weeks later Laurent Fabius, only 37 years old, became France's youngest ever Prime Minister.

Norman Tebbitt would go on to become Chairman

of the Conservative Party and one of Prime Minister Margaret Thatcher's staunchest supporters. He had a higher public profile and would become the butt of satirical TV programmes, such as "Spitting Image", which portrayed him as a street-fighting skinhead or as a Rottweiler. He suffered dreadfully in the IRA's bombing of the Conservative Party conference in Brighton in 1984, which nearly killed him and Mrs Thatcher. It left his wife with very serious injuries and an invalid for the rest of her life.

Another of my duties was to chair the Security Committee on Electronic Information Processing (SCEIP). It was my least satisfactory task. I felt uncomfortable because too often I felt out of my depth when some of the highly technical issues were being discussed. However, it was a good learning experience for me because I had to accept that, as an administrator, I would often not be able to contribute substantively to the issues under discussion, but had to rely on those around the table who were more knowledgeable. My job was to steer these discussions to a satisfactory conclusion. We laid down guidance to government departments on the handling of electronic information. Its membership was drawn from departments with a strong security interest, such as the Ministry of Defence, plus experts from GCHQ at Cheltenham and MI5. They were a high powered bunch.

A much more enjoyable duty was serving on the computing and telecommunications committee of the Organisation for Economic Cooperation and Development (OECD). This met twice a year in Paris in the spring and the autumn. What could be better? I thoroughly enjoyed these trips and the discussions were generally worth the journey and time spent. For some reason the U.S. delegation always comprised three or four women whereas most countries had just one representative. It also soon became apparent that some of these women had other things on their mind than work. I think I could have had five or six flings had I risen to the bait.

This committee also arranged an annual conference hosted by each country in turn. There is a certain amount of competition between countries to lay on the best conference. When I joined DTI in 1983 it was our turn and we held the conference in Church House in the grounds of Westminster Abbey, whose ambience and atmosphere the delegates lapped up. The arrangements had all been made when I arrived so I had little to do except welcome the delegates. We also laid on a very fine reception in Lancaster House, the early 19th century mansion which adjoins Green Park. The delegates were stunned by this setting. The Grand Hall and Great Staircase, designed by John Nash, are reckoned to be the finest in London. Queen Victoria certainly thought so. She considered it to be a finer palace than her own. Kenneth Baker was there to welcome the delegates and it all went very well. When I attended my first committee meeting a few weeks later in Paris the chairman thanked the UK warmly for laying on such a memorable conference and there was generous applause.

The next year it was Spain's turn and they chose to hold it in Siguenza, an ancient town some 100 miles north-east of Madrid. The conference and our accommodation were in a fabulous 8th century castle which had been converted into a Bishop's Palace in the 18th century and modernised more recently. The Roman

Catholic hierarchy certainly knew how to live well. It really was quite special with external walls some 6ft. thick and a cavernous interior. This definitely put Spain one up in the conference competition stakes. It is now a Parador, I believe, and would be well worth a visit.

In my third and final year at DTI there was a move, led by the U.S.A., to get me elected chairman of this OECD committee, but I opted out, knowing that I would not be in my present job much longer and no longer a committee member.

At the time I was there DTI was a "sponsor" department of particular industries, which boiled down to fighting their corner in trade negotiations and encouraging the development of new products. We would fund these, within the boundaries of what was allowed by EEC rules and other regulations. Ministers and officials were bombarded with invitations from companies to visit them or agree to a meeting in which they could plead their case for support. You had to respond to these because companies needed to feel that you were on their side, which we were. I paid scores of visits and had even more lunches and dinners with their chief executives or managing directors. I gained a reputation for being positive and helpful, which I tried to be.

One such sector within my purview that was particularly important at the time was telecommunications. It was on the threshold of the digital revolution. The old telephone exchanges would soon become obsolete as small printed circuit boards replaced huge racks of valves housed in serried ranks of metal cabinets. The two leading telecommunications manufacturers in the UK were Plessey and GEC, which had decided to cooperate on the development and manufacture of their own technology. They looked to DTI to support their efforts at every opportunity.

I paid visits to both their factories. Plessey were based in Liverpool. Des Pitcher, its Managing Director, took me out to supper on my first visit there. The restaurant was only half a mile or so from my hotel, but Des was insistent that I should be taken there and back by their company car. He explained later that it was too dangerous to walk in that area late at night. Liverpool had a very bad crime record at that time.

What both Plessey and GEC needed badly was to be awarded a contract by BT for its replacement systems. The favourite was Ericcson, the Swedish company. I accompanied Kenneth Baker to a meeting, followed by dinner, with Sir George Jefferson, the head of BT, and his senior staff. The question of what replacement system they would choose was discussed at length. Ericcson was clearly the favourite. I argued the case for Plessey/GEC to be considered and it was eventually agreed that there would be a follow-up meeting at which the companies themselves could argue their case. Sir Jeffrey Sterling did a good job in steering this discussion, but the upshot was a decision in Ericcson's favour. I had done my best to get the UK's case heard, but to no avail.

One of my more tiresome duties was to represent the UK on the EU's Computing and Telecommunications Committee, which met several times a year in Brussels. This usually entailed getting a flight from Heathrow, after a long day's work, arriving just in time to have a very late meal at a restaurant in the city centre. My favourite was a Greek restaurant where the traditional

Greek dancing was accompanied by the smashing of crockery on the marble floor as the music got faster and faster, ending in a loud crescendo and a round of applause - great fun, which made the journey worthwhile. That was the high spot of the trip.

I would flop into bed after midnight and have to be up for an early pre-breakfast meeting with the UK's permanent representative in Brussels, who would brief me on the agenda and on any developments that I should be aware of. Then off to the committee meeting, which was conducted in French in those days, so I had to wear headphones to pick up the translation. I found it so tedious. There would be preliminary meetings, too, where the French would try to dominate proceedings, as always, and I learnt to time my interventions in order to get my voice heard and my points across.

I think it was this experience, and others like it, that would later determine my vote to leave the EU in the UK's EU Referendum. The EU is a bloated talking shop, dominated by the Commission and the two countries which spawned it, France and Germany, who regard it as their institution to fulfill their needs. The UK's voice gets smaller and smaller as the EU's membership grows. Better out than in, I reckon.

Walking down Victoria Street one day to a meeting at the Cabinet Office Kenneth Baker said to me "there's a lot wrong with education, don't you think, Brian?" What did I think? Did he mean primary, secondary or university education? My four children had all been to Applecroft, which was a very good junior school. Three of them were now at university and all four had been to Stanborough, which was the old grammar school and was still a good comprehensive school. All of this was flashing through my mind when he told me what he thought. He clearly saw the need for big changes and would soon get his chance to make them when he was appointed Secretary of State for Education and brought in the National Curriculum and much else. He will also be remembered for introducing "Baker Days". He would later become Chairman of the Conservative Party and a target for the satirical TV series "Spitting Image", in which he was portrayed as a slug. It was a clever joke, triggered by his copious use of Brylcream on his hair, but unfair.

I went on two quite different overseas trade visits. The first was to Tokyo with a group of businessmen and senior DTI colleagues. We stayed in the green and pleasant area close to the Imperial Palace. The first thing you notice is how tall you are compared to the local population. I went out one evening to the Ginza shopping district to buy something for Ann and Graham. Standing at the roadside waiting for the traffic lights to change I felt like a giant in Lilliput, the hordes of people around me hardly coming up to my shoulder. Getting there and back on the underground was a bit of an initiative test, trying to interpret the station names and get off at the right one – I resorted to counting the number of stops. It was all good fun.

We spent one evening being entertained at a Geisha House by the equivalent of the UK's Confederation of British Industry(CBI). The setting was extraordinarily colourful, as were the painted Geisha girls. We sat, most uncomfortably, cross-legged on large cushions on the floor being served traditional Japanese fare by the Geisha girls, who were adept at brushing their breasts firmly against your arm every time they offered you something. I wondered at one point exactly what we were being offered. The food itself was not at all to my liking, but I had to eat it lest I offended our hosts. It was an evening to remember.

Most evenings, however, were spent working late in meetings, which were held in one of several tall tower blocks. We would take a break to get something to eat in one of three restaurants in the basement. They were packed with people also working late. When we went back to the meeting room and looked over to the other tower blocks, where lights were on the offices, most of them had someone working there. I said to a colleague "how can you ever beat these people? They are so dedicated and determined". It is said that we have the flair and the innovative skills which Japanese lack, but they know better than us how to put those ideas into money-making products.

I had to make a very early start one morning to visit the NEC headquarters, which was some miles out of Tokyo, at the invitation of its Managing Director. We toured the plant and had a good discussion, but I could have done without this because it meant having to work even later that evening to complete the negotiations in Tokyo. I had also been pressed by Taiwanese civil servants to break my return journey home in order to visit Taiwan, but I declined, not wishing to jeopardize Anglo-Chinese relations.

The second trip was to Canada. Roy Croft, my Deputy Secretary, had invited me to accompany him. This was much more relaxing. We visited Toronto and Ottawa, both of which I liked very much, especially Toronto. Ottawa is very different and has a very English feel to it. It is green, has a lot of trees, and an absence of high rise buildings. Although it is the seat of government it is a very unpretentious sort of place. We talked to government officials and visited various companies, at their invitation, but nothing concrete came out of it. Given the workload which would be waiting for me on return I did question whether this was time well spent.

Geoffrey Pattie replaced Kenneth Baker in September 1984. He was a totally different kind of Minister. He was not a man on a mission, as Kenneth Baker was, but took things at a slower pace, which certainly suited me and my team. I got on with him extremely well. Soon after becoming Minister I accompanied him to an OECD conference in Berlin, where he was giving the opening address. I had written his speech and was holding a copy whilst listening to him in the conference hall. Next to me sat Shirley Williams, one of the original Gang of Four which left the Labour Party to set up the Social Democratic Party, before merging with the Liberals. She was one of my all time favourite politicians and we had some interesting discussions during the conference. When Geoffrey Pattie had finished she asked me if I had written the speech and I said yes. "Well done" she said, "Very good." If she genuinely meant it, rather than just being polite, then that was welcome praise.

I went with her for lunch where Prof. Kenneth Galbraith, the renowned Canadian economist, joined us. We talked about the Berlin Wall, which was close by, and agreed to walk out afterwards to see it. Looking across the barren stretch of no-mans-land to the wall on the other side you could see the watchtowers manned by soldiers with machine guns, ready to mow down anyone who dared to try to cross, as many had. "It won't last" he said. "The people won't tolerate it forever". He was right. It came down four years later. Ann and I visited Berlin recently and saw the bits that have been kept as a reminder of that horrific past. "Never again" should be its motto.

Meanwhile my family was growing up fast. Despite having four children to care for Ann still did not stop me playing cricket for Welwyn Garden City at the weekend, which I now find quite astonishing. Modern marriages do not provide for this. As the children got older they would spend time with me at these matches. Helen, Bruce and Benj would all become scorers for the club. Helen scored for me when I captained the second team, tugging at my hand and pleading to go home if I had stayed too long drinking with the opposition after the match. She and Benj would spend many a cold afternoon huddled in the scorer's box. Bruce was a wonderful scorer for the first team when Malcolm Bateman was captain. He would use a variety of coloured pencils for each bowler and record not just the runs scored, but each ball faced by each batsman – a complete record of each batsman's innings – magic! They got some pocket money for their efforts.

When Helen was older still, she would sometimes do a spell of bar duty at the club to earn more pocket money. Graham would play for the club as a junior and was in the WGC team that got to the National Under 15 Club finals in 1985. He was a good cricketer, captaining his year's team at Stanborough School and also playing in various regional county matches. As a batsman, though, he says he never quite got over his fear of the hard ball, not surprising considering the lousy wickets on which he had to face fast bowlers. He also played with me in my last two matches for the club, which I really enjoyed. Having scored fifty in one match and taken five wickets in the next I decided that, at fifty years old, I should stop playing whilst my reputation was still intact. I would play in some less demanding cricket matches for ten more years, but not club cricket.

The years in which Helen and the boys changed from being children to young adults and developed their own personalities were happy ones for them and rewarding ones for Ann and me. It was easier for me, though, because I was only with them at the weekends and in the holidays and (briefly) in the evenings. Ann had the hard bit. They had a lot of friends, who were always welcome at our house, and they have been very successful since in keeping those friends right into adulthood. I think that says a lot about what well-rounded individuals they have become.

As a family we have always done a lot together, and still do. Sport was one of the interests we all shared and I encouraged it. We played tennis at Dellcott Family Club, just round the corner from our house, where Ann and I ran "tea and tennis" tournaments for the adults and other knockout tournaments each year for the juniors. In the school holidays Helen and the boys would often be there all day. At Stanborough School they played in football, cricket, tennis and hockey matches against other schools. In practice it was the same handful of boys and girls from which all the school's teams were picked. Helen and her tennis partner were unbeaten. Graham also played for the school at rugby and narrowly missed out on playing in some county school matches. The boys also played for local football clubs, where over-excited parents would growl at their offspring from the touchlines and blame the poor referee for everything: it was taken far too seriously by some – it's only a game.

Over the years I would take the boys to football, rugby and cricket matches. We stopped going to watch football at Watford in the late '70s after hooligans supporting the opposition started ripping up seats in the stands and throwing them around. It was a troubling time for football clubs. I got a surprise when I took them to watch Leicester City play Leeds. I was cheering Leicester, as were the rest of the spectators around us, but Bruce and Benj were shouting "come on Leeds", because that was the club they had always supported. It raised a laugh from the home fans.

Watching the Leicester Tigers match on Boxing Day was a regular fixture if we were in the Midlands over Xmas, as we often were, but rugby was not really Bruce and Benj's game.

The whole family would go to Wimbledon, which was often a memorable experience. We were there in the year that the long-haired seventeen year old Bjorn Borg burst onto the tennis scene mobbed by his ecstatic fans and also when a fiery, young John McEnroe made his entrance. Wimbledon was far less crowded then than it is now and it was possible to move easily from one outside court to another and be very close to some of the star players. It is a different game seen from ground level to the one you try to follow perched high up in the stands.

I would take the boys to Test Matches at Lords and The Oval. At one match against the West Indies at Lords Graham and I had seats close to the boundary ropes, but Graham chose to spend most of the match sitting on the grass amongst the young West Indian supporters, having a great time. You would not be allowed to do that now.

The children did not just do sport. From an early age each of them had music lessons, learning to play the piano and one other instrument, and they all reached a high standard, but inevitably in their late teens their commitment waned as other interests took over. Nevertheless that grounding has given them a good appreciation of music generally. Helen played the clarinet, Bruce the cello and both Benj and Graham played the violin. They all played in the Stanborough School orchestra, which was quite strong in their day, but has since fallen away, I believe, which is a pity.

The children grew up at a time when pop culture and pop concerts really took off. The Glastonbury Festival was the pick of the bunch and they would go there and to some others. Some years Glastonbury was a sea of mud and very challenging, particularly for pitching your tent, and in others it was baking hot sunshine. Whatever the weather they all loved it.

They each had there own specific interests, though, which I tried to encourage, transporting them to and from their various venues. Bruce's was fishing. He built up quite a collection of rods and other equipment out of his earnings as a paper delivery boy and other jobs, plus his pocket money. I would take him early in the morning to some river bank or lakeside and collect him in the evening. I would ask him how the day had gone, to which he would always say "great". If I asked what he had caught he would often answer "nothing", but he still enjoyed being there.

Helen's passion was horses. She would spend weekends and holidays helping to groom the horses and muck out the stables at Mill Green. She then acquired an old horse, Banner Boy, to look after when a friend moved abroad. It was kept in a field near to the cricket club to which I would take bales of straw and feedstuff. She loved it. Her friend, Kate Farlie, helped her, but she was the victim of a tragic accident and was killed by a car which mounted the pavement. It was a dreadful shock to Helen and to her parents, who we knew.

Amongst our many friends Catherine and Len Hall were the closest during these years. Our children got on well together and Catherine was a great friend to Ann. She was a good tennis player and partnered me in some League tennis matches playing for Dellcott. I also partnered Len in some local tennis tournaments, but without much success. I was his weak link. He was a lovely man and a great competitor despite having a heart problem. He taught me to play squash, but I struggled to get a single point against him for a long time. He had been a champion in Berkshire in his younger days and was still very good. We have to thank Catherine and Len for introducing us to the delights of the Isle of Wight and, in particular, to Freshwater Bay and the Farringford Hotel, where we would have many happy holidays. It was Alfred Lord Tennyson's former home and was quite charming. It had an old-fashioned, relaxed air about it, which was just what we needed for a restful holiday. We would go back there many times as our family grew, enjoying its golf course, tennis courts, bowling green, croquet lawn and walks up to nearby Tennyson Down. It was a place in a time warp, which we loved.

Until they moved abroad after ICI closed its W.G.C. factories we spent a lot of time with John and Jean Sefton and their three boys. We have to thank them for introducing us to the glorious beaches and cliff top walks of Pembrokeshire. We went with them on some organised walks there, discovering the Iron Age settlements along the cliff's edge and, on one quite memorable day, the source of the giant "Bluestones" which were transported over land and sea, with great difficulty, from the Preseli hills and used to build Stonehenge in Wiltshire. What an amazing feat. We would go back to Pembrokeshire many more times with our growing family.

Smiths on the right and Seftons on the left on Druidstone Beach

One by one Helen and the boys went off to university. Helen chose Sussex, at Brighton, Bruce went to Surrey, at Guildford, Benj to Loughborough, partly influenced by its reputation for sport, and Graham to Reading. It was the practice at the time to have a year off before starting your course and they did this. They used it in different ways, taking advantage of the offer to students to travel around Europe for a month on a budget railcard. I wish it had been available in my day. Helen and her friend Caroline, who was waiting to go to Oxford, went to work at a private school on the Swiss/French border, which Helen described as a growing up experience. I didn't ask for details. Benj worked in the parks and gardens of a local authority in a small town in France.

With his sister and brothers all at university we had Graham all to ourselves for four years before he, too, went off. I enjoyed that. Having passed his driving test he asked if he could take over our old Mini and renovate it. With the help of Bruce, who was living with us at the time after completing his university course, and Graham's friend, John, he set out to transform it into a high-powered Mini Cooper, completely rebuilding it from top to bottom. Graham does nothing by halves. He did a great job, but it all came to nothing when he was involved in an awful crash, completely smashing the whole front of the car. A large van had done a sudden U-turn in the road and Graham could not avoid it. My heart was in my mouth when we got a call from the police to say that "they were cutting the boys out of the wreckage". It was a dreadful sight when Bruce and I got there. Graham was in the ambulance, but tried to reassure us that he would be OK, despite lots of blood on his head. He was a very lucky boy to escape with relatively minor injuries and cuts, thanks to the racing harness he had thankfully been wearing. Had he not, his life might have been very different and he might even have been killed.

Graham (right) and Matt (left) off on their European trek

Back at work my final contribution before I moved on from DTI was to produce a comprehensive report on the implications and issues raised by Direct Broadcasting by Satellite (DBS). Space Division felt that it should be doing the work, but Alasdair MacDonald, my Deputy Secretary, agreed with me that it was not the manufacture of satellites that was the key issue, but the use that would be made of them to deliver information in all its forms. One of the key questions was the communications protocol to be used and there were a lot of competing options, each championed by different interested parties, both in this country and abroad. It was a major topic in the EEC Committee that I attended in Brussels. It had still not been settled by the time I left DTI. I had well over a hundred meetings in a whirlwind last few weeks. Some of my findings were surprising. In meetings with the BBC, including with Michael Checkland, it's Finance Director, who would shortly afterwards become it's Director General, I discovered that it had no plans to introduce DBS. It had a comprehensive land-based communications network, which it planned to keep. That would change.

With my secondment from the Treasury due to end soon I got an unexpected call from Jimmy Clarke, who had been the Principle Establishment Officer at DTI and was now in a similar post at the Securities and Investments Board (SIB), the newly created City regulator. His boss and Chief Executive was Roy Croft, who I knew well from my time at DTI. During our recent visit to Canada together I had mentioned that I was unsure what to do when my secondment to DTI came to an end. Jimmy asked if I would be interested in becoming SIB's Director of Information Services, with responsibility for all its computing needs and for providing various public information services. I would report to Roy, who I got on with very well. I went to see them and liked what I heard. However, I would have to resign from the Civil Service, because SIB was not a government body, so I would no longer enjoy that security. Also, how long would SIB last? This would not be the first time I had been in at the start of a speculative new venture. Joining IOR and moving south with a young family twenty two years ago had been a big act of faith. However, I did not see this move as posing similar risks, so I accepted the job.

I had thoroughly enjoyed my time in the Civil Service and look back on it as a very creative period. I was fortunate to be in posts where I could make some changes for the good. It was probably the best period of my working life, although I have been lucky to have had several others which run it close. It was consistently hard work, which may surprise outsiders whose images have been forged by "Yes, Minister" and similar parodies.

I said my farewells to Whitehall and headed for the City. Would I find it to my liking?

Chapter 14

The City
Birth of a Regulator

I arrived at the SIB in March 1986 feeling exhausted from my frantic efforts to complete the report on Direct Broadcasting by Satellite and leave a number of other matters at DTI in a satisfactory state. I really needed a week's holiday, but Roy Croft, my new boss, was insistent that there wasn't time. The 1986 Financial Services Act (FSA) was due to come into full force on 29 April 1988 requiring all firms carrying on investment business to be authorised by us, otherwise they could not trade. One of my main tasks was to set up and maintain a Public Register of such firms. I had little time to recruit staff, decide how to provide this Register, choose and install hardware, develop appropriate software and make arrangements with thirteen regulatory bodies to provide the data needed before the Register went live. Roy also wanted me to embark on an immediate whirlwind tour of regulatory and other bodies in the USA and Canada in order to learn from their experience and to get a better understanding of the financial services world.

Initially I was a bit deflated. At the CCTA and DTI I felt I knew everything there was to know about the IT and tradeable information sectors and just about all the movers and shakers in them. I knew nothing about the City and hardly anyone of significance in it. The sole exception was Reuters, which I had seen reinvent itself over the past six years from a company whose main focus was international news to become a leading provider of financial data to firms in the City. These feelings would soon dissipate, however, as I grew into the job, but in mid-1986 I wondered for a while if I had made the right move.

The need for a new Financial Services Act (FSA) stemmed from Mrs Thatcher's decision to open up our financial markets to competition, from both home and overseas. Her friend and mentor in the USA, President Ronald Reagan, had already done so and London's leading role in finance was being threatened by New York. In this new competitive world UK retail banks could now merge with or take over investment banks and could now sell investment products, mortgages and insurance. Building Societies could become banks. Everything was up for grabs. The London Stock Exchange also made two significant changes, allowing its member firms to be owned by other financial institutions, including overseas companies, and on 27th October 1986, known as "Big Bang", screen-based trading in remote offices replaced noisy open-outcry trading between buyers and sellers on the Stock Exchange floor. Once-busy streets and restaurants outside the Stock Exchange were suddenly empty, as the long City lunch break gave way to eating sandwiches in offices, tied to computer screens. The result of all these changes was a flurry of takeovers and mergers and a huge influx of overseas investment, leading to a complete transformation of the financial services marketplace. It was this new world that SIB had to regulate.

The FSA set out SIB's responsibilities. Its first task was to ensure that firms carrying on investment business were authorised to trade by an appropriate regulator. SIB authorised very few firms directly itself, setting very high fees to discourage applications. Instead, SIB set the rules by which four Self-Regulating Organisations (SROs) and nine Recognised Professional Bodies (RPBs) could authorise and regulate firms within their scope. The four SROs were IMRO, SFA, LAUTRO and FIMBRA, each one regulating different types of investment activity. The nine RPBs authorised accountants, actuaries, insurance brokers, solicitors and lawyers to carry on investment business. Investment Exchanges and Clearing Houses also needed to be "recognised" by SIB before they were allowed to operate.

Although SIB had a big job it remained a small body throughout its life. When I arrived in 1986 there were less than twenty staff, about a half from the Civil Service or the Bank of England and the rest from the private sector. Ten years later there were still less than 200. Most had financial services expertise. There were some ex-DTI staff in key senior posts but it did not feel like a Civil Service organisation. It was commonly thought that SIB was a government body run by civil servants. Not so. It was a private body, the high-powered Board having applied to the government to be designated as the Agency to administer the FSA. It raised its income by levying fees on those it regulated. This was to prove a running sore throughout my time there. The industry and the other regulators constantly complained about our costs and the complexity and toughness of the regime we created. Fortunately, that did not apply to my area, as I will explain.

Sir Kenneth Berrill was SIB's full time Chairman. He was a stocky individual with a large head which you felt was bursting with brain power, which it was. He was quietly spoken with the demeanour of an academic, as befits someone who was a Fellow in economics at Cambridge, but he was sharp and businesslike, too. He had just completed four years as Chairman of Vickers da Costa, the City stockbrokers, and had worked under three Prime Ministers as Chief Economic Adviser to the Treasury and head of the Central Policy Review Unit in the Cabinet Office. He seemed the ideal choice as Chairman. He would only occasionally involve himself in my activities, leaving that to Roy Croft, his Chief Executive, but in practice Roy left me largely to my own devices. I would get the agreement of the Management Committee or the Board on specific issues, when needed, but I had almost no direct oversight. I enjoyed the freedom.

In those early days SIB's main pre-occupation was with producing a book of rules firms had to meet in order to become authorised to trade. SIB's senior staff were locked in long debates and arguments about how best to translate the complex legislation into a workable rulebook. It was an onerous task. Prof. Jim Gower, the architect of the FSA, provided insight and advice on how to interpret the legislation. The lawyers clung on his every word. Ken Berrill, Roy Croft, the other Directors and I would meet in brain-storming sessions to try to resolve key sticking points, starting in the afternoon and going on well into the evening. At about 6pm the drinks trolley would be wheeled in. I'm not sure that it improved our decision-making, but it was very civilised and relaxing.

There was a lot of brain-power and expertise around the table. Kate Mortimer, on secondment from Rothchilds, was Director of Policy. She had previously been at the World Bank and in the Policy Unit at 10 Downing St. She was very sharp and made most of the running. Three ex-City practitioners injected practical expertise into the arguments. Having no particular financial services expertise, my contribution to these discussions was largely confined to issues related to the Public Register or to general issues. I did chair one of the sessions when we all went off for two days of brain-storming at Kings College, Cambridge. Ken Berrill had been Bursar there and knew well the secrets of the wine cellars. We drank well, including an absolutely wonderful 1949 Sauterne, quite the best sweet wine I have ever tasted.

SIB was very much on trial. The politicians would be watching closely to see how we administered their legislation and the industry would be ready to tell them and us if they thought we had got it wrong. Michael Howard, Parliamentary Under Secretary at the DTI with responsibility for the financial services industry, paid us a visit. Ken Berrill, Roy Croft, the other Directors and I lined up for his inspection, for that is what it was. He fixed each of us in turn with a penetrating stare and offered a limp hand. I didn't know whether to kiss it or shake it. Some ten years later, when he was Home Secretary and hoping to become leader of his party, Ann Widdecombe made a damning speech, saying that "there was something of the night about him", which brought back memories of that piercing stare.

My main focus was on creating and disseminating the Public Register and, most immediately, in recruiting some staff. I appointed Ross Hopcroft as my Head of Systems and he took up his post just in time to join me on the trip to the USA and Canada. He was a great asset and we got on very well. He was captain of Tabard Rugby Football Club, based in Radlett, and a towering second row forward. However, when we landed in Washington in July the temperature was over 90 degrees F (32 degrees C) and the humidity about 90%. Ross wilted like a dehydrated flower. He had difficulty breathing and found the next few days in Washington and New York very uncomfortable, but he perked up when we moved on to Chicago and Toronto. We did all of this in just one week. Although I was jet-lagged, I loved it. The British Embassies had done a great job, drawing up a non-stop schedule of meetings with all the key regulators and Exchanges. We soaked up their experience and learned a great deal. The British Consul and his wife gave us a very enjoyable dinner at their official residence.

The excitement and frantic activity on display made our visits to the various Exchanges memorable. The Chicago Mercantile Exchange was a riot of colour and a cacophony of noise as young men in exotic jackets shouted their requirements and waved their arms to get noticed whilst others tried to get their response heard and accepted. A huge display board registered the latest prices for pork bellies and other products we saw traded. It was a place of enormous energy and vitality.

We did not have time for sightseeing, but on one evening I did manage to introduce Ross to Georgetown, the lovely old part of Washington, with a flourishing restaurant scene. Georgetown had been started by the English in the mid 18th century and the old part still retains a certain English feel to it. It was a popular place for politicians to live, including past Presidents Thomas Jefferson and John F Kennedy. I came back invigorated and clear about the way forward. Ross was a bit bewildered and I am not surprised.

I decided to provide public access to our Register via PRESTEL, the on-line information service, which was already used in the City. This was long before the days of the Internet, mobile phones and universal access to information, but there were a few examples of simple public access information systems and BT's PRESTEL service was one of these. By modern standards it was very unsophisticated, but it did allow for interactive enquiry, albeit in a somewhat clunky fashion.

I needed a gateway service to PRESTEL and decided to use the Datasolve bureau, which was part of the Thorn-EMI Group, partly because I knew Sir Colin Southgate, Chief Executive (and later Chairman) of Thorn-EMI, from my time at CCTA and DTI. We had served together on the Cabinet Office's IT Committee, one of the National Economic Development Council's "Little Neddies". I liked him very much. He had a most engaging personality and was physically impressive – tall and broad with curly, almost blond hair. He was genial, relaxed and always positive - a great guy to spend time with. Colin hosted a lunch to cement the signing of the contract with Datasolve.

I chose COMPEL to supply our hardware. It was owned and run by Neville Davis and based in nearby Hatfield. We were to become one of COMPEL's biggest customers and certainly their most prestigious, on which they would capitalise. They ran an article on me and SIB in their company magazine and I featured on the front cover standing by the Thames with St Paul's and the City in the background, trying to look commanding.

Ann & I (top left) with Datasolve at the Computer Industry's Annual Dinner

The Central Register was launched publicly on 29 April 1988 by Lord Young, Secretary of State for Trade and Industry. It was a very big day for SIB because it heralded the Financial Services Act coming into full force, but even more so for me and my team, since we were the star attraction. I decided on a high risk strategy of inviting the press, radio and television to a live launch at BT's headquarters, close to St Paul's. The large conference room was packed, such was the intense interest in the new regulatory regime. It was my show and it had to go well, otherwise SIB's reputation would have been destroyed from the start. I prepared carefully to ensure that it did go well and it did. In fact it went very well.

I welcomed everyone, explained how the enquiry service would work and invited Lord Young to press the button and set off a live demonstration, which was projected onto a screen for all to see. After questions I invited the audience to try the new service themselves using various PRESTEL terminals in the room. Louise Botting, the ebullient main presenter of Radio 4's "Money Box", was sitting with Ken Berrill and called out for "that lovely man Brian" to help her use the service. It all went off without a hitch and I got plaudits from Ken Berrill and my senior colleagues. Later that day I also gave an interview for Channel 4 News in which the presenter tried repeatedly to get me to confirm that the Central Register was effectively a "black list", which it wasn't – it was a "white list" with some warning messages. I took the team out to celebrate. That same day Roy Croft and colleagues used their investigatory powers for the first time by interviewing Peter Clowes, of Barlow Clowes, in the Boardroom. He was subsequently charged and imprisoned for ten years for a £17m investment fraud. He was the first of many. The Financial Services Act was up and running.

The euphoria did not last long. The next day Ken Berrill asked to see me. He showed me a brief footnote in 'The Daily Telegraph' referring to the Central Register of Authorised Persons – "CRAP". It did not imply that it was crap, indeed the paper's financial pages were complimentary, but this was a little joke at our expense. Ken was not amused and neither was I. It had originated from a badly worded Press Release issued by our Press Office. With hindsight it would have been better to call it the Public Register.

Another problem hit us. We had no idea how many enquiries would be made, which made drawing up a contract with Datasolve to use their PRESTEL gateway service extremely difficult. We seriously underestimated the number, so that the first month's invoice was astronomic and well beyond my budget. We were the victim of our own success. Some 123,000 enquiries were made in the first two months, before settling down to about 5,000 per week. Fortunately I had built up a good relationship with Datasolve, and particularly with Colin Southgate, so that commonsense prevailed and I was able to renegotiate the contract.

The enquiry service performed well, but in the early days the quality was not good. The SROs, in particular, struggled to get their acts together and the data they supplied was often not bang up to date. I pressed them to put more effort into improving it. In theory we could have threatened to remove their status as a Recognised regulatory body, but that was a nuclear option that I was never going to use, and they knew it. Nor was it my style. I always preferred the carrot rather than the stick and spent a lot of time with my opposite numbers trying to understand their difficulties and agree ways of achieving the smooth flow of high quality data that was required by law.

I decided to get closer to the SROs. I brought them all together to share experiences and resolve any current concerns. It worked well. It also helped later when I wanted their cooperation in tackling initiatives in which I took the lead, such as the Shared Intelligence Service. I got to know each of them individually and some became particularly good friends. I made a point also of meeting each SRO's Chief Executive regularly, which gave them a chance to let of steam about their latest grievance about the SIB. As a result of all this interaction I became well known across the SROs and was viewed as one of the good guys, whereas my colleagues faced a lot of hostility.

Over the next few years the Central Register became an integral part of the fabric of financial services regulation. Investors could check if a firm was authorised to trade, identify the firm's regulator and its unique SIB Register Number. It also told them how to claim for compensation under SIB's Investors Compensation Scheme if an investment company failed. It was a very useful source of information for investors. A firm's SIB Register Number became a standard for use in business transactions. Some 35,000 firms appeared on the Central Register in 1989. By July 1992 the total number of enquiries made had reached one million and by 1994 we were handling about 100,000 enquiries a year via PRESTEL and another 50,000 by telephone. It was also a useful source of income, bringing in over £400,000 a year from providing copies of the register on magnetic tape, which went a long way to recovering my Division's costs. Whatever else might be said about SIB's performance as a regulator it was widely acknowledged that the Central Register was a success story. Recognition of this also came from it being nominated for the British Computer Society's

'Application of the Year' award. It did not win, but we were buoyed up by the publicity it received.

However, the reaction of the financial services sector to SIB's new regulatory regime was universally hostile. SIB's rule book was seen as too legalistic, over complicated, expensive to implement and unworkable. The SROs, in particular, were furious. Relations between them and SIB were not good. Heads had to role and Ken Berrill was replaced in June 1988 by David Walker, a Bank of England Director and seen as a safe pair of hands.

David was quite different from Ken. He was tall, slim, broad-shouldered, athletic-looking and an extrovert. He talked with enthusiasm. In fact, he was known as "Walker the talker". I found him very easy to get on with. On arrival, he summoned all the senior staff to a meeting and proceeded to lay down the law. The quality of our work was simply not good enough, he said, and must improve. He went on to lecture us at length, deliberately over-stating his case in order to shake us up. His Chief Executive, Roy Croft, had to bite his lip. We were all a bit apprehensive about how our work would be perceived and I was soon to find out. A week or so later I presented a paper on which I wanted colleagues' agreement and a decision. David decided to take it first, which was ominous. I feared he was about to tear it to shreds and hold it up as an example of all that was wrong with our work and, in the process, destroy my confidence. On the contrary, it was exactly the standard of work he was looking for, he said, and to which the rest of SIB should aspire. Phew, what a relief!

David Walker's priorities were to tackle the much criticised rulebook and to mend SIB's fences with the regulatory bodies, particularly with the SROs and the firms they regulated. He introduced the "new settlement" whereby the rule book was revamped and detailed rules specified for particular types of investment business on which the SROs would take the lead. The new rule book was well received by the industry. It was hailed as a positive step forward and SIB's image immediately improved. This was also helped by allowing each SRO to produce its own annual "self-assessment" report, thus reducing the amount of routine monitoring and checking carried out by SIB staff, which these bodies had found so irksome. Personally, I was doubtful about the wisdom of this. In my view a "hands-off" regulator was a contradiction in terms, but I could see why David Walker wanted to do it.

At about this time Roy Croft invited me to become Director of one of the other Divisions in order to improve relations with one of the SROs. Although I had enjoyed my policy-making days at the DTI I was not keen to take on a similar role at SIB, mainly because of my lack of investment expertise, so I declined. Also, I was quite happy where I was.

Informally, relations with the SROs improved. I started a programme of annual cricket matches against each of them, playing on the Bank of England's lovely sports ground at Roehampton. I played in all of them, right up to my retirement. They would start in the late afternoon and go on into the evening. Senior staff from SIB and the SROs would turn up for the closing stages of these games and stay for a drink afterwards, which undoubtedly helped to thaw the frosty relations between 'us' and 'them'.

Life within SIB also became more relaxed. Ross Hopcroft persuaded four of us, including my brilliant secretary, Jenny Cusack, to run in the annual race in Battersea Park for people who worked in the City. Our numbers grew each year to reach over thirty - not bad out of fewer than 200 staff. We went there by coach and had something to eat and drink after the race, usually on Clapham Common, where the atmosphere on a summer's evening was great. I loved lining up at the start with the other runners, most of them "young bucks", who would try to start as near to the front as possible and dash off as if they were running the 100 metres. I would stay nearer the back, knowing that my natural pace for such a long race would be nearer 8 minutes per mile. As the race progressed I would pass literally hundreds of these flagging early starters, which was quite satisfying for someone in his fifties and, later, early sixties.

From quite early on the SIB also had its own bridge team in the London Business League. My partner was Roger Purcell, the new Finance Director, but if he was not available I would sometimes play with Arthur Selman, a Deputy Director. Arthur was extremely good. He was an Irishman and played at the famous ACOL Club in Chelsea, often winning big money prizes there. He had a fantastic memory and could reel off every card played by each player in the match. I was very impressed and a bit over-awed, but he was easy to play with. The team did very well. We started in the sixth division and were promoted each year until we settled into the second.

After two years I had begun to settle into life in the City, which initially I had found to be a very bleak place, almost completely treeless and with very little colour. The streets were teeming with men in dark suits, rushing from place to place, like the White Rabbit, as if they were constantly late for their meetings or their trains home. There were few residents in the square mile, with the exception of the Barbican and the neighbouring area around Bunhill Row, so there was an absence of children and mothers and the noise that would accompany them. There were some women, of course, but the predominant impression was that this is a male environment, focussed on making money. What I did begin to appreciate were the relics of old London sitting cheek by jowl with new developments.

I worked from five different locations during my fifteen years there. The first was right in the heart of The City, just behind the Royal Exchange and only a few steps to the Bank of England. The Royal Exchange, opened in 1571 by Queen Elizabeth 1, has served many different trading purposes over the years. It was the birthplace of the embryo London Stock Exchange, but from the 17th century stockbrokers were barred from operating there because they were considered too rowdy. They moved to neighbouring coffee shops in order to forge their deals. It has a much more mundane function now as a place to indulge in the modern preoccupations of eating and shopping.

The Bank itself is a strange looking building. Aesthetically, it has very little going for it, but once inside it is a different story. You get an impression of space and elegance that you might associate with a grand country house - high ceilings, beautiful doorways and massive walls covered with large, old pictures. The messengers and doormen in pink coats and scarlet waistcoats added to the feeling of being from a different age. I would have many meetings in there over the next few years.

We weren't in those offices long. We moved out to the unlovely and unloved Paternoster Square, an expanse of dull, grey, monotonous, utilitarian buildings, completely lacking any charm. This area was home to several well-known publishers before the war, but was completely destroyed in the Blitz and rebuilt in a style better suited to East Berlin. Its only redeeming features were that it was within easy walking distance of St Pauls and had a beautiful bronze sculpture, "Shepherd and Sheep", by Elisabeth Frink in one corner. It seemed so out of place in such bleak surroundings, but to see that every morning lifted your spirits for the rest of the day. There was one other bonus. Because it was a vast, flat open space it was also used by lots of frisky young women playing netball, which brightened up many a lunchtime.

Prince Charles was one of those calling for the Square's redevelopment, describing it as a carbuncle and a monstrosity. He was right. It has now been transformed and the London Stock Exchange has moved there.

Our next move was to Moor House, one of those anonymous tall, glass towers that have come to dominate city skylines everywhere. We were on the 17th floor and I made it my daily ritual to get my heart racing by climbing the stairs rather than take the lift. Located close to Moorgate station, it was ideal for me because my train from W.G.C. now terminated there after the line was electrified. Moor House was at one end of London Wall. At the other end was the Barbican.

I can remember coming to this area in 1960 for a computer programming course when it was still a huge bomb site. Its redevelopment was controversial at the time. The Barbican was built with dark reddish-brown brickwork and its three tall residential blocks stood out in stark contrast to the traditional London stonework. It was also the butt of jokes about how impenetrable it was. Visitors were advised by its detractors to take a large ball of string so that you could mark your way in and retrace your steps out, otherwise you would be stuck in there forever. I loved it. Some 6,000 people live there, so it does not die when workers go home to their suburbs. It is a great arts centre with a concert hall, cinema and theatre, library, art galleries and is home to the Royal Shakespeare Company. Its internal design has similarities with the National Theatre in that it works on lots of different levels and offers constant views across into other spaces, which makes it feel more alive. It works for me and I never tired of going there at lunchtime for a walk through The Curve, an open art gallery which mounted new displays every few weeks. If you went there via London Wall you could also see the few remnants of the City's old Roman wall and gatehouse which Hitler's bombs failed to destroy.

Our third move was to Bunhill Row, enabling SIB to be reunited as one unit, which was much more satisfactory. It was still within easy walking distance of the Barbican and was surrounded by houses, schools and other non-business activities, which made it much more congenial. Just down the road were Bunhill Fields, the ancient burial ground which housed the remains of many famous people. It was first used in 1665 as a place to bury victims of the plague. It is now maintained as a public garden and is well visited by those curious to see where John Bunyan, Daniel Defoe, William Blake and others are buried. John Bunyan's monument is a full size effigy lying on top of an attractive stone tomb. Daniel Defoe has a tall, elegant obelisk as his monument, but William Blake only managed a simple headstone.

Finally, I spent the last few years working from Canary Wharf, to which many of the leading financial institutions migrated in the late '80s and '90s. London's docks had been the largest and busiest in the world in the 19th and 20th centuries, but by 1981 they had all closed and new docks were developed further down the Thames. I learned some years later, on a holiday on La Gomera in the Canary Islands, about the origins and demise of Canary Wharf. It was dedicated to handling goods from the Canary Islands, hence its name. The Olson family grew bananas and tomatoes on La Gomera and transported them to Canary Wharf by ships of the Fred Olsen Lines. It was a flourishing market until the European Union outlawed their bananas because they were too small. Both the trade and the banana plantations died and so did Canary Wharf's role. Hans Olsen, a descendant of Fred, was scathing about the way the French, and particularly President Sarkosy, had engineered this outcome. Personally, I think the smaller bananas from La Gomera are much tastier than the larger ones grown elsewhere and Hans explained how they were also more nutritious because of the way they were grown and harvested - just one more reason to be annoyed with the interfering and restrictive EU.

It was a brave and risky decision in the early 1980s to pour money into regenerating Canary Wharf, a huge area of derelict land, and for a while it looked like a bad one, as the property market collapsed and the original owners went bankrupt. It now looks like a very good decision. The property market picked up and the whole area has been transformed, but what has been created does not lift your spirits. With its huge skyscrapers, mostly of glass, it is bleak and anonymous. The only thing I liked about the place was the journey there, initially via the Docklands Light Railway (DLR) and later by underground on the Jubilee Line extension. The DLR was fun. It's small, rickety, driverless carriages sat up high above the ground and the surrounding water, so that you had a good view of East London, one of the poorest parts of London. Older residents, who can remember the days when there was lots of work there for the ordinary working man, now live cheek by jowl with rich young City workers occupying the many up-market housing developments round the old dock basins. They may be in the same space, but they occupy different worlds.

Extending the Jubilee Line was what really made the difference to Canary Wharf's fortunes. It was completed in 1999 in time for the new millennium celebrations in The Dome at Greenwich. That became another iconic symbol of London, but was for a long time the butt of jokes and ridicule. It was started by John Major's Tory Government as the main venue for the year 2000 celebrations. When Tony Blair's government took it over in 1997 the media's attitude to The Dome changed. The right-wing press, which accounts for about 85% of newspapers sold, were predictably scathing, taking every opportunity to undermine the Labour Government. It was said to be in danger of not being ready on time. Since it was to be the focus of the celebrations on New Year's Eve this was potentially a disaster in the making. Confounding its critics it was, after all, ready on time and the celebrations went ahead, as planned, and were spectacular.

Ann and I went there afterwards and thoroughly enjoyed it. The Dome itself, designed by Richard Rodgers, has a tent-like domed roof held up by metal "guy ropes" attached to enormous metal spears, which pierce the skyline. It is still there, renamed O2, and used for big concerts and sporting events and is very much an accepted and liked feature of the London scene. The underground station at Canary Wharf, designed by Norman Foster, is well worth the journey to see it. It is a true work of art, cathedral like in its scope and impact.

Life outside work was also pretty busy during these years. In 1986 I played my last season for Welwyn Garden City Cricket Club, aged 50. Graham, who was then sixteen, played alongside me in my last match, which really pleased me. Having scored fifty in one match and taken five wickets in the last I decided that it was a good time to stop. It had been a good innings, starting at my Junior School in Leicester and playing for one team or another for over forty years, including twenty two years for W.G.C., but I did not want to hang on and become a liability.

It was during my City years that Helen and the boys completed the transition from school to university and into the world of work. They would also find their long-term partners. After graduating with a good 2.1 degree, Helen stayed on in Brighton with her friends, Louise and Liz, living in a rundown flat one street back from the seafront. It was here, on the night of 15/16 October 1987, that they felt the full ferocity of the Great Storm that hit the south coast and headed north until it reached Hertfordshire and then turned east through Cambridgeshire, Norfolk and Suffolk. Hurricane-force winds of 120 mph hit Brighton and the effect was frightening. Helen thought the windows would be blown in, which they were in a nearby house where an elderly couple was trapped in their room and unable to open the door to escape downstairs.

The hurricane swept north through Welwyn Garden City, leaving a trail of fallen trees. Our road was completely impassable to traffic. In the UK some 15 million trees were uprooted and the damage to property, railways, power and telephone lines caused massive disruption. It was estimated to have cost the insurance industry £2bn. The night of 15 October has gone down in BBC folklore as the night they got it all wrong. Their weatherman, Michael Fish, reported that the rumours of a hurricane were misplaced and that the lady who rang the BBC should stop worrying – how wrong can you get?

The late '80s were a difficult time for Helen to find a job. The country was going through another of Mrs Thatcher's economic downturns. Helen decided to become a volunteer at a school for disabled children in Brighton in the hope that it would lead to a paid job there, which it did. The woman who ran this school spotted a born teacher in Helen and encouraged her to take it up, so she moved to Manchester, where Benj was living, to do her teacher training. It turned out to be a very good move. Not only did she find that teaching really was her vocation, but she met her future husband, Andrew, there and they have lived happily together in Manchester ever since. There was an even happier event in 1994 when our first grandchild, Joe, was born. His brother, Ben, followed three years later. They would prove to be the first of ten grandchildren.

Mum and I dancing at Helen and Andrew's wedding

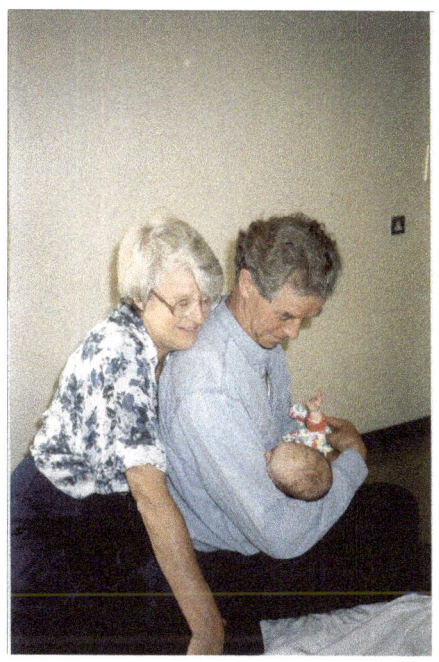

Ann and I with newly born Joe

Bruce did not move away, but got jobs locally with manufacturing companies in St Albans and W.G.C. He lived with us for a while before sharing a flat in Hatfield with his friend, Nick Reeves. Then he had a stroke of luck, meeting Orla, a lovely girl from Belfast. Eventually they married and settled down in the attractive old part of St Albans, close to the cathedral. There were plenty of old pubs in the neighbourhood, including "The Garibaldi", a few yards down the road. It had a younger clientele than most pubs and they were up for playing games. Carrying on the Smith tradition, Bruce raised a football team and a cricket team to take on other pubs and persuaded Benj and Graham to play in them. I got a lot of satisfaction from cheering them on from the touchline or the boundary and also when I joined their team in quiz nights at the pub. Bruce left manufacturing industry for far more lucrative work in the City where he plies his considerable computing and analytic skills. It pays well, but is demanding and stressful work.

Benjamin, or Benj, as the family call him, had a bumpier ride. Having done Materials Engineering at Loughborough he started work at a manufacturing company near Manchester. He was unlucky to fall foul of the asset-stripper, Hansen, who cut jobs mercilessly, including his. It was a bad time to be out of work. Unemployment was sky high and he had a hard time finding a new job. His one stroke of good luck was meeting Maria, a breath of fresh air from Spain. She was supposed to go back to Spain to do her law degree, but the tug of love was too strong and they settled down together in Levenshulme. However, the housing market had collapsed and they decided to buy a smaller, cheaper terraced house in nearby Stockport. They lost a lot of money on the Levenshulme house and we helped make good their loss so that the sale could go ahead. It gave them a chance to make a fresh start.

Benj decided to retrain, taking a course in computing. His luck changed, thanks to the kindness and generosity of his brother-in-law, Andrew, who by now was a Managing Partner of a very successful market research company. Andrew found him a job and he has never looked back. He is now highly successful in his new field, having moved south to live initially with Graham in London, then in St Albans and finally settling close to us in Welwyn Garden City. Benj and Maria got married in 2004, so Ann and I have all the benefits and pleasures from living close to them and their lovely family.

In 1987 Ann persuaded me to become involved in the running of the local Citizens Advice Bureau (CAB), for which she was a volunteer advisor for twenty seven years. I became its Chairman, succeeding the legendary Allison Bellack. Gil Bomber, the current Manager, was a large, jovial lady, originally from Czechoslovakia, who commanded a lot of loyalty from her workers. Welwyn Hatfield had gained a reputation as one of the best CABs in the country under her and Alison's leadership. The pressing problem in 1987 was how to deal with the huge number of debt problems that the advisers had to handle. The country, reeling under another of Margaret Thatcher's economic experiments, was going through yet another prolonged period of financial turmoil, as house prices soared, interest rates and mortgage rates followed, housing repossessions mounted and people got into serious financial difficulties. They came in droves to the CAB for advice and help. In 1988 Welwyn Hatfield alone was dealing with £500k worth of debt.

What was needed was a full time, paid adviser, dedicated to dealing with these problems, but how could I bring this about? With a little bit of luck I found a solution.

CAB got most of its income from Welwyn Hatfield Council. Securing a satisfactory settlement each year was a tortuous and disheartening process. Historically, our relations with the Council had not been good and its Treasurer, Fred Clarke, in particular, was not a friend of ours. When the time came to negotiate our next annual grant I decided to get directly involved. I led the CAB team which met the Council in the Council Chamber. We sat miles apart, on opposite sides of the Chamber, as if we were having a debate rather than a business meeting. It was bizarre. There were no introductory words of welcome. The Council just asked Gil Bomber to explain the proposed budget. It was as if Gil was simply regarded as a Council employee. I intervened, saying that I would like to introduce my team and to ask the Council to introduce theirs. I then went on to make a statement about what we were seeking before asking Gil to give more details. We had a good exchange and I felt that we had made a good case.

Then we had a big stroke of luck. Fred Clarke retired and the Council's Chief Executive left, to be replaced by David Riddle. Gil Bomber and I decided to seize our moment. I invited David to have supper at our house before going on to our AGM as guest speaker. He had come from Camden, where he had been a great supporter of its CAB. We pressed our case and, in due course, we got the funding we needed and Di Mellish became our first full time Money Adviser.

The CAB service is such an important safety valve for our society. Thousands of people come through its doors every day with a wide range of problems, some of them very sad and tragic. Ann would often come home with tales of hardship and despair, wishing that she could do more to help them, sometimes wanting to give a homeless person a bed for the night. CABs have very few paid staff, relying mostly on volunteers, so their operating costs are extremely low, but they set themselves high standards and are very professional in the way they operate. Despite the constant pressures on public finances, it is vital that they are supported.

Back at SIB I continued to build up contacts with a wide range of people engaged in IT in the financial services world, whilst others, such as The Federation of Software Suppliers, sought my help in establishing contacts with City regulators and companies engaged in financial services activities. Some old contacts sought me out, too, often because I could be useful to them in my new role. One of these was Gerald Watson, my old boss and Director at the CCTA. He had left the Treasury to join Ernst and Young, the accountancy and consultancy firm, where he specialised in financial services work. I liked Gerald and he seemed to enjoy my company. He took me and Ann to Covent Garden followed by a really special meal at Bibendum, the up-market restaurant in the old Michelin Tyre building, with its spectacular Art Nouveau design.

Belonging to the Butler Cox Foundation was a great help. They arranged conferences, business meetings, lunches and dinners, bringing together key individuals and relevant speakers. I found them stimulating and enormously useful. Because I was a key member of the City's newly-formed regulatory body I found myself invited to many of these gatherings. They were often held in the ancient halls of City Livery Companies or in the Guildhall itself, when it was a special occasion, and the atmosphere created was often memorable. Butler Cox had real style. They did everything well and attracted an extremely high quality membership. I was able to take Ann with me to one of their international conferences at Burgenstock, Switzerland. Our hotel sat high up on the mountainside overlooking Lake Lucerne and was quite beautiful. It had a swimming pool with a huge picture window at one end, which created the illusion of being able to swim straight into the lake hundreds of feet below.

Another Butler Cox occasion was nearly life-changing, or even life ending, when I was involved in a serious car crash whilst travelling to its conference in Dorset. It was late on a Sunday night when I stopped at the roadside, under a street lamp, to check where I was going. The next thing I remember is being helped out of my car by an ambulance crew and a policeman. A young man, drunk and on drugs, had hit me at high speed in a large Volvo estate car and pushed me into the street lamp, crushing my car, a large Ford Granada, to the size of a Mini. The Volvo, his father's, was uninsured and untaxed. He came to see me a few days later to mumble an apology. I never saw his face. I was ten days in Poole Hospital recovering from damage to my back, head and kidneys. I was lucky not to have been killed. What a different life Ann and the children would have had.

The City is steeped in tradition and I had a taste of it in 1988 when I became involved in the creation of the Worshipful Company of Information Technologists, the 100th City Livery Company. Livery Companies have a long history. The first was the Mercers, founded in 1394. They were essentially trade associations, controlling who could ply that trade, as well as providing support to their members in sickness and old age. Over the years they have raised huge sums for charities, run almshouses and supported good causes. A Trust set up by Richard Whittington, a Mercer who was four times Lord Mayor of London and died in 1423, still operates today - he was the original "Dick Whittington". The driving force behind our new Company was Alan Benjamin, one of Kenneth Baker's old IT Advisers, whom I knew well. He persuaded me to become a Freeman and one of the original founder members. I took part in a quaint ceremony in 1989 to become a Freeman of the City of London. I swore allegiance to the Queen and promised to obey lots of rules, which are laid down in a little red book entitled "Rules for the Conduct of Life". It was all very medieval. I'm not sure if I have transgressed any of those rules, because the little red book is enclosed in a glass-fronted frame, which Ann kindly had made.

As well as providing the Central Register I had responsibility for providing all other IT systems and services to enable SIB to carry out its functions. As a service provider I placed great store on keeping all staff and Board Members informed about what we were doing, outlining our plans for the future and providing a progress report on new developments. My chatty newsletter proved very popular. There was something in it for most people and it became part of the glue that held SIB together.

I got a very welcome break from my SIB duties when I attended the International Organisation of Securities

Commissions' (IOSCO) conference in Venice in September 1989 with our Chairman, David Walker, and Roy Croft. It was Roy who suggested I should go as a reward for helping to prepare one of the presentations. In practice it was a five day holiday in luxurious surroundings, blessed with the best Italian food and wine. We stayed at a gorgeous five star hotel, a former palace, on the Grand Canal opposite the church of San Giorgio Maggiore. The gondoliers would stop outside my window and sing their songs at full blast. The first time it was delightful. By the fiftieth time I could have shot the singer.

The boat ride from the airport to the hotel is still etched in my memory. Nothing quite compares to the stunning entrance to the Grand Canal and the first sight of the beautiful pastel patchwork of 15th and 16th century buildings on either side, basking in early autumn sunshine. I have travelled extensively since and I would rate this as top of my list of best first impressions. The Italian organisers had gone to great lengths to make this the best IOSCO conference so far, similar to the way successive Olympic venues try to out-do each other. The closing banquet was lavish in the extreme. The papers I had helped prepare went down well and I met some interesting people, but I got little out of the conference otherwise. Perhaps David and Roy did. It was an opportunity for them to foster good relations with other regulators, but I am sceptical about the value of such events. I have similar reservations about OECD jamborees, too. Nevertheless, for me, it was a very pleasant interlude.

However, life for Ann and me was about to take a turn for the worst.

Chapter 15

The City
Troubled Minds

When Graham went off to Reading University in October 1989 to read Electronic Engineering, following his two brothers in pursuing an engineering course, the last of Ann's brood had flown the nest and she was left alone with me. She still had a very busy and active life, as an adviser at the Citizens Advice Bureau and as a fund-raiser with Crossroads Care, which provided respite care for carers, and she played tennis, golf and bridge. We had a lot of good friends and did a lot together, so there would seem no reason why she should start to feel anxious and then depressed, but she did. She had fallen victim to the "empty nest syndrome".

It is ironic that, having coped well with all the stresses and strains of raising the children, Ann would then suffer the first of several bouts of severe anxiety and depression over the next thirty years. She would have long periods in The Priory, the leading private psychiatric hospital in Southgate, in 1989, 1995, 2009 and 2017 and in an NHS psychiatric hospital in 2017/18. I have agonised about whether I could and should have done more to ease the burdens on her and why I was unable to see these episodes coming or help prevent them becoming so traumatic, but mental illness is not like physical illnesses and, even now, we are not at all clear about the underlying causes and what triggered each episode. Your gut instinct tells you that it must have something to do with your relationship, because that has been the common denominator over the years, but Ann insists it is not and that the cause lies elsewhere, possibly in her childhood and the high expectations placed upon her by her father. As a result, Ann's confidence and self-belief are brittle and always liable to evaporate without much warning. Doubts sown in the formative years are very hard to overcome.

The first episode started when we went on our first holiday abroad since before we were married. We went on a walking holiday in Greece with Ramblers, one week in Delphi and one on the island of Euboea. Ann was very frightened of flying. I had persuaded her to go, but at the airport she was petrified and refused to board the plane, but eventually did. When we reached Athens and she saw the white city below against a clear blue sky she burst into tears, a mixture of joy and relief. The holiday itself was lovely, particularly the ancient ruins of Delphi in their breathtaking setting on the slopes of Mount Parnassus. I ran on the 100 metres track used in the Pythian Games, which preceded the Olympic Games. The walk down to the Gulf of Itea, through the largest olive grove in Europe, was memorable. Despite all of this, Ann was dreading the flight back, could not relax and slept badly.

Soon after getting home we went to Reading to have lunch with Graham and to see how he was settling in.

Ann did not want to go. She was very agitated and anxious throughout the visit and over the next few days became very depressed. Her G.P. referred her to a consultant psychiatrist, Dr McClure, a lovely, big bear of a man, whom Ann found very comforting. She was admitted to The Priory. It was based in Grovelands, an impressive 18th century house designed by John Nash. Tall columns framed the imposing entrance and large picture windows overlooked Humphrey Repton's grounds and parkland. The entrance hall was very grand, too - two majestic winding staircases swept up to the first floor to where Dr McClure had his consulting rooms. The original estate had been split up, with the local council maintaining Grovelands Park. Patients from the hospital would be taken into the park every morning for a walk round the lake, as Ann and I would when I visited her. Ann had a large room with a picture window and TV. It was a very pleasant place in which to recover, well decorated and carpeted throughout. It had a comfortable lounge in which to play games or just read and a lot of comfortable settees and chairs in the wide, spacious corridors. It cost our insurer a great deal of money, but I was glad she was there rather than in an NHS hospital, whose psychiatric departments had a bad reputation.

Ann responded well to the anti-depressant drugs and after a few weeks was having conversations with other patients there and playing cards after dinner with me and another patient. I visited her after work every day in time to have an evening meal with her and other patients. I stayed all day at weekends. The hospital placed great emphasis on getting patients to eat well and the food there was excellent. She recovered well and was discharged on Christmas Eve. Helen and the boys were due to come home for Christmas and, to my astonishment, Ann was determined to do Christmas dinner as if nothing had happened. She showed tremendous guts and determination. To my great annoyance the local butcher had sold our turkey by the time we got there at lunch time, but we managed to get another and had a better Christmas than had seemed remotely possible a few weeks earlier. The boys and I played our traditional tennis match on Christmas Day morning, having tucked into the traditional Smith Christmas breakfast of Melton Mowbray pork pie, Stilton cheese, ham, piccalilli, pickled onions etc. I was, however, very tense throughout.

The strain of worrying about Ann, driving to and from Southgate each day to be with her after doing a hard day's work, then trying to fit in washing, ironing, cleaning, shopping and preparing for Christmas, took its toll and I became increasingly stressed. It had manifested itself earlier when Neville Davis, Compel's Chairman, had asked me to speak at their annual conference at nearby Brocket Hall in early December. William Keegan, Economics Editor of 'The Observer', gave the opening keynote address and I followed. As I listened to him I was so stressed I could easily have walked out, but managed to control my anxiety and give the talk. I have never felt particularly nervous about speaking, no matter how large the audience or how important the event, providing I am clear about what I want to say. I usually enjoy the experience, the actor inside me coming out, but not this time. I knew something was seriously wrong.

Over lunch with William Keegan and Neville Davis I relaxed a bit. Neville offered to show me round the house. It is very grand, but has a homely feel to it. There had been a house on this site since the early 13th century, but the current Hall, designed by Sir James Paine, was built in the mid 18th century and is a grade 1 listed building. Two prime ministers, Lord Melbourne and Lord Palmerston, have lived here and Lord Byron had a scandalous affair here with Lady Caroline Melbourne.

Neville and I went into the snooker room where the current owner, Lord Brocket, was playing. He was young, fresh faced, very friendly and approachable, and offered to complete the tour of the house. He had financial problems and was trying to make the house and estate more profitable. The cows had gone and had been replaced by a golf course. He was marketing the house for conferences and weddings and it would later be turned into a hotel. That, however, was not all he was doing to increase his income. He tried to claim insurance for the theft of several vintage cars that he and his manager had, in fact, hidden. He was caught, charged and convicted of fraud. He went to prison and, on release, re-invented himself as a celebrity, taking part in the TV show "I'm a celebrity get me out of here". You would never have foreseen any of this from my brief encounter with him.

On returning to work after Christmas Roy Croft asked how Ann was doing and also how I felt. I said that Ann was OK, but I was shattered. He told me to take a few days off to recover, which I did, but it had the opposite effect. I completely collapsed. I would lie in bed unable to stop shaking. My GP prescribed sleeping pills, but I got worse and became seriously depressed. I was given the same anti-depressant as Ann and eventually it worked. After a month or so I started to get slowly better, but it was a very scary experience. People talk of feeling depressed when they really mean that they feel unhappy or a bit low in spirits. Real clinical depression is a different animal altogether. Your body's chemistry goes haywire and your nervous system is in shreds. You cannot function as a person. I couldn't go out, talk to anyone or focus on anything. I was as taut as a violin string and felt that I could snap at any moment. I felt one step away from going mad.

Eventually, after six weeks, I had improved enough to consider returning to work, which I did, but only because I feared for my job if I stayed away any longer. I was far from ready to engage with people or do meaningful work, but my secretary, Jenny Cusack, and the other staff were very understanding and supportive. I was able to coast for the next two or three weeks, but I could not hide away completely. I needed the Management Committee's agreement to an important policy change and I prepared a paper for it. I asked Roy Croft if it could be the first on the agenda so that I did not have to sit waiting my turn and getting increasingly fretful. He kindly agreed, knowing what lay behind it. Slowly I mended, but it was the worst period of my life.

As we both returned to normality Ann and I decided to have a holiday. Despite the traumas of the holiday in Greece, Ann's appetite for travelling abroad had been whetted and we decided to go walking again with Ramblers, this time in the south of France, but to get there by train and ferry because Ann was still frightened of flying. This was before the days of the Channel Tunnel and Eurostar so getting down to Montpelier by overnight sleeper took nearly 24 hours, but it was worth the effort. Our first week was in the Cevennes, a range of thickly wooded hills, mostly horse chestnut trees. This was where Robert Louis Stevenson undertook his "Travels with a Donkey" and we stayed at the same Hotel L'Orange in St John du Gard where he ended his journey. The mother and daughter running the hotel endeared themselves to the party. Not only were they very good cooks, but they were Anglophiles, an unusual species in France, who took their holidays in Cheltenham. Ann loved the food and the games of bridge with a doctor and his wife after the day's walking.

The second week was in St Remy de Provence where Van Gogh had been a patient in the local asylum, which we passed on our way to Les Alpilles, a range of jagged limestone mountains that Van Gogh often painted. Negotiating these mountains was not easy and our leader, Dick Berger, was not up to the job. On one very hot day, with the temperature in the mid-thirties, we lost patience with him and I told him to give me the maps and compass. I eventually found the right paths and got the party back safely, but it could have been a disaster. It was apparently his first experiencing of leading for Ramblers and the party's members vowed to make sure it was his last.

Ann decided that she must tackle her fear of flying if we were to have more holidays abroad. She showed great guts by enrolling on a British Airways course at which pilots, hostesses and psychiatrists addressed people's fears and tried to convince them that flying was safe. It worked. After the course Ann and I would sit in our car outside the perimeter fence at Heathrow and watch the planes land safely every one and a half minutes. It reinforced the messages she had got from the course and opened up a whole new world for us. Ann now looked forward to flying and made over twenty flights in one year. Over the next twenty five years we would travel extensively in Europe and round the world. Many of these visits have been on walking holidays, often in search of wild flowers. We particularly enjoyed walking on the islands of the Mediterranean in springtime, when the flowers are spectacular - Crete is hard to beat. We went several times a year to Amsterdam when Graham lived there. We could have done none of this had Ann not confronted her flying demons.

Ann and I on a mountain top in Tuscany

With three of the children no longer living with us and Graham at university Ann decided to offer one of the bedrooms to young foreign teaching assistants who were working at Stanborough School for a year. Two were French and one German. The first was Lawrence, who was a real Anglophile. She and her boyfriend would spend their holidays travelling round the UK on an enormous motorbike which seemed to be twice as big as her. After she finished her teaching year they would come back and stay with us en route to another part of the UK. They liked Scotland, in particular. They still keep in touch. Ann had a shock when the second girl, Karin, a German, turned up at the CAB where Ann was working and announced that she was a vegetarian. Ann had not reckoned on that, but she adjusted and we learned to go without meat for our main meal, which was fine for a few months. The third one was Geraldine. She was a delightful French girl, who still sends us cards and letters many years later.

When Graham graduated in 1992 the UK economy was still struggling, so finding a good job was difficult. He worked for a short time in Reading before gravitating to London and the City where both Bruce and I worked. After a successful spell at Coopers and Lybrand he moved to ABN Amro, the Dutch bank. By then he had met his future wife, Beth, on a sailing holiday in the Mediterranean and they settled down together. They were well matched, both having a sense of adventure and a get-up-and-go approach to life. Beth is a very accomplished performer in her own right, having qualified as a ski instructor in France and being an expert water skier, too. Before starting to raise a family they went off on a long round-the-world adventure holiday and a gruelling trek in the Himalayas of Nepal,

When ABN Amro offered Graham a move to their HQ in Amsterdam he jumped at it. This opened the way for Ann and me to make many enjoyable trips there over the next few years. Graham and Beth went out of their way to ensure that we had a good time with them, showing us the sights and treating us to some lovely meals out. We had plenty of time to ourselves, too, so we got to explore Amsterdam and the nearby towns. Amsterdam is perfect for tourists because everything is reachable on foot. There is an absence of traffic, which is a big plus, but you have to be very alert to avoid being mowed down by cyclists or treading on dog mess, which is a pain. We liked Amsterdam and got to know it well. The architecture is very different. The Dutch had to make good use of their precious land, which had been reclaimed from the sea, building very tall but narrow terraced houses, which meant that you were forever going up or down stairs in them. Simply walking beside the canals was a great pleasure, but top of my list would be visits to the Van Gogh Museum, housing over 200 of his paintings and 500 drawings.

Delft, only a few minutes from Amsterdam on the super-efficient railway, was the pick of the nearby towns. The old town is very little changed from its 14th century origins. It is famous for its blue pottery, of course, and also for being the home of Vermeer. He painted only a few pictures, but they are all exquisite.

As they settled down we saw a lot more of Helen and the boys and their partners, either at our house or on visits to theirs. Christmas was usually celebrated as a family at our house, if we were not in Manchester with Helen and Andrew, and we would all get together as often as we could at other times, enjoying many relaxing meals in our garden. Then the family started going on summer holidays together, initially staying in the grounds of the Farringford Hotel on the Isle of White, and then in cottages on the south coast (in Devon, Somerset and Cornwall). Ann's mum, Ida, would join us when she was alive, and Nigel and Sue. These were immensely enjoyable occasions, which I look back on with enormous pleasure. As their families grew we would continue these get-togethers, either in the UK or France, which the grandchildren loved.

Lunch in the garden
Ann, Derrick and Andrew (left). Maria, Helen, Nigel and Benj (right).
Me at the far end and young Ben at the front.

Back at SIB my Head of Systems, Ross Hopcroft, decided to leave in 1991. He had been a great asset, not only in his approach to the work in hand, but in the cheerful way he dealt with everyone. He was well liked and I was very sorry to lose him. He had made a significant contribution whilst with us.

Alan Futter was Ross' replacement. With Alan's arrival we reviewed our IT strategy and decided to leave the Datasolve bureau and run our own systems. We became much more cost-effective and technically resilient. We could now provide other regulators with direct access to our Central Register and other systems, and provide a much better service to SIB's own staff dealing with 50,000 Central Register telephone enquiries a year from the public. We supported many of SIB's other functions. After Allied Equity went bust in 1989 there was general praise for the way SIB handled investors' claims under the Investors Compensation Scheme, which was in large part due to the effectiveness of our systems. We received many visits from overseas regulators. The Chairman of the USA's Securities and Exchange Commission and Board members of both the Hungarian and Portuguese regulatory bodies were all impressed with the Central Register and with the cost-effectiveness of our IT services generally. The latter vowed to go home and copy our approach.

Ann and I continued to meet our friends, Jill and Ray Rundle, two or three times a year. When in Alford we enjoyed some lovely walks in the Lincolnshire Wolds, which were very close to where they lived. It is completely unspoilt countryside, just a few tiny hamlets nestling in the folds of the hills. Years later I would introduce John and Jean Sefton and our walking group to this largely unknown and undiscovered gem.

With Jill and Ray in the Lincolnshire Wolds

After Ray and Jill Rundle retired they moved south to Oundle in Northamptonshire so that they were nearer to their two daughters. They settled in very quickly and Jill was soon running various University of the Third Age (U3A) groups and starting others whilst Ray got involved in the Bridge Club and in local history. The place was tailor-made for their retirement. Northamptonshire has always been one of my favourite counties, with its big country estates, prosperous farms and mellow, honey-coloured stone villages. I only knew the north of the county and it was a pleasure to discover the beauty of this part, too. Jill wished they had moved there years earlier.

When Jean and John Sefton moved back to the UK from Belgium they settled in north Yorkshire, close to the Cleveland Hills and the North York Moors, an area which is largely unknown to southerners. It is a gorgeous bit of England and we enjoyed some very happy visits there. Later, when John retired they were torn between staying there or moving back to Welwyn Garden City. John would have been happy to stay, having put down strong roots there, but Jean was not so committed to the area and they chose to move, which meant that we saw more of them, but could no longer enjoy those lovely visits.

John Sefton (left), Catherine and Len Hall (right), Jean Sefton and me (centre) in North Yorkshire

David Walker completed his four years as Chairman of SIB in 1992 and deservedly got his knighthood. He would later become Lord Walker. He had restored a degree of confidence in the regulatory regime, improved SIB's relations with the other regulatory bodies and the firms they regulated, and enhanced the City's reputation internationally. Whilst there was still a lot of discontent and unhappiness with SIB, particularly about its costs, the noise was a lot less than before David had become

Chairman. However, there was a sting at the tail-end of his Chairmanship when Robert Maxwell, the flamboyant ex-MP, publisher and entrepreneur, fell off his yacht in the Atlantic and was drowned. Subsequently, huge discrepancies were found in his companies' finances. In particular, he had raided the Mirror Group pension funds of hundreds of millions of pounds in order to shore up other parts of his ailing empire. Two of the companies that managed these funds were authorised and regulated by IMRO. The media turned the spotlight on both IMRO and SIB. Why had IMRO not spotted that this was going on and what was SIB doing to ensure that IMRO was fulfilling its regulatory responsibilities properly? Were they both asleep on the job?

Andrew Large took over from David as Chairman. His first task, set by the Chancellor of the Exchequer, was to review the way SIB carried out its regulatory responsibilities. He concluded that IMRO had serious weaknesses and needed to undergo major reforms, including changes in personnel. Its Chief Executive, John Morgan, was replaced. I was sorry to see him go. He was a true gentleman and I had got on very well with him. IMRO's procedures were radically reformed. The two fund management companies that failed had only been inspected once every two years - this was changed to twice a year, and the inspections made more rigorous.

On the wider review Andrew Large was scathing about SIB's performance so far. He concluded that the industry did not really understand what SIB's role was. It was widely thought to be simply a rule-making body. He proposed that SIB should make it clear what it stood for by publishing its objectives, setting new regulatory standards and enforcing them rigorously. From now on

SIB would develop more bite and become an enforcer. Out would go "self-assessments", whereby each regulatory body judged its own performance, and in would come a hard-hitting system of direct inspection visits by SIB staff. I was glad to see this, for I had never believed in the old regime, introduced by David Walker. It was a sop to the SROs, made at the time in order to quell their criticism of SIB, but it was a cop-out and would lead, sooner or later, to the kind of situation we had with IMRO. The Chancellor accepted Andrew's Review report and its recommendations, and Andrew set about making it work.

I found Andrew to be a very intense and serious person. In the four years I worked closely with him I cannot recall him making a joke or even smiling very much. He was determinedly focussed on the job in hand, which he did very well. I got on well enough with him. He was always perfectly civil, but not warm. Given the remit he had been given and the solutions he had proposed you might imagine that he could become overbearing and intolerant, but he did not work like that. His strengths were his sharp, analytical mind and his determination to finish what he had started. He started by replacing Roy Croft, who was approaching retirement, bringing in John Young as his Chief Executive. I had thoroughly enjoyed working with Roy, going back to our days at DTI, and would miss him. He had helped me enormously when I had problems following Ann's illness. I wondered what would happen next and so did everyone else in SIB. We would soon find out.

Andrew and John called a meeting of all senior staff and announced that they would be creating a totally different organisation and staffing structure. All staff, without exception, would have to apply for the new positions and convince John and Andrew that they were the right person for that job. We were warned that there would be several people who would not find a place in the new SIB. That was a bombshell for everyone. I made a comment, in response to a question from John, to which he said "Now there's a positive view from that grand old trouper, Brian", for I was the oldest person there. I thought that was either a promising sign or an indication that I was too old for the new set up. We all left the meeting and waited.

John sent for me the next day. To my great surprise he said that he wanted me to be his Head of Operations - effectively Chief Operating Officer, but he didn't like that title. There would be three other Divisions. I would join the heads of these plus John Young and Andrew Large on the Board's Executive Committee. I would keep my current responsibilities and take on Finance, Administration, Personnel and Training. I had resisted taking on more responsibilities under Roy Croft, but I had no hesitation in taking up this offer. John said that I still had to convince Andrew that I was the man for the job, which I did.

The next three years were challenging, but very satisfying. I loved the job and, in particular, working with John Young. He was a most rewarding boss, always ready to encourage and praise. He had been one of my sporting heroes in the 1950s. He was a brilliant runner, winning the AAA 100 yards in 1956, and playing on the wing for Harlequins, England and the British Lions. He made no mention of any of this, as many would. He was very modest. He would not have done so well in modern rugby, though, where you have to be 16 stone and over six feet tall to stand any chance of selection. He was small, slight in build and a chain smoker, but very likeable.

Before taking up this new post I completed the development of the Shared Intelligence Service to enable staff in SIB's Enforcement Group and other regulators to find out quickly if anything adverse was known about particular individuals and firms. It was accessible via direct links to 27 regulatory and other bodies. Tony Whitfeld garnered the data from SIB, 3 SROs, 9 RPBs, 6 Exchanges, 1 Clearing House, the Bank of England, Lloyds of London, DTI Investigation and Insurance Divisions, plus financial services overseers in Guernsey, Jersey and the Isle of Man. I held regular meetings with all these to encourage them to contribute relevant data. Eventually the system would hold over 1.5 million entries and handle about 85,000 enquiries a year. It has been a great success story for SIB, enhancing our standing in the eyes of the other regulators. During the course of this system's development I had a number of meetings with the newly-formed National Criminal Intelligence Service, exploring the possibilities of tapping each others' intelligence databases. On a visit to their HQ I was astonished at how few staff there were to tackle some of the most infamous criminal networks, such as the Mafia and the Chinese Triads – just one man and a desk, it seemed: very scary.

Over the next four years the newly-fashioned SIB worked very hard to help Andrew Large achieve the aims set out in his Review. Andrew was a very hands-on Chairman. He would go off in his car late on Friday to be driven to Tal-y-Bont, his home in mid-Wales, laden with papers and reports for his weekend reading. If he wanted to query or discuss something he would telephone you, no matter that it was the weekend. On Mondays, if I saw Michael Blair, our Head of Legal Affairs, he would invariably ask if I had been "Tal-y-Bonted" that weekend, because he would certainly have been.

SIB stepped up its enforcement work and published the standards to be met by other regulatory bodies, markets and firms. In the four years from 1993 to 1997 SIB opened 2,267 investigations into unauthorised investment business and 162 cases of fraud were referred for criminal investigation. SIB became a force to be reckoned with.

My immediate tasks were to complete SIB's reorganisation, implement a staff training programme and tackle the problem of SIB's costs. Sue Proctor was Head of Personnel and Training and Roger Purcell was Head of Finance. I knew them both well, which made relationships easier, and we worked well together. Sue and I worked on completing the reorganisation and sadly making some old colleagues redundant, including Bruce Bennett, my long-standing Computer Operations Manager, which really upset me. He had been with me from the start, but I had to do it. Andrew Large's Review had proposed a cap of 200 on SIB's staff numbers for the next year, despite the extra work that he foresaw. Job titles and salaries were a problem. There was no grading or salary structure across the organisation. We introduced one, attaching a salary range to each new job title and grade. Some staff were well outside these ranges and we had to make significant adjustments, which were very unpopular, as you can imagine.

We then embarked on a training programme for the whole organisation, starting at the top. This had been one of Andrew Large's Review recommendations so we had hoped that Andrew would join the rest of us on the Board's Executive Committee at the first sessions, but he opted out. That was a pity because it was as much about bonding the new team together as it was about learning new ways of doing things. It went very well and we felt more like a team afterwards. That would appeal to me and John Young, who came from sporting team environments, but it was new to our other three colleagues and they got a lot out of it.

Another of Andrew's Review recommendations was that SIB should be more transparent about its costs, which were a sore point with the industry and with the SROs, in particular. SIB's costs were not that high. We did not pay ourselves silly salaries, nor were we in lavish accommodation or our other overheads high - our computing costs, in particular, were very modest. The truth is that our costs would have been resented whatever they were. Nevertheless, I decided that we had to meet the criticisms head-on and try to still them. I called a meeting of all the SROs and the Bank of England at which Roger Purcell set out in great detail how our charges had been arrived at. I persuaded Roger that we should hold nothing back and allow them to probe whatever they felt like. It worked. It was astonishing how their distrust and anger evaporated. They went away satisfied that they understood what they were paying for. We had other meetings, but that first meeting set the tone and relationships changed for the better from then on.

In 1993 a huge IRA bomb in Bishopsgate sent shock waves through the City and galvanised those trying to find a peaceful settlement to "The Troubles". Its impact was devastating. Because it was set off on a Saturday, and warnings had been given, only one person was killed and 44 injured. On a weekday it would have been a massacre. The target was the NatWest Tower, then the tallest building in London. It was badly damaged and the costs of rebuilding were enormous, but the psychological impact was just as great. Seeing that huge building, standing high above the London skyline, unused and with its windows blown out was a constant warning to everyone that there was danger afoot whilst the conflict went on unresolved. I went there the following Monday and saw windows blown out of almost all the buildings, right down to Liverpool Street Station. A nearby church had collapsed.

There had been another huge bomb the previous year when the Baltic Exchange was destroyed and we had got used to living with this constant fear, but this felt particularly threatening. The City was such a huge contributor to the country's wealth that the government had to react quickly. It could not afford to let these threats frighten business away. John Major, the Prime Minister, has since said that these events only hardened the government's resolve and did not hasten an agreement with the IRA, but the facts speak for themselves. The IRA suspended its bombing campaign whilst negotiations took place and declared a complete cessation of its military operations in August 1994, seventeen months after the Bishopsgate bombing. The whole country was mightily relieved, but none more so than those working in the City.

John Young had another surprise in store for me when, in mid 1995, nine months from my planned retirement, he asked me if I would take on the work to deal with two applications from CRESTCo, newly created in a great hurry by the Bank of England. It had applied to SIB to be Recognised as a Clearing House and Approved as the Operator of a 'Relevant System' for electronically transferring and storing legal title to securities – effectively doing away with the need for share certificates and other paperwork and handling the buying and selling of investments via computers. The work on these CRESTCo applications was currently being handled by John Serecold alone, and he was struggling, but I was not keen to get involved. I thought it would be a bed of nails and I already had a heavy workload.

John Young was disappointed, but didn't press me too hard. Instead he came back a few weeks later with a much firmer proposal and an appeal to my sense of public duty. He knew how to push the right buttons. He stressed how the whole viability and future of the City was at stake, which it was. It hung crucially on whether CREST, the proposed new computer system, could be made to work by CRESTCo. For SIB, too, it was a severe test - how it handled CRESTCo's applications was an important and highly visible test of its regulatory credibility. There were a lot of rumblings of discontent from the Bank, CRESTCo and the Treasury about SIB's handling of these applications so far. John had to do something and he had a radical solution. He asked me to consider standing down as Head of Operations, without loss of pay, in order to work full time on the CRESTCo applications. Rod Whittaker, who had worked for Andrew Large before, had been identified as my possible replacement. I agreed to do a quick assessment of what was needed.

I went to see Jeremy Heywood in the Treasury. He was responsible for financial services policy and, in particular, for developing the legislation that created the new Regulations. He described the latter as the most difficult and intellectually challenging task he had yet undertaken. He would have far greater challenges later when he became Cabinet Office Secretary and Head of the Civil Service. He clearly had direct feedback from others about the way I operated and said he would welcome my involvement. I told John Young that I would take it on provided that I got someone with direct experience of stock markets and settlement systems. He agreed and the very capable John Aarons joined my team.

Rod Whittaker took over from me as Head of Operations and I got stuck into this new challenge. It was a bumpy ride.

Chapter 16

The City Honoured, Ma'am

My new task was to decide whether to recommend to the SIB Board that it should give legal recognition to CREST, the new computer system being developed by CRESTCo for settling the sale and purchase of financial investments. CREST was the Bank of England's response to the failure by the London Stock Exchange (LSE) to build a replacement for Talisman, their current system. It urgently needed replacing if the UK was to provide services that met modern international standards. There was a real risk that business in the UK's financial services markets would move elsewhere, with devastating consequences for the City and the UK economy. Many millions of pounds had been spent on the development of a replacement for Talisman, but it had proved to be a bitter and expensive failure. I had represented SIB on one of the LSE's development committees, chaired by Alan Harvey, for whom I had a very high regard. When he left the LSE to set up his own systems consultancy I engaged him as an adviser, monitoring the development of the CREST computer system and giving me detailed weekly progress reports. He was superb -- tenacious and undaunted in the face of fierce resistance from CRESTCo to his legitimate demands for hard evidence of progress.

The Bank moved fast to set up CRESTCo as a separate company to develop and run CREST. It was doing its duty, stepping into the breach to save the City's reputation and secure its future.

The services to be provided by CREST were a major step forward. Out went paper share certificates to be replaced by the holding and transferring of transactions in electronic form. July 1996 was set as the target date for CREST to go live. It was a daunting task for CRESTCo and a very demanding one for SIB, too.

Pen Kent, a Director of the Bank, also became CRESTCo's Chairman and Iain Saville its Chief Executive. Iain had been heavily involved in the sterling crisis of 1992 when, on "Black Wednesday", the UK was finally forced by the market to abandon its policy of shadowing the deutschmark. He liaised closely with Jeremy Heywood, who was then the Principle Private Secretary to the Chancellor, Norman Lamont. I reckoned that this bond between Iain and Jeremy would probably work in CRESTCo's favour when disputes with SIB arose, so I took steps to tip the balance the other way.

Jeremy Heywood agreed to have lunch with me at SIB at regular intervals to review progress and talk informally about current problems and concerns. This worked well. He was serious but not intense, an astute listener and very easy to get on with. We formed a good working relationship enabling me to contact him to discuss any difficult issues that arose, so that he had our side of the story as well as CRESTCo's. This was particularly important as we approached the planned date for CREST's inauguration by the Chancellor, Kenneth Clarke, when I was still refusing to give Approval and Recognition to CREST until a large number of outstanding issues had been resolved. Iain Saville was furious and we had a heated telephone exchange ending with him threatening to get the Governor of the Bank to call the Chancellor and put pressure on Andrew Large, my Chairman, to get me to shift my ground. I rang Jeremy Heywood immediately and explained the importance of the outstanding issues. I would not give Approval and Recognition, I said, until these issues were resolved to my satisfaction, even if that meant having to cancel the official launch by the Chancellor. I had good reason to think that Pen Kent would not have sanctioned such action by Iain. After one of the regular review meetings that Andrew Large, John Young and I had with him and Iain Saville, Pen Kent took Andrew aside and said "You are giving us hell. Keep it up." Iain's threats never materialised. I felt vindicated.

Since CRESTCo remained under the wing of the Bank until after CREST was inaugurated it felt as if we were dealing with an application from the Bank itself, which created constant tensions. Relationships were often confrontational and sometimes bruising. My task was to ensure that the law, and investor protection principles implicit in it, were upheld and given due weight in the many difficult issues that arose. CRESTCo saw SIB as nit-picking, bureaucratic, obstructive and expensive.

CRESTCo welcomed my appointment even though I made a lot of changes to the way we worked. I introduced formal review meetings every two weeks plus regular sandwich lunches with Iain Saville, alternating the venues, so that we could speak frankly and off-the-record about anything which concerned us and so gain a better understanding of the key sticking points. As a result, although relations were strained to breaking point at times, we managed to remain on constructive speaking terms over the next seven months. Crucially, Iain also agreed that our staff should have direct dialogue on specific issues rather than channel everything through him. As a result, we made much better progress on key issues, some of which had previously seemed intractable at times.

CRESTCo submitted its formal applications for the Recognition and Approval of CREST in January and March. They were mammoth documents, each over 2,000 pages long. The first application was rather poor and incomplete and we had to ask for additional material, much to their great dismay. The Treasury announced that the Chancellor would inaugurate the new service on 15 July. The pressure was on for both CRESTCo and SIB.

CRESTCo had set out to keep CREST's design simple and to minimise the use of rules. It aimed to be tough with everyone, including SIB, in order to achieve this. This gave rise to a lot of tensions with us and also with CREST's users. In one dispute CRESTCo resorted to taking Legal Counsel's opinion to try to persuade us to shift our ground, but it failed. In another dispute the London Stock Exchange, the London Clearing House (LCH) and other Exchanges could not agree with CRESTCo on how rules requiring firms to report and settle trades within given times would be enforced and who would be responsible. When it was clear that no agreement was forthcoming I got everyone together over a working lunch. This formula worked well, drawing CRESTCo into the regulatory net, improving personal relations and changing CRESTCo's attitude on key issues.

In May, when the Board considered the application for Recognition as a Clearing House, there were still eight significant unresolved issues, and a month later there were still five. The figures for the application for Approval as an Operator were much worse. Less than two weeks from the planned launch date, there were still twenty unresolved issues. The pressure on CRESTCo staff was enormous. The last big issue, the contract between CRESTCo and SWIFT, was not settled to our satisfaction until a signed copy was faxed from Tokyo just two hours before SIB's Executive Committee met on 11 July to consider the applications again. Even then not all the outstanding issues had been resolved, but we judged that those that remained did not constitute a sufficient reason for withholding our Recognition and Approval. I reported to the Executive Committee that the system was ready to go live. We judged that any remaining issues posed no significant risk of system failure. I recommended that CRESTCo should be granted Recognition and Approval. The Executive Committee, acting on behalf of the Board, agreed.

I telephoned Iain Saville and Jeremy Heywood immediately to convey the good news. I also wrote to Iain, congratulating him and his staff, saying that they "deserve all the plaudits that will deservedly come your way". I also wrote to Jeremy, attaching the two Orders made by the Board and a Press Release.

Apart from a farewell lunch those were my last dealings with Jeremy Heywood. It was no surprise to me that he rose to the very top of the Civil Service and was knighted. On the way up he had been Tony Blair's Principle Private Secretary in 1999 and head of the Policy Unit at no. 10 when Gordon Brown became Prime Minister. They have both been fulsome in praising Jeremy's contributions – "incomparable" according to Gordon Brown. Jeremy went on to serve in David Cameron's office when he became Prime Minister and was appointed Cabinet Secretary in 2012.

There was a sad postscript, however. Jeremy died suddenly in 2018 whilst still only in his late fifties. I wrote to him, on learning that he was seriously ill, and wished him a full recovery, but he died very soon afterwards. He was made a Lord just before he died. He deserved a fuller life, having given so much for his country. I was invited to his private Memorial Service in Westminster Abbey but could not attend because Ann was seriously ill again. The Guardian newspaper recognised the importance of the occasion by devoting its two centre pages to a photograph of Theresa May, the current Prime Minister, and her four predecessors seated on the front row of the congregation.

Iain Saville and I met one more time for a farewell lunch, after which I handed over responsibility for supervising CRESTCo to Andrew Whittaker.

CREST was launched by the Chancellor, Kenneth Clarke, on 15 July 1996. There were some early hiccups, as I had warned the Board there might be, but it came through them, as a said it would. It has gone on to be a rousing success story and to secure the City's future.

Andrew Winkler was promoted to Chief Executive when John Young took early retirement because of his wife's serious ill-health. Sadly, she died soon afterwards. I had thoroughly enjoyed working with John. He was very supportive at all times, backing me on the many substantive changes that I introduced. He had drive, commitment, good judgement and an engaging personality. He was also a great persuader. I can see why Andrew Large wanted him as his Chief Executive.

Andrew Winkler asked me to stay on in order to tackle some specific assignments and I was happy to do so. Over the next three years I worked on a range of problems, including a review of the London Metal Exchange; on the so-called "millennium bug"; on the implications for regulators of the Internet; and advice on the Financial Fraud Information Network. I gradually reduced my working week from full time to two days and stopped when I felt that work was interfering with my play.

Anticipating retirement I had joined Welwyn & District Bowls Club and, after a while, found that I was quite good at it. I got the bug, got drawn into playing more for the club and in competitions of various kinds, and by 2001 began resenting having to go to work rather than playing bowls or spending time engaged in various activities with Ann, including walking holidays abroad. I can vividly recall when I first started working four days a week. I played bowls that day for the club. It was a strange feeling, not being at work, but I also had a tremendous feeling of optimism and relief at the prospect of being able to do this instead of work for the foreseeable future. I was probably more relaxed in that match than in any other since and, as a result, played incredibly well: so well, in fact, that my "skip" rang me that night to congratulate me on how well I played. That did not happen again!

Now that Rod Whittaker had taken over from my old job I was no longer involved in Butler Cox Foundation events, which I had enjoyed so much for about twenty years. It was a lovely surprise, therefore, when they offered to host a farewell lunch for me. I was asked to choose the guest list and the venue. I named about a dozen of the most senior IT practitioners in the country and was delighted when they all came. It was a lovely gesture. I really appreciated that.

The last few years before I finally retired were very enjoyable. No stress, no racing to meet deadlines. I could relax.

My work on SIB's Review of The London Metal Exchange (LME) is worth a brief mention because it provided fascinating insights into another part of the complex jigsaw that is the City of London. I had not had any direct dealings with it in my previous ten years, so it was virgin territory. The Review arose because, back in July 1996, the Japanese company, Sumitomo, announced heavy losses of $1.8bn over a ten year period as a result of unauthorised trading in copper by an employee, Mr Hamanaka. These revelations posed serious implications for the operation of the copper market operated by the LME, which accounted for some 95% of the world's trading in copper.

The City of London is an amazing place, which never ceases to surprise me. It is full of hidden gems and the LME is one of them. Tucked away in an unassuming building is this highly successful international marketplace. It is the world's leading centre for trading base metal "futures contracts" (which specify in precise detail what metal would be delivered, when and at what price). The prices at which futures contracts are traded on the LME form the basis for trading in physical metal throughout the world. Trading is carried out in "open out-cry" sessions on the Ring Trading floor by sixteen Ring Dealing Members, sitting opposite each other in a ring, shouting to attract each others attention in the way that traders shout their wares in an open market. Physically and visually the trading floor does not carry the same excitement as the Mercantile Exchange I saw in Chicago, because it is on a smaller scale, but it is still a lively spectacle.

Led by its charismatic and much respected chairman, Raj Bagri, the LME had been a great success story. Trading increased more than six-fold between 1988 and 1996. It was not all sweetness and light there, however. There were growing tensions. Ring Dealing Members held half of the positions on the Board and, since the Chairman was always an appointed Ring Dealing Member, they were always in control. They argued that it was their practical expertise, commitment and commercial acumen that had brought this success, and they should, therefore, retain their controlling voice on the Board and in key committees. The non-Ring Dealing Members, however, whose numbers have grown five–fold in ten years and now outnumbered the Ring Dealing Members by six to one, saw this as unfair and felt that the Board was out of touch with its changing membership. There was a clear case for changing the present arrangements and I proposed several. It all added up to a fascinating assignment.

Then, in November 1996 I got a very big surprise, a letter from 10 Downing Street saying that the Prime Minister was minded to recommend me to the Queen for an OBE – the Order of the British Empire - and would I accept. Ann thought I might decline it, because she had often heard me complain that awarding honours was such a flawed and arbitrary process. I had no such doubts, however, and rushed to get the acceptance letter in the post. It was the kind of recognition that I needed. Although I am an eternally optimistic and pro-active person I do need my ego stroked and my confidence boosted from time to time and this was very timely, as I approached retirement. We had to wait until the Honours List was published on New Years Day before we could tell friends and family, but at a New Year's Eve party with friends Ann produced two bottles of champagne and they all toasted my good fortune. A few weeks later Ann was happy to tell fellow walkers on a Ramblers holiday that I had got this award.

I was particularly pleased to receive congratulations from other regulators that I had worked with. They all seemed genuinely pleased. Apart from the Chairmen of SIB getting their knighthoods this was the first honour to a financial services regulator, so it was significant also in recognising the contribution of SIB itself.

The investiture took place in March. I could take only three visitors, so Ann, Benj and Graham joined me. I wished Helen and Bruce could have been there, too. I was a bit nervous and tetchy with Ann, which was a pity on such a day. I felt very grand, in a silly kind of way, wearing my morning suit and driving up to the gates of Buckingham Palace in my white Audi estate car through large crowds of onlookers. After a security check by the army we went into the courtyard. I had always thought Buckingham Palace to be a charmless building. It is from the outside, but inside it is very grand indeed and every inch a palace, with very wide corridors, huge ceilings and colour from floor to ceiling. Even the gents' toilet was impressive.

Ann and the boys went off to sit in the ballroom whilst I was ushered into a large room full of oil paintings. We were given a short talk on where to go and how to behave when in the presence of the Queen – "speak when you are spoken to and remember to retreat by stepping backwards. Enjoy yourself: this is your day".

I stood there for about one and a half hours before it was my turn to leave. I was absolutely dying for a drink. The Arsenal and England goalkeeper, David Seaman, was there to get his MBE and Ned Sherrin his CBE. I was in a group next to Ned Sherrin's, but I could not really move in order to talk to him. He was very tall and broad, a surprisingly large and physically dominant man. He was holding forth to the group around him and I was dying to be there. I had long been a fan of his, since he burst on the show business scene with "That Was The Week That Was" in 1962. He was also one of the first celebrities to be openly gay. I wished I was in a lounge suit, like him. It would have been much more relaxing.

Then it was my turn to go. I was ushered through various corridors to reach the side entrance to the ballroom, where I stood until my name was called out in a loud voice. I walked into the huge ballroom, turned left to face the Queen, gave a short bow and walked forward. She was smiling. She looked very small even though she was on a raised platform. Her demeanour was immediately relaxing. She pinned the medal on my coat and said "Financial services regulation – sounds terribly complicated". I said "Yes, ma'am. It is a bit". "How long have you been doing it?"- a standard question, I imagine, for those to whom she cannot easily relate. "Eleven years, ma'am", I replied. "Oh" and she held out her hand to shake mine, which was the signal to go. I had expected longer and, in my haste to get away, I forgot, for a moment, to take a step backwards - not a hanging offence, but I felt a bit foolish.

I rejoined Ann and the boys in the ballroom and watched as others got their awards. The band played alternately soothing and stirring music and then struck up "God save the Queen". We all stand. The Queen leaves and, in a flash, it is all over. Benj manages to get David Seaman's autograph, which made his day. We have formal photographs taken outside and took some of our own. It was all a bit unreal, like a Hollywood film set rather than real life. I drove to "Nico Centrale" in Gt. Portland Street, one of my favourite restaurants, where Bruce and Orla, and Sue (Graham's girl-friend) joined us for a very enjoyable lunch, which even Ann, the fiercest critic of restaurant food, thought was good.

Displaying my OBE medal - Graham, Ann, me and Benj

I'm glad I've got this award, although in practice I have not broadcast the fact. There was a slightly embarrassing situation when I first became an officer of the bowls club. The Chairman, Gerald Papworth, had got an MBE and this was printed on the club's stationary and on members' fixture cards, which went out to other clubs. Should I follow suite and reveal mine? I decided that I should, rather than hide the fact. It caused a slight stir in the bowling community. The only other bowler I know who has an OBE is Tony Allcock, Chief Executive of Bowls England and former World Bowls Champion, so I was in good company.

In May 1997 Ann and I were on a walking holiday in Crete with Ramblers, so we missed the excitement of the Labour Party securing its landslide General Election victory. We had plenty of our own excitement. Our leader had refused to take us on a twelve mile walk through the famous Samaria Gorge, much to the annoyance of the whole party. It was traditionally opened on the 1st May, but he judged it to be too dangerous because the water levels in the river were still high, and he castigated the authorities for opening it too soon. We learned later why he had been so angered. He had been the leader when two walkers in his party had been drowned crossing the river, swept away by the water running down to the sea. He must have been utterly devastated. It was surprising that he could still take on the job as leader, but he was very good and Ramblers had apparently persuaded him to carry on. He took us on a walk instead through the nearby Imros Gorge, not as spectacular as Samaria, but still very impressive. On another day we climbed up the mountain to the top of the Samaria Gorge with the river over a thousand feet below. As we climbed up a huge eagle with an animal in its talons swept very low over our heads, its menacing shadow causing us to duck down as it passed. On reaching the top we spotted it again through a telescope feeding the animal to its young perched on a nest on the cliff face on the far side of the gorge. That was some compensation for being unable to do the walk through the gorge.

At breakfast everyone was talking about the election result. The whole party, regardless of political persuasion, seemed to welcome it. The country was ready for a change. Despite John Major's efforts to reverse their fortunes, the electorate was tired of the Tories and wanted them out. It had sent them a decisive message: "don't come back for some time", and they didn't – not for thirteen years. Although I was no longer active in the Labour Party I was delighted. Tony Blair seemed to offer real hope of a new beginning and an end to sleaze and drift and "boom and bust" policies. For the next few years he could do no wrong in the eyes of the electorate. The Guardian newspaper, always ready to criticise even those it would otherwise champion, could not understand it and dubbed him "Teflon Tony", because nothing adverse ever stuck to him.

He undoubtedly did a lot of good, reversing years of decline in the public services, particularly health and education. Extra teachers were recruited so that class sizes went down from the upper 30s to a maximum of 30, which delighted Helen so much that she cried when it was announced. Crumbling and makeshift schools were rebuilt. Antiquated hospitals were similarly replaced, more doctors trained and more nurses recruited. Waiting lists went down and patients were seen more quickly. The decision to provide free access to museums and galleries epitomised for me the change in political philosophies: whereas the Tories had favoured only those who could afford to pay, the Labour government reckoned that everyone should be able to see the nation's treasures, even the poorest. I was particularly pleased also by the new powers given to Local Authorities to maintain and enforce Public Rights of Way, encouraging the public to get out into the countryside.

The Blair government was a reforming government, introducing a minimum wage, tackling child poverty, bringing peace eventually to Northern Ireland and devolving powers to Scotland and Wales. It delivered eleven years of unbroken economic growth, full employment, and much more. It also took a crucial decision not to join the Euro, which proved to be a blessing years later when the Eurozone got into such difficulties. He certainly did not get some things right, though. The failure to tackle the country's housing problem was a disgrace and has now escalated into a severe crisis. Too few houses were built and a major factor was Margaret Thatcher's earlier veto on Councils replacing their depleted housing stock, as a result of her "right to buy" scheme. House prices are now beyond the reach of young people and the outlook for them is dire. He also left a ticking time-bomb as a result of the policy of allowing immigration to rise unchecked. When the European Union expanded to take in Poland and other eastern European countries the UK welcomed them at a time when other countries imposed restrictions. As a result our population has rocketed, putting pressure on schools, housing and health services and making immigration a toxic issue in many parts of the country.

His eventual downfall, after three election victories, was his identification with America's "War on Terror", following the devastating attack by Al Qaeda on the twin towers in New York, killing over 3,000 people. He threw in his lot with President George Bush and took us into long and bloody wars in Afghanistan and Iraq. The Iraq war, in particular, split the country and there were several marches in London and elsewhere to protest against it. It also split families and threatened friendships. Helen felt very strongly that the arguments for war did not stack up and she went on protest marches in London and Manchester.

On a visit to stay with our friends, Michael and Mary Jackson, in the Lake District we got into a very heated argument lasting well into the night. Michael, who was a retired senior civil servant, thought that Blair was a liar, who knew that the claims that Saddam

Hussein had weapons of mass destruction were false. They were simply a smokescreen to justify the invasion, he reckoned. I thought that it was not that clear-cut. Blair claimed to have evidence that Saddam Hussein had weapons of mass destruction which he would use if not deposed. I had just seen an interview on the BBC's "Newsnight" programme between the respected reporter, Susan Watts, and Dr Wright, one of the UK's own weapons inspectors on the United Nations team, who was quite convinced that Saddam Hussein did have them, so perhaps Blair was right, I thought. Even if he did have them, however, I was still ambivalent on the merits of removing him. Clearly he was evil, having poisoned some 3,000 Marsh Arabs in his own country, and invaded both Iran and Kuwait, and would almost certainly wreak more havoc in the Middle East, if left unchecked, but getting rid of obnoxious national leaders per se would lead you down a very slippery slope. Where do you stop? Eventually Tony Blair's luck ran out and he decided it was time to hand over to Gordon Brown after an unedifying period of backstabbing and dirty tricks between their two rival camps.

In 1997, however, when Tony Blair and Labour swept to victory, the outlook was one of optimism. Gordon Brown immediately made the Bank of England independent and announced his intention to create a super-regulator, the Financial Services Authority (FSA), to replace SIB. It would take over the Bank's responsibilities for regulating banks and all the responsibilities of the SROs, RPBs and other bodies which regulate investment activity of all kinds. So, it was the end of the two-tier system of regulation. This new monster of 3,800 people and costing £177m p.a. would do the lot.

It made a lot of sense, if it could practically be made to work, but it was a daunting task. There would be no need for companies which carried on multiple types of investment activity to be authorised and regulated by several regulatory bodies. The new body would regulate with a light touch, it was said, which sounded to me like a recipe for disaster, and so it proved. The Labour Party had fallen in love with the City and saw it as one of the few remaining bits of our economy in which we could lead the world and be a source of sustained economic growth. The idea was to make the UK attractive to overseas companies and make London the centre of global investment business.

It all went swimmingly until the whole global system collapsed in 2008, starting with Lehmans Brothers in the USA and spreading with lightening and frightening speed to the UK and the rest of the world. Economies throughout the world went into meltdown, ours included. Gordon Brown earned some credit internationally for his efforts to save the banking system from collapsing, but domestically he was a broken man and he paid the price at the polls in 2010, where Labour lost heavily and a new Conservative/Liberal Coalition Government was formed. Commentators and the general public were all asking the same question - "Why did the regulators in all these countries not see this catastrophe coming?" It is almost unbelievable that so many supervisors did not see how over-exposed and precarious these firms were – so much for "light touch" regulation. Had they learned nothing from the earlier Robert Maxwell and IMRO experience?

By 2014 the economies of the UK, the USA and Germany had all started to recover, but they were still saddled with mountains of debt, which would take years to clear. In the UK a programme of austerity and massive reductions in public expenditure left millions of poor people in dire straits. The churches and various charities started food banks to alleviate their suffering - what a terrible indictment for such a rich country as ours. The situation in some other countries, particularly Greece, was even worse, with no sign of recovery in sight. All of this came about because regulators here and abroad, particularly in the USA, failed in their prime task of investor protection. What a dreadful catalogue of incompetence. I don't broadcast too loudly that I was part of the original system. Of course, had the SIB still been functioning when the financial crash came it would have been the Bank of England, which regulated banks, and not the SIB which would have felt the full force of the public's wrath. In its latter years, under Andrew Large's chairmanship, SIB could never be accused of being a "light touch" – quite the contrary.

Returning to 1997, Andrew Large completed his term at SIB, which was wound up, and Howard Davies took over as Chairman of the new Financial Services Authority. Andrew had tried to make the two-tier system work, but there were still serious defects, he felt, and the case for reform was overwhelming. Andrew got his knighthood, which he had certainly earned, and went on to be Deputy Governor of the Bank of England.

I started my last major assignment at SIB. It is hard to imagine now a world without the Internet, the World Wide Web and e-mails, but that was the position in the mid-1990s. It was clear that these developments could have significant implications for financial services regulation and I was asked to carry out a review for the

Board. I consulted nearly one hundred firms and organisations in the UK and overseas and built up a detailed picture of how this phenomenon had developed, how businesses in the UK and overseas were currently using it, where it was all headed and what problems it posed for regulators – there were plenty of them.

It all began in 1969 when US academics produced ARPENET, a network of dispersed computers that could continue to operate in the event of a nuclear attack. They developed electronic mail as a way of communicating. These networks grew and coalesced and the term Internet was adopted in 1989, at which time an Englishman, Tim Berners Lee, invented the World Wide Web, again for research scientists to use rather than commercial companies. However, as soon as it went public in 1992, commercial companies started to recognise its potential. With the sale of personal computers growing, overtaking TVs in 1996, and better software becoming available, the Internet really took off.

The Internet is now a truly global marketplace, potentially posing huge problems for regulators. It is a network of networks with no single owner or controlling agent. You can communicate with a web-site thousands of miles away but only pay communication charges at local call rates. It is a bonanza for the consumer. It was growing at a phenomenal rate with network increasing a thousand-fold in the next three years. What would be the implications for the way financial services business was conducted and for regulating it?

Many suggested to me that the Internet was all hype, but I could see that this was not so. It was here to stay and would transform the way businesses and individuals operated. E-mail, I predicted, would become the dominant means of communication, although many in SIB and elsewhere found this hard to believe. Investment companies were gradually setting up web-sites, mostly for advertising at this stage rather than for making transactions - secure systems for taking payments did not then exist, but these would soon follow. The marketplace was changing amazingly fast. If one competitor made a move then others had to follow suit, for fear of being left behind, thus creating a snowball effect. However, if an investor wanted to do business with an investment company or intermediary how did he know it was legitimate? A prudent investor would check a company's authorisation status on SIB's Central Register. Even so, the scope for fraud and scams was enormous.

I identified a host of issues on which the financial services community urgently needed guidance and on which SIB needed to take the lead. All of this, however, was overtaken by the sudden winding up of SIB and its replacement by the all-singing-and-dancing Financial Services Authority, which would itself come crashing down a few years later.

Back in Welwyn Garden City I had taken on another role. In late 1997 Anthony Roe made a bee-line for me one day in town. He had been my deputy when I was Chairman of the Board of the Citizens Advice Bureau (CAB) some ten years earlier. He was now its Chairman, but coming to the end of his term and looking for a successor. He asked if I would rejoin with a view to taking over from him. Ann encouraged me to take it on, so I agreed. She was still an adviser there and was soon to receive her award from the National Association of CABs (NACAB) for her twenty years of service. She was very happy there, still serving under the charismatic Gil

Bomber, but then Gil announced her retirement after seventeen years at WGC. She was an enormous loss to the bureau and to the CAB service more generally.

I chaired the sub-committee to find Gil's replacement. We had a pedantic NACAB Regional Adviser on the sub-committee, who was a pain, insisting on political correctness at every turn. I would have appointed a young man with no CAB experience, but well qualified otherwise. Instead we ended up with another very large Gil Bomber look-a-like, who had loads of experience, but turned out to lack the necessary motivational and management skills. She was a poor choice. She lasted a while, but was eventually replaced.

Following a very good talk from a NACAB adviser on the need for CABs to find alternative sources of income I suggested to Anthony that my time might be better spent setting up and running an active fund-raising committee than taking over from him as Chairman. He agreed and in January 1999 I formed the Friends of Welwyn Hatfield CAB and became its chairman.

Before the Friends could get properly started, however, the Board had to deal with an acute financial crisis. Unless it could raise £10,000 by 1 June 1999 the WGC office would have to close. We had just two months. Anthony Roe, Clive Gibson and I made contact with scores of firms in the area. John Lewis, which had always been supportive of the CAB, because of the helpful advice we had given to their staff over the years, made a generous donation. Some, such as Marks & Spencer and Tesco, said they were bound by Head Office restrictions on supporting local causes, which did not endear them to us. The largest contribution came from June Redgrove's sponsored London Marathon run, which raised a magnificent £1,630. As a result I was able to report to the Board in June that sufficient funds had been raised to keep the Bureau open and to thank everyone for the efforts made.

I turned my attention to setting up the Friends. I did not want simply to send out appeals for money, in the way that national charities generally do. I wanted belonging to the Friends to be fun, both for those supporting us and for those doing the fund-raising. I set out to form an active committee of doers rather than talkers, and to mount a programme of money-raising ventures. I wanted to give Friends good value for their money so that they spread the word to others. I persuaded three friends and neighbours, Alison Daniels, Bev Stewart and Colin Leeson, to join the committee. Two WGC Bureau workers, Lynda Cowan and Clive Gibson, volunteered to join, as did three Board Members and a former Manager of the Hatfield Bureau, Joan Bensley. These were the core of the Friends Committee. We gelled as a team and had a lot of creative energy.

We set ourselves a target of raising £25,000 in three years. The money raised would not simply be absorbed into the Bureau's running costs, which might result in the Council's grant to us being cut, but used to make one-off purchases or improvements to the Bureau's operations. We decided to launch ourselves in September and to link it with our Diamond Jubilee Appeal. We held a Gala Evening at the University of Hertfordshire at which a large audience were given a fascinating talk on "Lying and Deception" by Dr Richard Wiseman. The evening was a great success and we were launched.

In order to raise our profile, and hopefully bring in more funds, I decided to invite some prominent local people to become Patrons. I put a lot of effort into this and was more successful than I could have hoped. All seven agreed.

Viscount Cranborne, now Lord Salisbury, who lived in nearby Hatfield House, was very supportive. He spent a whole morning with me at the Hatfield Bureau finding out what we did and how we did it and he became a regular donor. Lord Laming, a former Director of Social Services, although busy on two major Government enquiries (the notorious mass murderer, Dr Shipman, and another), nevertheless found time to act as host for the day at the House of Lords as one of the prizes in our Diamond Jubilee Raffle, raising over £700. Prof. Neil Buxton, Vice Chancellor of the University of Hertfordshire, helped secure the use of the university for our Gala Evening and launch. The Rev. Ron Ingamells, vicar of Lemsford Church and a golfing friend of mine, laid on a magnificent golf day at nearby Brocket Hall, raising over £2,250. I spent two delightful mornings with David Kossoff, the actor and raconteur, who lived in Hatfield. He owed a debt, he said, to the CAB for help in times past and wanted to say thank you. In addition to a generous donation he presented "An Evening with David Kossoff" at the Barn Theatre, which was a delight, full of wry Jewish humour. It raised over £900. Finally, Melanie Johnson, our MP and a supporter of the CAB service, agreed to be our guest speaker at the Bureau's AGM. It helped enormously to have these Patrons prominently displayed in our literature, showing their support for us and encouraging others to follow suite.

Over the next two years we laid on a variety of well attended events, which helped us to recruit new Friends and secure more donations. A supper and musical evening was particularly well liked. Clive Gibson, his wife Pat and their friends excelled themselves with their catering at this and other events. Colin Leeson secured £6,000 from two generous donors and organized a highly successful business lunch, which brought in yet more donations. Ann and I completed the annual 14 mile sponsored walk round the Garden City, organised by Rotary, and raised £350, the highest total. We were invited to a Rotary lunch to receive an award for this. By 2002 we had easily reached our target of £25,000 and the money raised was making a real difference to the Bureau. Then it all fell apart.

The Bureau's financial problems would not go away. Basically, the grants from the Council and others were not enough. Although most of the workers at the Bureau were volunteers, like Ann, there were a few paid staff, most of them working part-time, and there was not enough money to pay them. Nevertheless, they still worked long hours, unpaid, out of loyalty to the Bureau. The Deputy Managers, who supervised the volunteers, were under tremendous pressure and suffering from stress. The Board was very concerned. The new Manager simply could not cope and eventually left.

Coupled with this was an ultimatum from the Council to vacate its premises within six months and free up the space occupied by the Bureau. Alternative locations in WGC were considered, but the financial problems seemed intractable. Dr June Redgrove, the new Chair of the Board, proposed closing the WGC Bureau and consolidating in Hatfield. Since the WGC Bureau dealt with the larger part of the 14,000 clients seen annually, and was regarded within the CAB service as one of the best in the country, it seemed perverse to close it and keep Hatfield open. The attraction of Hatfield, however, was that it had space and was cheaper. It was decided to move to Hatfield.

The advisers at WGC rejected the Hatfield solution and produced their own analysis of the problems facing the Bureau. Roy Jacklin, John Cropp and Clive Gibson mounted a campaign to keep the WGC office open, but Dr June Redgrove rejected it, arguing that the future lay in one office and greater dependence on a telephone-based enquiry service. The move went ahead. It was very acrimonious. Anthony Roe, former Chairman, described it publicly as "a moral indignity and absolutely disastrous". John Lewis expressed its concerns. Ten volunteers, including Ann, resigned. I resigned from the Board and as Chairman of the Friends and several Friends Committee members resigned, too. The Friends limped on for a while, but was eventually wound up, which was a tragedy. We had shown that we could raise something like £10,000 a year and that was now all lost to the CAB.

However, without the Friends to worry about I could put more time into other voluntary activities that I was involved in. One of these would also prove controversial. Throughout my time at SIB I had become involved again with The Tavistock Institute of Human Relations. Mike Aldrich, who I knew well from my time at CCTA and DTI, had become Chairman of the Institute's Council. In 1989 he invited me to lunch, ferrying me to and from the restaurant in his chauffer driven Rolls Royce, and asked if I would consider becoming a member of the Council. He knew of my former involvement with the Institute when at IOR and thought my experience and expertise would fill a gap. I agreed.

Sir Louis Blom-Cooper QC was also joining the Council and Mike took us both to lunch before the first meeting to give us a feel for the current issues and how he saw his role and ours. Given my earlier experience of how researchers in the different units in the Institute vied and bickered with each other I speculated that Sir Louis might be perplexed and irritated by much of what he would have to deal with and soon leave, but I was quite wrong. In fact he out-stayed me. Mike had none of these misgivings: he was very understanding of their behaviour and seemed to accept that the kind of work they did threw up these kinds of fractious, argumentative personalities. Whilst he would often bemoan their lack of financial discipline he was extraordinarily supportive of the work they did and was always full of encouragement and praise, but this happy relationship would end on a sour note in 1998.

It was clear that the Institute had changed considerably since my first involvement with it over twenty years earlier. Although one or two of the old guard were still around the big guns had mostly retired or left. The nature of the work carried out had changed, too, but some key planks still remained. It was still the managing editor of "Human Relations", the influential and internationally renowned journal for social science research.

There were a number of financial crises in the ten years I was there and Mike Aldrich spent a lot of energy and time trying to adopt more effective administrative and management practices. This was not at all easy because there was no single "Director" of the Institute, but a number of semi-independent units, which did not always see eye to eye on how to proceed. What motivated the staff and exercised the managers most of the time was the research work they carried out - administration and finance were second and third order issues.

After seven years on the Council I agreed to take over as Chairman of the Institute's Pension Trustees from Sir Pat Lowry, who was another Leicester Grammar School boy, but he went to Wyggeston, the better one that I did not get into.

In 1997 The Institute would be 50 years old and we decided to celebrate it in style and to generate publicity from it. A full programme of events was agreed. The celebrations ended with a party for staff and guests in the highly atmospheric Garden Room at The Barbican at which I gave a brief welcome on behalf of the Council. My feelings were that these celebrations had been a great success and would have a unifying effect on the Institute. That hope was to be quickly shattered.

The rosy glow from these events had been overshadowed towards the end by a staff disciplinary matter, which rocked the Institute and led to a serious rift between staff and the Council. A senior member was accused of gross misconduct and a Disciplinary Sub-Committee, chaired by Mike Aldrich, was set up in October 1997 to consider the charge. He took legal advice. The charge was upheld and the accused was informed that they would be dismissed. An appeal was lodged and I was appointed to a three man Appeal Panel, alongside David Glassman and Prof. Robin Wensley. After a formal hearing and mountains of legal and other documents from both sides, we decided in June 1998 to reject the appeal.

Throughout this whole process there were numerous expressions of discontent from staff and from some Council members. We were bombarded with letters setting out their grievances. One Council member, Prof. Enid Mumford, resigned, as did two senior staff members. It was all very damaging. Mike Aldrich decided that enough was enough and gave up the chairmanship. He described the last six months as disastrous. He did not deserve to go out on such a low note after the tremendous efforts he had made over a nine year period. Four months later, in July 1998, I decided that I, too, would leave. I was doing less work in London, so it would take a special journey to attend Council and other Institute meetings. I had done my bit and it was for others to pick up the pieces, however messy. I received a kind letter of thanks from the Institute's Secretary, John Margarson, for my contribution over several years, but it was a sad note on which to leave.

In 1998 Ida, Ann's mum, died. Towards the end of her life she had become increasingly frail and Ann's sister, Janet, travelled some distance by bus each day to care for her. When Janet and Alan went on a long holiday abroad Ida came down to stay with us. We converted the TV lounge into a bedroom and tried to make her comfortable. Ann persuaded her to walk the short distance each day into the lounge to have her breakfast looking out over the patio and into the garden, but after a while she refused to move. She stopped eating and drinking and appeared to have made up her mind to die. We got a doctor to examine her, but decided not to take action to force her to eat and drink. She died within two weeks. All the family came to see her and say their goodbyes. Graham sat and held her hand and talked to her for ages, but Benj found it very upsetting and could not stay with her for long. It was a very emotional and sad time for us all`.

I was very fond of Ida and we got on well together. Surprisingly, given their different backgrounds, she also got on very well with my mum. They had both stayed together at our house many times and enjoyed their outings with us. They regarded these breaks as holidays and got a lot of pleasure from them. Ida rarely complained and was very undemanding. She was the kind of person you wanted to please or make happy, which is not a bad epitaph.

My mum (right) and Ann's mum, Ida, at Wisley

My final assignment at the FSA, in 1998/9, was to help prevent the so-called "millennium bug" causing computer systems to fail, creating chaos throughout the financial services sector. When 1 January 2000 arrived computer systems had to interpret that change of date correctly. Failure to do so would bring big problems. I helped Martin Owen evaluate the risks posed for each business sector, monitoring the progress being made by businesses to test and modify their systems. FSA's contribution was only part of a massive effort by government and just about all parts of the private and public sectors. The effort paid off because the change-over proved painless.

That was the end of paid work for me. Andrew Winkler tried to persuade me to carry on, and had other assignments lined up –"why stop now? You're good at it", he asked. However, I was conscious that my knowledge-base was rapidly becoming out of date and I did not want to ruin my reputation by attempting one assignment too far.

There was no great fanfare when I stopped. The key figures that I had worked closely with, such as Sir Andrew Large, John Young and Roy Croft, had all gone and the new FSA was in different hands. I said my goodbyes to those colleagues who were still at FSA and Andrew Winkler took me out for a farewell lunch and then that was the end of my working life. The next stop was full-time retirement and lots of fun, or so I thought.

Chapter 17

Welwyn Garden City Leisure Time

The year 2000 was not just the start of a new millennium, but the beginning of life after work for me. It began well. I got a surprise invitation to the Millennium Service for England in St Paul's Cathedral on 2nd January, attended by the Queen and Duke of Edinburgh, Government Ministers and lots of other dignitaries. It was a big occasion, broadcast on TV. St Pauls is a huge building with a very long nave. Ann and I were near the back, a long way from the pulpit and the choirs, so we could not see much, but we had no difficulty hearing everything. We saw more on TV when we got home. The Archbishop of Canterbury, Dr George Carey, gave the sermon and led the service. He was as hard-hitting as always on our failure to deal with the problems that afflict our society. There were interesting readings by Ben Okri, the Nigerian writer, and by Patricia Hodge, famous for her TV parts in "To the Manor Born" and "the Good Life", and by Richard Griffiths, who brought Alan Bennett's "The History Boys" to life at The National Theatre. There was some lovely music and singing by the Children's Choir. The sounds soared in that great cavern of a building. It was an uplifting occasion and a good start.

With Ann and Ray on the new Millenium Bridge

Our friends Jill and Ray Rundle came to stay with us in June and we went into London to go to the National Theatre. The new Millennium Bridge, spanning the Thames from St Pauls on the north side to Tate Modern and The Globe on the south, opened that morning and we were amongst the first on it. We were also the last off it, as it turned out. Its design and construction is very modern and a complete break with the past. It looks very insubstantial, a lattice-work of interconnected metal poles suspended over the water. We took a few photographs and then started moving towards the St Pauls side, but it became very crowded as hundreds of people on a charity walk came across. Suddenly, it was difficult to walk without feeling that you would fall over. The bridge seemed to wobble and the wobbles got worse. All my aircraft industry experience of elastically unstable structures, such as the Tacoma Narrows Bridge, Washington, went flashing through my mind. Before I could get too worried, however, policemen appeared and started clearing the bridge. We were the last to reach the north side. It was closed for two years whilst they sorted out what was wrong and strengthened it.

The year 2000 also marked the start of George Bush's disastrous two terms as President. We were in the USA in November when the election took place. We were on another memorable Ramblers holiday, walking through the deserts of California and Arizona. It was fascinating, so forget your preconceptions about deserts being boring.

We watched the election results unfold on TV. It was extraordinary - so much razzmatazz and simulated excitement. Each of the networks, CBS and NBC, tries to outdo the other in its "race to the White House" soap opera. Each of them does its own predictions based on exit poles. It's a winner-takes-all electoral system whereby the winning party of any one State is allocated all the seats for the Senate or Congress. Each TV channel tries to be the first to "declare" the winner of each State. There is no patient waiting of the votes to be counted and the results announced officially by Returning Officers, as in the UK - this is show business and the facts must not be allowed to get in the way of a good show. By the time the votes are actually counted and announced the next day the whole contest has already been decided by the media. Only this time it was not so straightforward. One State, Florida, was highly marginal. The TV networks actually changed their mind on who had won it. It was the key to who would win the overall election and become the new President. In a further twist, the Governor of Florida was Jed Bush, George's brother. The Republicans were eventually declared the winners of that State and George Bush became President, but there were many accusations of serious irregularities in the voting, and the whole episode left a sour taste. The rest is history, and what a sorry history.

Back at home the Board of Gosling Sports Park dropped a bombshell in April 2005 by announcing its intention to close the bowls hall in order to build a Fitness Centre and Health Spa. Some months earlier John Beech, the Vice-Chairman of the Board, who I knew from playing tennis at Dellcott, had asked me to his house to discuss bowls. It was clear that he had formed the view that Gosling Bowls Club, and bowls in general, were in serious decline. I disagreed and said he was being over-dramatic. All sports have peaks and troughs. The number playing there now was still high, about 600, of whom 500 were members of the Club and the rest used the two public rinks. It was not as well run as typical outdoor clubs, including my own Welwyn & District B.C., of which I was then Secretary, but it was still a thriving club with all six club rinks used from

9.30am to 10.30pm every day. It was also a very competitive club with a number of members playing for the County, including me. At no time during this meeting did John hint that closure was on the cards. I thought that he wanted to find ways of increasing the income from bowls. I was furious when I learned that his real reason for talking to me was to find some ammunition to support his plans for closure.

Some 300 members attended an emergency meeting called by the Bowls Club's management. It was just before the General Election, so the two main contenders for the Welwyn Hatfield parliamentary seat, Melanie Johnson and Grant Shapps, were also there plus Dennis Lewis, our leading local Conservative councillor for over 30 years and an old friend of mine. I knew Melanie, our sitting MP and a Treasury Minister, from my time as Chairman of the Citizens Advice Bureau, but not Grant Shapps. Feelings were running high, but the club's management did not have much to say except to ask what we should do. Gus Edwards and I made impassioned speeches, denouncing the proposals and arguing that we should fight them. The three politicians offered support, but I wasn't sure then if this was not just gesture politics. In the event they did provide some practical help, but nothing that would prove significant in resolving our problems. It was agreed that we should put up a fight and a Save Gosling Indoor Bowls Club Challenge Group was formed.

By coincidence, I was due to play in the club's competition finals later that day. The morning's emotional meeting was not the best preparation. It was hard to get my mind back in gear, but I managed to win an absolutely superb game 21-20 to become the Gosling Bowls Club's last Men's Champion.

I rang John Beech. He argued that the sports facilities at Gosling Sports Park were increasingly expensive to maintain and without a substantial injection of regular income its future would be in jeopardy. I decided to write to him and his Board members. I copied the letter to Dennis Lewis. Apart from being our leading local councillor over the past few years, Dennis was also Chairman of the newly formed Welwyn Hatfield Alliance, set up in response to the government's wish to see Local Strategic Partnerships established, bringing together all sectors of a local community. They had just published their first glossy Community Plan and, under the heading "Helping people to enjoy life", was a full page picture of a bowler at Gosling. Oh dear, what bad timing. Dennis could not avoid getting involved.

My letter argued that the Board's proposals could not be reconciled with its remit as a Charitable Trust to meet the sporting needs of the whole community. Closure would deprive some 700 people with access to a sport that enabled them to meet people and engage in a healthy competitive activity. It would be an enormous loss for many, especially those who had lost a partner and regarded the bowls club as a place to fill that void. Moreover, bowls was one of the few activities at Gosling which made a very healthy profit. I urged the Board to reconsider.

We explored the option of building a new bowls hall and sought a loan of £550,000 from the Council, which was rejected outright, and the plans were shelved. It was clear to me that those who currently ran the club had lost the will to keep it going and a few months later it was finally wound up. The only hope now was for The Challenge Group to overturn the Gosling Board's decision, on legal grounds, and for us to take over the running of a new club.

Melanie Johnson telephoned to say that she had obtained the Gosling Sports Park's Articles of Association, which she sent to me. It was her last involvement. She lost her parliamentary seat at the General Election a few days later and Grant Shapps became our MP. The Challenge Group spent most of its effort arguing publically that the Board's decision was illegal as well as morally wrong, and probably financially unsound, too. We targeted the local press, which had reported the story of our protest meeting, but was thought to be on the side of the Gosling Board. I wrote to Terry Mitchinson, the Editor of The Welwyn Hatfield Times, setting out our case. We also issued a Press Release. Neither of these was published. I decided to write a personal letter to Terry Mitchinson reminding him of what he had said at a Rotary Club lunch some three years earlier, at which he was guest speaker and I was also a guest. He spoke then of the great satisfaction he got from championing local causes. Why was he not championing this one, I asked? To his great credit he published my letter, even though it was critical of his newspaper, under a very large headline "Not Bowled Over By Your Coverage".

I moved a motion at the AGM of the Gosling Members Association in October calling on the Board to reconsider its decision because it was wrong and would deny a vital sporting outlet to an important section of the local community. The meeting room was packed, with scores standing at the back, including John Beech and Stephen Hailey from the Gosling Board. The largest numbers there were bowlers, but there was a good representation from other sports clubs at Gosling.

I reminded the meeting of the vision of the early pioneers. When Gosling became a Charitable Trust in 1969 it explicitly declared "... it shall be deemed an **overriding principle** that the activities to be undertaken shall be such as will further the social welfare of the community of Welwyn Hatfield District and its neighbourhood ...". That charitable objective was central to the decision to provide indoor bowls in 1989. It had been a great success. By closing the bowls hall the Board was breaching its charitable status. I asked the meeting to send a strong, clear message to the Board. It did. Our resolutions were carried overwhelmingly.

It was all water off a duck's back. When the Board next met it rejected the Members Association's resolutions. What it boiled down to was that bowls occupied the space they needed for their new facilities and they had concocted a set of arguments to get their way. I wrote back, on behalf of the Members Association Committee, not accepting their basic point that the redevelopment would meet the Trust's charitable objectives. The Board simply did not want bowls on its site any more.

I realised at this point that the game was up unless we were prepared to engage in a bitter struggle with the Board and the Charity Commission. Although we went through the motions for another year or more we all knew that we were getting nowhere. We wrote to the Duke of Kent, who had opened the Tennis and Bowls Centre in 1991, asking him to use his influence, but it got the predictable reply. We had a meeting with John Dean, leader of Welwyn Hatfield Council, but it got us nowhere. He maintained that the Council had no jurisdiction over or influence with the Gosling Board, even though it had provided the grant to build the bowls hall. He said he was sceptical of the financial viability of the proposed redevelopment and the Board would get no loans from the Council, should it seek one. He maintained that the Council would remain neutral about the development, but it provided the Gosling Board with an extended lease without which the Board could not have secured the loans it needed.

We wound up the Challenge Group two years after it was formed. Grant Shapps wrote to me, commending us for putting up a good fight and criticising the Gosling Board for the shabby way it had treated us. I thanked him for his support and bemoaned the way Charitable Trusts seem to operate in an as self-centred a way as any private company when it suited them. The Charity Commission is a toothless tiger. He agreed and said that the Public Administration Select Committee, on which he served, was looking into such issues. The country seemed to be run by QUANGOs, he said, without proper public accountability, which was ironic because it was Mrs Thatcher who had resorted to setting up QUANGOs in the 1980s as a means of reducing the cost of the public sector as a proportion of GDP and, in the process, removing Ministerial accountability. The Conservatives came full circle in 2010 when they formed a Coalition Government with the Liberal Democrats and set in train a massive culling of these bodies.

Work on the new Fitness Centre at Gosling started in October 2007, two years after the bowls hall was closed. Duncan Kerr, Gosling's Chief Executive, did not stay long. He had achieved his goal of closing the bowls hall. Some of those who bowled at Gosling, mainly the more competitive players, moved to other clubs at Hatfield or Hitchin. The majority stopped bowling. Over the next few years thousands of others will have been denied the chance of even starting. Their health and quality of life will have been the poorer for it. What a tragedy.

Grant Shapps has since gone on to make a name for himself, not all of it as he would like. He became Housing Minister after the 2010 election, but had no answer to the country's chronic housing shortage, which had pushed up house prices, particularly in London and the south east, to levels which were unaffordable for first time buyers. The previous Labour government had wasted thirteen years in which it could have done something constructive, but failed dismally. It was particularly difficult for young people who needed a council house to rent. Mrs Thatcher's policy of allowing council tenants to buy their houses at subsidised prices proved very popular, but had the inevitable effect of reducing the pool of houses for future tenants, particularly as she stopped Councils using the proceeds of sales to build replacements. The pool simply got smaller - three million less, in fact. What was needed in 2010 was another Harold MacMillan ('SuperMac') to get a grip of the housing problem.

Grant Shapps' fortunes have ebbed and flowed. He has proved to be a very good publicist and was so frequently in the local paper that there was a case for renaming it "The Shapps Times". He is an effective MP, though, bringing a lot of energy and skill to resolving local issues. He has an engaging personality, too, utterly unlike any other politician and Minister that I have dealt with. He has a boyish charm, informal and modern in dress and in his dealings with you. His political rise continued until he was talked about as a future leader of the Party and Prime Minister. He was appointed Chairman of the Conservative Party, with a seat in the Cabinet, but his past then threatened to derail him. He was accused of operating a dodgy get-rich-quick internet scheme before he entered politics, marketing himself in the USA under the name of Michael Green, and of failing to acknowledge this properly in the Register of Members' Interests. He denied this when challenged and threatened to sue the challenger. He survived and helped to deliver an unexpected Tory victory in the 2015 General Election. You might have expected that success to lead to a significant promotion, but it did not. You could not keep him down for long, though. He is a significant politician and soon bounced back, securing a seat in Boris Johnson's Cabinet after the 2019 General Election.

Around this time we stayed with Graham and Beth and their growing family at their new holiday house in the French Alps just outside Morzine. They had often been skiing near here and had spotted an old and very large wooden-framed farmhouse which was up for sale. Property in France is much cheaper than in the UK, so they bought it with the intention of possibly moving there at some future date. They had it completely gutted and rebuilt, transforming it into an up-market guesthouse, with seven bedrooms and a very large, well equipped kitchen in which a professional chef would have been proud to work. We had the benefit of staying there in the years after it was finished, but they then decided to let it out to visitors for most of the year, so our little vacations came to an end. We had thoroughly enjoyed the ones we went on, including one with Helen, Andrew, Joe and Ben. Its location, sitting above a fast-flowing mountain stream, which tumbles down the valley from a large lake above, is idyllic and the countryside around is spectacular. It is perfect for walking in the summer and skiing in the winter.

In 2006 John and Jean Sefton invited us to join them and four others on a long distance walk in northern Spain along the Camino de Santiago, the famous Pilgrims' Way which starts in France and traverses the High Pyrenees before finishing at Santiago de Compostelo. We did the last 203 kilometre stretch from Ponferrado. It is a well-trodden, popular route on which walkers would greet each other with a cheery "Bon Camino". We would keep passing one young woman, who was built like an Amazon with legs like tree trunks which seemed to extend to her arm-pits. We dubbed her "thunder thighs". It was a great experience, well organised by John, and we resolved to do another walk next year.

I organised that one, which was along St Cuthbert's Way, another Pilgrims Way, this time starting in Melrose in the Scottish Borders and finishing 100 kilometres later at Holy Island, off the Northumberland coast. It was a walk of contrasts. We started by climbing the Eildon Hills and stared down at fishermen in the river Tweed below. It was an idyllic scene and John asked "why do we ever bother to go abroad?" We followed the Tweed, traversed the Cheviot Hills and finished by making the crossing at low tide along the causeway to Lindisfarne on Holy Island. Everyone said how much they enjoyed it. We have had several more walks since, taking turns to organise them. The only difference now is that we are older and the walks are much shorter!

Chapter 18

Welwyn Garden City
Black Clouds & Silver Linings

2009 was supposed to be a year of celebration for Ann and me, but it was quite the opposite. Our 50th wedding anniversary was in September and we made arrangements for a big lunch at Tewinbury Farm for family and friends. Christmas in 2008 was at our house with all nineteen members of the family present – Sofia was not then born – and Ann coped very well. Early in the New Year, however, she started to get very anxious and panicky. Dr McGhee prescribed Diazepam to relax her, but it didn't. She became more anxious and the panic attacks became more frequent and more severe. They were very frightening for her and very distressing for me. She was prescribed sleeping pills, but they did not bring her much sleep. We tried to carry on life, as normal, but it was increasingly difficult for her. She said she would not be able to go to Malta in March on a wildflower holiday, so we cancelled it. She was becoming depressed, so Dr McGhee prescribed one of the modern anti-depressants, but changed it after a few weeks when Ann said that she still felt terrible. That didn't work either and, when Ann told Dr McGhee that she felt "lethally depressed", the alarm bells rang and he said that she must go into a psychiatric hospital immediately. That is what Ann wanted and she readily agreed to go back to The Priory again.

We still do not know what triggered this new bout of depression, even after months of talking to psychiatrists, psychologists and counsellors. Ann's theory is that it started on a recent holiday in Nepal when we were trekking high up in the Annapurna Range in the Himalayas and she had become very frightened at being in such a remote and dark place. She had said then that she wanted to go home, but it was impractical as we were four days hard walking from the nearest mountain road. She survived and quite enjoyed the rest of the holiday, I think. It was absolutely memorable for me.

The Priory Hospital had changed. It now took in NHS patients as well as private ones and the age profile was much younger, so Ann had fewer people of her age to relate to. It also ran a big recovery programme for addicts of various kinds – drugs, alcohol, gambling etc- and there were a lot of these. They sat together at a large table in the dining room and were very noisy in contrast to the more subdued and older patients at other tables. Ann recognised one famous young actress from the "Eastenders" TV programme. Then Susan Boyle was admitted. She had just startled the world with her singing of "I dreamed a dream" on the "Britain's Got Talent" TV show and had immediately had some kind of breakdown. She was a rather plump, plain young woman and unlikely star material. She had a room near to Ann's and would sit slumped on a chair outside with her head in her hands, deep in her thoughts.

I said good evening and good night to her, but got no response. Until she left a few days later the entrance to the Priory was besieged with reporters and TV crews, blocking my way in. She has since gone on to be very famous, as well as rich, I imagine.

Ann did not like this new-look Priory, which did not help her recovery. Dr McClure had retired and her new consultant, Dr Michael Beary, was completely different. Whereas Dr McClure was a softly spoken, big cuddly bear, Dr Beary was tall, angular and thin as a rake, with sharp features and a more brisk style of interaction with patients. On visits to Ann's room he would rap out instructions to his junior doctor for changes in medication. Ann did not immediately warm to him, but over the next few years we got to appreciate his sense of humour and kindness and his sharp insights into the human condition.

The other big change at The Priory was the adoption of Cognitive Behavioural Therapy (CBT), one of the so-called "talking therapies" in which patients would meet in groups to talk through their feelings about themselves and others and to confront their fears. Dr Beary thought it would appeal to Ann, but she got very little out of it and found it quite stressful. I thought it was not much more than basic commonsense dressed up as a breakthrough in psychological treatment. There was a small army of staff trained in this approach, almost all women, and I thought some were a bit too self-important, strutting around The Priory like the new queens of the psychiatric world.

Dr Beary changed Ann's medication and very slowly she improved. As in her previous stays there, I would get to the hospital every weekday after Ann's group therapy sessions had finished, have supper with her and leave at about 10pm. In the first two weeks she was agoraphobic and frightened to leave the hospital, but later on we were able to walk around the lake in Grovelands Park and afterwards sit in the lounge, doing crosswords, before I returned home. I was no longer working, so I was not under the same degree of stress as in Ann's first stay at The Priory, but it was nevertheless still a very stressful situation. Ann's condition, however, was much worse than in previous episodes and she was not on the same drug, Doxepin (renamed Dosulepin), that had worked so well before. I had questioned Dr Beary about his reasons for not using it and he said that it was not suitable for someone of Ann's age and other modern drugs were superior. I had to bow to his judgement.

After four weeks she came home over the weekend, but felt very anxious. The following weekend was a little better, but still not great. It was a big surprise, therefore, when Dr Beary said that, after six weeks, Ann should go home. Neither of us thought she was ready. I realised afterwards that this was all geared to the limit set by our insurer for in-patient stay, even though I was quite prepared to pay the £4,500 per week cost myself, if necessary.

At home Ann tried to get back to normal, but found it very hard. She was on six different medicines, had lost a lot of weight and found it difficult even talking to and seeing her own family. She agreed to go as a day patient to The Priory on three days a week to attend group CBT sessions, which she found quite distressing. Whereas previously The Priory had always been a sanctuary, a place in which she felt safe, she now hated going there. She was not sleeping and having to take more and more pills. On 1 July I sent an e-mail again to Dr Beary, ahead of our next visit, asking him how confident he was that the current medication would eventually lift "the black cloud" hanging over Ann and expressing surprise that he was not using Dosulepin, which had worked so well before. I needed to see some light at the end of this long, dark tunnel, I said. Before that meeting took place, however, events moved on quickly and I was in touch with Dr Beary every day.

When Ann's panic attacks and depression became impossible to cope with she was readmitted to the hospital. Fortunately, it was a new insurance year, and we were eligible again for BUPA to pay for in-patient treatment, so I did not have to worry about that. She was immediately put on a huge dose of Lithium, a very old-fashioned drug, and a kind of last resort for psychiatrists. It knocked her out so that she could not get out of bed or walk for a day or so. Eventually, however, it did make a significant difference and she improved over the next few weeks until she started talking herself about wanting to come home, in part because she disliked being in The Priory. Nevertheless, it was still a surprise to me when she was again discharged after six weeks. She was in a very fragile state and still on heavy medication.

Sadly, we had to cancel our planned 50th wedding anniversary lunch. The hotel kindly waived a large part of the charge we were due to pay, but it still cost us £800. I had not thought about taking out insurance when we had booked it nearly a year earlier. It is astonishing how quickly your fortunes can change. One minute the world is a good place to be and the next it is a nightmare. Take nothing for granted, I have learned, and make the most of the present. Nor could we go on the holiday to France with the whole family, which we had paid for as part of our celebrations. We were so looking forward to that. They sent us a photo by e-mail of their lunch together at our favoured restaurant in Pujol, which was kind, but made us feel very sad.

Nor could I go later with the boys and their friends for our annual golf weekend in which the Smiths took on the rest of the world for the Coppa Cup. At the time it felt as if I would never be able to do that again, but thankfully I did. It was such an enjoyable experience for us all, but particularly for me because I had time with the boys. Benj set it up as a mini Ryder Cup. Bruce and I had a memorable game the previous year, coming back to win from three down with four holes to play. We were clapped in by the opposing team when we came in for the evening meal. That was a good memory to cling on to in the dark days that lay ahead.

During all this time I was trying to keep family and friends in touch with what was happening. I would often come home after visiting Ann to find as many as twelve messages on the answer phone. Benj, who now lived and worked in the town, would come to the house at lunchtime to see how we were and that helped a lot. Friends also came, some occasionally and others frequently. Derrick Swann, however, who had painful memories of his own depression, found the whole experience too distressing and it would be over a year before we were in touch again. Jean Sefton and Beryl Povey came most often, at least weekly, but when Ann was at home, and not in The Priory, they had to stay in the hall to talk to me because Ann felt unable to talk to them. She would get very agitated if she knew they were there. I was very glad to see them and would pass on their good wishes to Ann. Sadly the many get well cards Ann received did not make her feel better. In her troubled mental state they frightened her because they were a reminder that she would have to face these people again when she got out.

The person who gave me the greatest support was my wonderful daughter, Helen. For well over a year she rang me every night. During the very darkest days that Ann was about to enter, from October 2009 to February 2010, those calls were absolutely precious and a lifeline for me. I was finding all of this very tough, particularly during that five month period, and being able to speak to her gave me great comfort and encouragement. She also passed on messages to the boys and others in the family about what was happening, which helped. She made an enormous difference and I cannot thank her enough.

When she was back home again Ann made brave efforts to see family, but found it very hard. We went on one or more walks every day, but she was reluctant lest she came across people she knew and had to talk to them. Catherine came to see her and I took her to Catherine's once, but that was about the extent of any interaction with friends. Graham's birthday was in late October but we could not give him the customary party for family and friends, so he held one at his house. We drove over just to wish him happy birthday, but Ann had to stay in the car because she felt so awful. She had become more and more depressed, unable even to watch TV because she felt so threatened by it. We spent hours doing as many simple crosswords as I could get my hands on. We went to see Dr Beary on the Monday following Graham's party and he increased the Lithium dose yet again to 1000mgs, getting close to the safe limit. Dr Beary said that we should trust him, because he had great experience of such medicines. Ann got much, much worse. She was awake early every night, having had only two or three hours sleep, despite taking sleeping pills. The panic attacks got worse. It was a nightmare to deal with.

I rang Dr Beary and we went to see him again. He increased the Lithium dose even more, stopped Flupentixol and added Sulpiride. It was absolutely disastrous. She developed Lithium poisoning, which is life-threatening, and became delirious. She said she felt she was going mad. She did not even know who I was, asking me where was that nice young man who was looking after her, meaning me, of course. I rang Dr Beary and arranged to see him the next day. However, this time I decided to confront him over Ann's medication and rang his secretary to ask her to let him see an e-mail I was about to send. In it I said: "It is quite tragic to see her now. She has become a frail, old woman, whereas at the beginning of the year she was playing golf twice a week and preparing for a strenuous walking holiday in May. Her friends and family are truly shocked". I asked what his prognosis was and whether he was confident that the current medication would eventually work or whether there was a case now for using Dosulepin, the one drug that had worked spectacularly for her before. I sent that off at about 4.30pm. At about 8.30pm that evening he rang me to say "OK, Brian, you win. We will change to Dosulepin". He wrote to Dr McGhee to confirm it. I was so relieved. I did not know if it was the answer, but it seemed to me to be worth trying, given that it had worked before. He also took her off the dreadful Sulpiride and reduced the Lithium dose.

The omens were not good over the weeks leading up to Christmas. In fact it was a total nightmare. It takes many weeks to move from one anti-depressant to another, gradually reducing one and building up the other. I kept meticulous records to make sure I got it right, because in my stressed and over-tired state I could easily get it all wrong. I would do the same throughout 2010 and 2011 until Ann would eventually rid herself of all these drugs except Dosulepin. It took several weeks before the Dosulepin took full effect, so this transition was very distressing. Ann refused to go out of the house at all, so I spent hours repeatedly walking her from one room to the next just to get some exercise. She developed weird hallucinations, convinced that someone was trying to drag her out of bed or off her chair. To make matters even worse she stopped eating altogether. I had seen Ann's mother, Ida, do this before she died, so it was a very alarming turn of events. Was Ann trying to die?

Over the next three months she lost three stone in weight and looked like a skeleton. She was just shrivelled skin and bone and could not walk unaided, partly because she was so weak, but also because she was over-medicated. We saw Dr Beary weekly and Ann asked if she could go back into The Priory, but he said that it would be better for her to be looked after by me. I was happy with that. I thought I could look after her better than nurses at the hospital. She needed 100% attention at all times of the day and night, and she would not get that in The Priory, however conscientious the nursing staff were. Eventually I persuaded her to have some soup, taken through a large straw, because she would not eat with a spoon, and after a few more weeks I got her to have some other very easily digested food, such as yoghurt, rice pudding, cheesecake or scrambled egg. It took another three months to get her eating normally again without feeling frightened.

We spent Christmas alone. Ann had soup and I had something pre-prepared from Waitrose. When the doorbell rang on Christmas Day we found Jean and John Sefton on the doorstep. They had been to the Service at St Albans Abbey. Ann agreed to see them briefly but could not engage with them., so they simply said hello and left. They were the first people Ann had seen, apart from me and Dr Beary, for many weeks and it was a very kind gesture.

Ann's difficulties continued throughout January, but then she started to eat some easily digested foods and eventually agreed to see some friends and family for a few minutes when they called, but she still felt depressed and frightened at times. We were confined to the house, doing very little, except the occasional crossword. I kept repeating that she would get better, but I don't know how much this registered with her. After a particularly bad few days, I became so convinced that she would, after all, have to go back into The Priory that I transferred some investments into our bank account in anticipation of having to pay for her stay there. I also drew up a long note for the nursing staff about Ann's eating problems and how best to deal with them. In the event, none of this was needed because Ann started imperceptibly to improve. The changes were so slight that I did not notice them at first, but Dr Beary did. The full effect of the Dosulepin was, at last, beginning to take effect. She gradually improved. What a huge relief that was.

Some weeks later, although she was far from well, she was very brave and went to have her eyes tested by our daughter-in-law, Orla, at Letchworth. Orla, who had not seen her for over a year, was shocked by her appearance and asked if I was sure she was getting better. I also arranged for a hairdresser to come to our house, after which she agreed to see some family members, so in late February Helen and Joe travelled all the way from Manchester by train just to see her for about an hour. It may have been only a short visit, but it had a marked positive effect on Ann's behaviour.

Dr Beary had stressed how important it was to get out of the house and go for walks every day and Ann agreed, reluctantly at first. I would drive to another part of town, in order to avoid Ann seeing friends or neighbours, and we would walk for just a few hundred yards. We would do that for a week or so and then we would walk a bit further. Building on this I devised short walks of about a mile and a half around some nearby villages and we would do two of these in a day. At times Ann was still confused about who I was, but by March she was no longer disorientated and the world was beginning to fall into place. Amazingly, she asked me to make an appointment at John Lewis with a fashion adviser to choose some new clothes, a sure sign that her self-esteem was returning. It was not a great success, though. The woman did not know how to cope with someone who looked so ill and frail, but Ann did manage to choose some clothes, which suited her very well.

By now Dr Beary was convinced that she was on the mend and we arranged to see him only every three weeks. I drew up a list of activities that I would try to get Ann to do until she was a fully functioning person again. Many were very simple, such as "washing up", "listening to the radio", "using the phone to talk to family", whilst others were much more demanding, such as "cooking" or "playing bridge". I ticked these off as they were done. The last one, "travelling abroad", was not until three years later. Helen and Ben came to stay for two nights at the end of March, then Bev Stewart, Catherine Hall and Lyndsay Robson each came to tea in April, and she started to read again and watch TV. We went to visit some friends in May, starting with Catherine Hall in Hitchin, Derrick Swann in Finchley and Jill & Ray Rundle in Oundle. Ann's first bridge evening was at the end of April with Simon & Jill Hunter, and eventually at our bridge club in May. We went a walk in a bluebell wood with Benj, Maria and their two children and the next weekend with Graham, Beth and theirs, followed by a pub lunch. It was an enormous relief for me to have this family contact.

The signs of improvement came more quickly now. In the summer we resumed visits to the Royal Academy and the National Theatre followed by our regular monthly visits with our friends to the local Barn Theatre, followed by supper. On a visit to Dr Beary at the end of August 2010 Ann declared that she was back to normal again, nineteen months after she had first been to see Dr McGhee. She started playing golf again in October and at Christmas that year we had the whole family at our house and it felt then as if we really had shaken off the dreaded illness at last. In the following May 2011 I had my first night not sleeping in our own house for over two and a half years when we resumed our annual walking holidays with Jean & John Sefton and other friends. It was my turn to organise it and I chose to walk the Norfolk Coast Path, but based this time in one location, the excellent Hoste Arms in Burnham Market, using the reliable Coasthopper bus service to get us about. It was a great success and Ann thoroughly enjoyed it, especially as there were no hills to climb!

During 2010 and 2011 Ann successfully withdrew from taking all the medication except Dosulepin. The last of these was Lithium, which I always regarded as a very scary drug and I was glad when she finally stopped taking it in July 2011. So Ann was now back to normal and we could do all the things we used to do before the illness struck at the end of 2008. In September we went to Cornwall for a week, our first holiday for three years. In May 2013 I could tick off the final activity on Ann's "to do" list when we had our first holiday abroad for nearly five years. Before Ann's illness we would go abroad two, three or more times a year, so we had missed out on a lot of travelling, which might be difficult to catch up on, given that we were approaching our eightieth birthdays. However, we had made a start and Ann achieved a lifetime's ambition to go to The Burren on the west coast of Ireland on a wildflower exploration holiday, which was quite memorable, not just for the flowers, but also for the glimpse into the relaxed Irish way of living.

Since then we have seen Dr Beary once a year and he has become something of general counsellor, being as much interested in my health as Ann's. He remarks from time to time how well regarded Dosulepin is now by the medical profession and how doctors are being urged to use it more. If only that had been the perceived wisdom back in May 2009 we might have been spared a lot of pain.

The start of Ann's illness was not the only setback I was faced with in 2009. In March my sister, Sheila, phoned to say that Mum had collapsed and been taken into Glenfield Hospital, Leicester and, to make matters worse, Sheila had also been admitted to the General Hospital, so I would have to deal with Mum without her help. It was at a time when Ann was becoming more and more anxious and panicky, but not yet totally depressed, and I did not want to leave her, but I had no option. I went three times in the next fortnight to see both Mum and Sheila. Mum was quite cheerful, but much more fragile. The hospital did a great job trying to get her fully mobile again, putting her through a series of tests to see if she would be able to manage on her own but, at a meeting I attended with doctors, nurses and others, it was decided that she would have to go into a Nursing Home. We had gone though a similar process two years earlier when it was decided then that she should remain in her flat, but not this time. As I left the meeting, wondering how on earth I was going to find a suitable place for Mum when I lived nearly a hundred miles away, a woman's voice said "I am here to help you". I could have kissed her. With her help and later with Sheila's, after she was also discharged from hospital, we found a very nice place, which Mum moved into and liked. We had to clear mum's flat and Ann came with me this time, but she was not at all comfortable doing it. Later, when Ann was in The Priory, I would travel to Leicester to visit Mum in her new home in the morning before coming back to see Ann in Southgate in the late afternoon. The staff at the Home were very caring and Mum settled in well, but sadly she did not enjoy her stay there for long. She died suddenly in October. She was 98. I hope that my end is as unpredictable and sudden as hers.

Sheila's daughter, Caroline, made the funeral arrangements for me, which was a great help. She had been an absolute rock during Sheila's many spells in hospital and would be again in four years time when we thought Sheila would not survive emergency surgery. Ann was far too ill to come to the funeral, so I travelled there and back as quickly as I could. Mum chose to be buried rather than cremated, so Sheila, Caroline, Robert, my boys and I stood round her open grave reflecting on her life. I knew how hard that life had been in the early years when she was raising her family, practically single-handed, and how much I owed to her. In her eyes I could do no wrong and I got her total, unconditional love. When I was young I took it for granted, of course, but in later years I began to appreciate how lucky I had been and tried to return her kindness. She had come to stay with us and gone on holidays with us regularly over the years and, after I retired, I had taken her on many walks in Bradgate Park or by the stream in Barkby Village, followed by lunch, which she always enjoyed. We had done this well into her 90s, using a wheelchair at the very end. I thought about all of this as we stood round the grave. I felt very sad, but most of all I was relieved that she had not had to endure a painful, lingering death.

Chapter 19

Welwyn Garden City
Close of Play

Ann and I were determined to put those dark days behind us and put our life back together again. We had played bridge at Shire Park Recreation Club for many years. It was the old ICI Bridge Club, which had flourished in its heyday, before ICI closed its factories there, but was now struggling. On some nights in the summer there were only one or two tables and the Chairman, Robin Burgess, thought we would have to close down. That would be a big blow to Ann, who partnered Beryl Povey, and looked forward to going. She had only recently begun to play there again after her long illness.

I agreed to take over as Secretary and set about persuading Robin and Roy Jacklin, our Treasurer, that we must modernise if we were to attract new members and survive. I did that by creating our own web-site and introducing automated scoring. It worked. Six years later, when I retired as Secretary, we were a flourishing club again, having successfully negotiated a move to the Welwyn Sports & Social Club when the Recreation

Club was closed down. It is ironic and sad that, having settled in there, Ann would soon afterwards become seriously ill again with the dreaded depression and unable to play.

When the Royal Bank of Scotland (RBS) took over ABN AMRO, where Graham worked in Amsterdam, he was offered a job at RBS' Head Office in London. He asked me to look at several possible houses for them to move to before finally deciding to settle down in nearby Hertford. With Benj and Maria also moving from Manchester to St. Albans and then on to W.G.C., and Bruce and Orla already in St. Albans, we now had all the boys and their families within a few minutes drive or a short walk from our house. This made it easier for us to get together at weekends or in the school holidays, when Helen, Andrew and the boys could join us. The family had grown and we now had ten grandchildren, who got on surprisingly well together. We continued to have summer holidays together, but now went abroad to France after Helen and Andrew had discovered a gem of a place near to Villeneuve sur Lot in the Dordogne. It was a very large, old farmhouse with converted outbuildings surrounding a cobbled courtyard plus two swimming pools and tennis courts. I organised tennis tournaments in which the family and other holiday visitors took part. Meals on the veranda with the sun beginning to set were blissful. At other times we would eat on communal tables at the "night markets", which took place regularly in neighbouring towns and villages. They were very happy times.

The whole family, minus Joe

The last part of this journal is punctuated, I'm afraid, with more accounts of illness and death, but there was a lot of happiness and enjoyment, too. Having got through the years of Ann's depression we were just starting to enjoy ourselves again when it was my turn to be seriously ill. In 2012 I was diagnosed with advanced and aggressive prostate cancer. It was only by chance that I discovered it, just in time to get treatment that would save my life. Our friend, Michael Jackson, had become very ill and he died soon afterwards with prostate cancer. It was a great shock to his wife, Mary, and a loud warning bell for me. Recently I had begun having to pee urgently and frequently, including during rounds of golf, so I decided to see Dr McGhee, my GP, who sent me for a PSA test. The reading was high, so I had another two weeks later, which was higher still. I was referred urgently to Prof. McNicholas, who took biopsies, and confirmed it was advanced prostate cancer with a score of eight out of ten on the Gleeson scale. At this level the cancer is either about to or has already escaped into other organs of the body and may not be curable. I decided to have immediate treatment, using my private health insurance, and went every day for eight and a half weeks to the Harley Street Cancer Clinic under the care of Dr. (now Prof.) Heather Payne. She was very reassuring and exuded confidence. They would kill the cancer, she said, and with luck avoid any complications in later years.

Well, she has been right so far. Over seven years later I have no cancer and no complications, so I owe a huge debt to her and her team. Although it was obviously a very anxious time I was buoyed by Heather Payne's gentle, quiet manner and paradoxically I began to enjoy the whole experience including the walk to Harley Street through streets familiar to me from my time at IOR. The staff operating the huge machines, which circled menacingly round you emitting powerful radiation, were a cheerful bunch - almost all Australians or New Zealanders and mostly women – so it seemed inappropriate to feel apprehensive or sorry for yourself in such company. Although I would feel extremely tired for several months afterwards I eventually resumed my old activities and I am alive to tell this tale. Medicine must be such a rewarding occupation.

We decided to celebrate Ann's 80th birthday in 2015 with two parties, one at the nearby golf club for the whole extended family and the other, a much bigger affair, for Ann's many friends plus her immediate family, at The Priory in Hitchin. At the first party there was a magician to dazzle the children with her trickery. At the second, held in a large marquee in the Priory's grounds, there was a whole lot more. I mounted a large display of photos going back over Ann's 80 years and made sure there was at least one picture of everyone there. The four youngest granddaughters put on simple dancing displays on a small stage – Katie and Sofia did solos, whilst Ines and Rosa did a duet. They were lovely. Andrew then introduced our guests to one of his challenging picture quizzes, which are regular features of Smith get-togethers, but new to most of this audience. Bruce then invited us all to toast his Mum's health, Ellen presented a bouquet and Ann found it hard to hold back the tears. After having to cancel our 50th wedding anniversary celebrations I was so relieved that this one went off without a hitch and everyone seemed to enjoy it. I did.

2016 was a year of highs and lows. The first high was celebrating my 80th birthday with family and a few friends in early March, but it very nearly did not happen. Ann and I were on holiday in La Gomera in the Canary Isles in mid-February, catching some winter sun, when we got a distressed phone call from Ann's sister, Janet, to say that Alan had just died at their hotel in southern Spain. He had been having medical tests for some time to find out why his blood pressure was so abnormally low and was due to have more at the end of their holiday. He was otherwise extraordinarily fit for a man nearing 80 years of age. He still went for a long swim every morning before breakfast, followed by a game of golf before lunch, and then either golf again or bowls in the afternoon. He was a phenomenon. Nobody could have expected this to happen and Janet was shell-shocked, as were her daughter and two sons. His life was recounted at his funeral by Ann's brother, Nigel, and Alan's son, Nick, who gave a very moving eulogy, but none of this did full justice to how extraordinary he was. I doubt if many of those present, except for close family members, appreciated the breadth of the man. I was just very glad that I had known him.

My first reaction was to cancel my birthday celebration, which Janet and her family were due to attend, but Helen and others all urged me to go ahead, so I did. The family all came, including Janet and Katy. It was a more sober affair than it might otherwise have been, but I am glad we did not cancel it. Jill Rundle made a very good speech about me, which she started by playing the song "We said we'd never look back" from Salad Days, which we had all seen and loved in the 1950s, and Jill knew was one of my favourite musicals. Unfortunately it produced floods of tears from Janet, Katy and others. Despite this it was the right decision to hold it, I think.

That was not the only unexpected funeral we attended that year. Andrew's mum, Pat McIntyre, died in hospital in Durham from multiple medical problems, from which she did not recover this time. Andrew was working in the USA and hurried back to organise the funeral, which was sad, but also memorable. It was a Catholic service, led by Father Colm Hayden, who gave a moving Homily, recounting Pat's extraordinary life. Pat was active in the Church and Father Colm's affection for her shone through.

Over 150 friends and family congregated afterwards in the Trades and Labour Club for three hours of remembrance and celebration of Pat's life. What a life. She was a lifelong socialist, who campaigned tirelessly for the cause from aged 13, when she joined the Labour League of Youth, until she died, aged 81. She served on the National

Executive of the Independent Labour Party for 25 years and afterwards on the Labour Party's Northern Region Executive. She was a committed activist all her life, campaigning against apartheid, nuclear weapons, and much else. In 1982 she got fourteen nominations to be the next Labour candidate for the parliamentary constituency of Sedgefield, but Tony Blair, with just one nomination, was selected and went on to win. He became Prime Minister fifteen years later. Instead of a life in parliament Pat enrolled as a mature student at Durham University and was awarded a PhD in 1992, at the age of 57. The celebration of her life was an experience to remember, with songs, tributes and old films of her following one after the other. We knew how well she could sing from the Xmas parties we had spent in her company in Manchester. Her husband, Vin, was visibly moved by the whole experience, but just about held his composure. He will sorely miss her. We will all remember her and count ourselves fortunate to have known her.

On a happier note, 2016 year saw Joe, Ben and Ellen all at university and William would follow soon after. Our youngest granddaughters continued to flourish and develop their skills at dancing and acting – Katie, Sofia, Ines and Rosa keep on winning awards at dancing festivals and are a joy to watch, whilst Ines and Rosa got involved with our local Barn Theatre, playing the two lead roles in Matilda, the musical, and as orphans in Annie, another musical. In 2018 all four of them did brilliantly in their local pantomimes at Hertford and Welwyn Garden City. It gives me so much pleasure watching them all and I hope I can live long enough to see their talents flower.

In 2016 David Cameron, after years of constant pressure from the right wing of his party, called a referendum on whether the UK should remain in or leave the European Union. There followed a very acrimonious and divisive campaign which split the country and divided families, including mine. I voted to leave, as did the country as a whole, but only Andrew of my four children and their partners felt the same. Bruce, Benj and Maria, in particular, were very shocked and incredulous. Maria, who is Spanish, felt it personally, as if Europeans like her were being rejected, which was far from the truth. I had first hand experience of the way the E.U. works during my years as a civil servant and then as a financial services regulator and had found the whole bureaucratic processes tedious and restrictive. I thought we could do better taking our own decisions rather than having to make poor compromises with 27 other states with quite different agendas and backgrounds. It was an expensive bureaucracy dominated by Germany and France, whose aim was to create a United States of Europe, which I did not want.

One small example captured for me the restrictive, controlling nature of the whole E.U. institution. It arose after I had retired and whilst on holiday on La Gomera in the Canary Islands. The Olsen family had developed huge banana plantations on the island and shipped them to England, where they were unloaded at Canary Wharf in London's docklands. It was a business that flourished for many years. Then, when the Common Market was created, the European Commission decided that these bananas were too small and did not conform to the standards they laid down. Exporting was stopped and the plantations withered, apart from a small area, and a hotel was built on the land. We stayed at that hotel and ate those bananas at breakfast each day. They were delicious. Hans Olsen gave guided walks around the hotel grounds and was scathing about the way they had been treated by the E.U. I thought of this and other examples of E.U. behaviour when I came to cast my vote. I may be proved wrong, but I think we can do very well on our own and still be welcoming to other Europeans.

The 2016/17 bowls season was an unexpectedly good one for me. You're supposed to get less physically able as you get older, and certainly when you pass 80, but I found quite the reverse. I was playing better and better, possibly because I was using my head more to determine how I played, plus my experience. Whatever the reason, I hit a winning streak. I won the men's club championship for the fourth time and played almost every week as a "skip" for Hertfordshire (i.e. captain of a rink), winning most of my games. The real surprise, though, was securing two "hotshots", one of them for the county and the other in a club match. I received a certificate, signed by the three greats of the modern game. To get a "hotshot" you have to get all your team's eight bowls counting (i.e. all nearer the jack than any of your opponents), so it is a very rare event. To do it twice in the space of a few weeks is unprecedented, I reckon. In both cases I had to play an attacking last bowl to remove all eight opponent's bowls, but without removing ours, so it wasn't a fluke!

I began writing this in 2009 when Ann was suffering from serious anxiety and depression. I am finishing it when Ann is once again struggling with this terrible affliction, having overcome potentially lethal Lithium poisoning and much else. It started in early 2017 and has already lasted well over two and a half years, involving treatment in two psychiatric and three general hospitals and now by me at home. It has been extraordinarily stressful for everyone, not least Ann. I could write at length about all of that, but I have decided not to. Instead I want to end on a note of optimism and hope, recalling the wonderful time we had with our family celebrating Xmas in 2016.

Christmas Day started, as always, with the usual Leicestershire fare of Melton Mowbray pork pie, Stilton cheese, pickled onions and baked ham for breakfast. The three boys plus Bruce's eldest son, William, went off to play tennis, as had been the norm on Xmas mornings for years, but now I was no longer taking part, which was sad. Ann once again did a scrumptious Xmas dinner and we spent the rest of the day eating and drinking, opening presents and playing the traditional Smith Xmas games. The ten grandchildren all entered into the spirit of Xmas and effectively took over the games, which in the past I would have organised. They did it very well. The mantle had passed to the younger generation. Everyone agreed that it was the best Xmas Day ever. So good, in fact, that it was unanimously agreed to repeat it all on Boxing Day, when our numbers swelled from 20 to 22. Ann rose to the occasion, once again. A fitting note on which to end, I think.

My story is done and my life is nearly over. All that remains is to restore Ann to full mental health, as we have done before, so that we can start to enjoy our remaining years together.

www.ingramcontent.com/pod-product-compliance
Lightning Source LLC
Chambersburg PA
CBHW061253230426
43665CB00027B/2928